SWEDISH FISH? I
HATE THEM THINGS

My Best Wishes

J A L A I L

ISBN: 0692989544
ISBN 13: 9780692989548

CHAPTER 1

Frankie Migliori, my Uncle, looks more like a calzone than a Corleone these days but what can I do about it. My mother, she tells me to watch what he eats, so I watch. I don't say nothing. The way I see it if the guy wants to grow a pot why shouldn't he. I mean, he is the Boss and he does what he wants.

My name is Vincent Pigra. I work for Frankie Migliori. I am thirty-five years old and I live with my mother. Why? She needs me, she is alone, I am her only son, and I'm scared to death of her. I can't move an inch. Not that she would let me if I could tell her I was moving out.

Where would I go anyway? I have no prospects, no money, no wife, and no idea how to cook a chicken. I have never had to do my own laundry or clean a dish. I don't have to make my own bed or cook a meal. Frankly I surprise myself every time I wipe my own ass.

My mother, Camille, she takes good care of me and it doesn't cost me a dime, but one time I wish I could have some private time, without being startled by a turning doorknob or being asked what it was I was doing with the door closed that I could't do with the door open.

At sixteen you expect that kind of attention. You don't like it, but you put up with it because you don't have a choice. Your parents make the rules and you try to break as many as you can before they break your balls too much, or make you get a job to get you out from inside their ass.

I can sit all day at a cafe drinking espresso until I piss my pants and it doesn't change a thing. Drinking coffee, and scratching my balls when they itch, is what I am good at.

The way I see it I got a few more years to get my shit together. After that I am what I am, an errand boy for a low-level gangster. No offense to Uncle Frankie but he is what he is, and he is not what he was.

Uncle Frankie has a grocery store, a bodega really. He sells old food for too much money, cigarettes to twelve-year olds, and lottery tickets to people who can't afford to pay their rent, but will throw away money on numbers that have never done them any good.

If any of these degenerates don't have a buck to give to the state lottery commission they can always play their favorite number the old-fashioned way and give a quarter to Tony Cretino who is a real douche bag if you know what I mean. So maybe if a number has got dog shit on it, it will make you a couple of bucks.

A douche or a douche bag? Italian, a doccia or conduit pipe, no help there. English, a device for washing out the vagina. Better, also the genesis. Key word, vagina. If a word can in any way be connected to a vagina you, as a young boy, will at any given moment be associated with that word. At least a thousand times before you have reached the age of maturity. And then you as an adult will use that word just because it is comfortable, it is familiar and it seems to fit almost any situation.

Stub your toe, yell douche! Drop your car keys while carrying a bag of groceries? Say douche but stretch it out. Your boss tells you that something you did at work was unacceptable, say douche under your breath if you don't care if you get fired, and when his back is turned if you do.

Douche is also fun to say, and it will accept any amount of stress you wish to put on it. You can squeeze it, flatten it out, sharpen it up, or dull it down, its yours own it.

And best of all, it is not actually a curse word, so you can get started on it right away, as soon as you can pronounce the word it is yours to direct. I believe that I was four years old the first time I said the word, and do you know what my parents did? They laughed. Latitude!

Parents can fall under the delusion that children want total freedom, ridiculous any child born with a brain realizes that autonomy before its time is failure. Eat their food, accept their love, be thankful for that roof they put over your head, live by their rules, but with some latitude there is room to grow, to develop a personality, and become an individual.

Do I think that saying the word douche a thousand times before you are an adult makes you a better person? No, but during those formative years it does free up some space between the straight and the narrow.

In the American definition, a douche is an obnoxious and contemptible person. I said that Tony Cretino was a douche bag if you know what I mean. He is an obnoxious and contemptible person.

If you were making book, taking numbers, etc., and so on, why would you want to make a dime for somebody else? For one thing you don't have to break a finger off an old man who doesn't fork over when the Giants don't cover the spread especially if that finger is the one that he pushes his morning suppository up his ass with. You don't want to shove a crooked digit up there. Or maybe you do. Whatever pops your cork.

I don't think Uncle Frankie ever broke a guys finger but the neighborhood pezzo di merda were all getting old so it would have come to that soon enough.

Sorry about the Italian words that is my mother's fault. She mixes her languages and I guess I picked that habit up along the way. Pezzo di merda means pieces of shit. I will try not to mix up my words too much.

So anyway Frankie gave over the numbers to Tony Cretino who was selling medical supplies from a step van at the time and was looking for a way to diversify his business.

Tony doesn't break fingers when the geriatrics stiff him, he breaks their hip. As Canes, crutches, and walkers, are all covered by Medicare. Frankie gets a piece of that.

Money coming in from the state of New Jersey for squeezing the life out of people who never seem to get tired of losing, Tony Cretino gives him money and maybe a half dozen other cows are getting milked regular and Frankie, what does he do? He gets pissed off at the state of New Jersey. Why? Not because he doesn't make enough money from Selling their lottery tickets, no.

Frankie is pissed off because they tell him to go fuck off when he asked for a handicapped parking space in front of his store. The locals, they put up a parking meter instead.

Now my uncle needs a handicapped parking space like I need a college education. It would be nice to have one, but it wouldn't do me any good and, well a salad and a Diet Coke he needs, a walk around the block he needs, less lasagna he needs, but a handicapped parking space he don't need.

The Mayor, "That fucking asshole douche bag," who Frankie failed to endorse in the last election, and who could have fixed the thing for him, but didn't, made matters worse by sinking a meter into the cement outside of Frankie's store.

Not that Frankie noticed all of the other parking meters lined up on his side of the street.

Did I mention that Frankie, and the Mayor, the Honorable James A. Murphy grew up together and at one time were very good friends?

That was until the Mayor, who wasn't the mayor at the time, purloined Frankie's girlfriend, one Lorraine Impaziente, and went and married her? This not only pissed off my uncle, but my mother as well, who had been wetting her bloomers over the guy.

Confusing, but if you lived in my neighborhood it wouldn't seem so strange. This kind of thing happened all the time, after the war, guys were coming back before other guys, and people were horny and shit.

The war I'm talking about isn't World War II, it's the Korean War. I know that World War II was a better received war and you are probably sick and tired of watching MASH reruns for what? The past forty plus years?

I like Alan Alda as much as the next guy, but come on enough is enough. This is not, by any means, a war story, give me five minutes and we will never go back there again. I promise.

The Mayor's wife, Lorraine, was very sweet lady who did about as well as she could do in this neighborhood.

She may have felt a pang or two of guilt, some mild discomfort, a desire for anguish and recovery, but Lorraine was tired.

She was tired of staying home at night, tired of not dancing with boys, tired of not holding hands with boys, tired of not kissing boys, and tired of being chaste, and chased without being caught.

Where was Frankie? Probably having sexual intercourse with every two Hershey bar whore he could find, and doing sex things with them while they were blowing him on his genitals.

The extent of Lorraine's knowledge of what happened when a penis met up with a vagina, or any other part of the female anatomy was limited.

Lorraine had been home sick with the chicken pox that prophetic day during her sophomore year when all was to be revealed to her in health and hygiene class. In other words she didn't know nothing about nothing.

Frankie had respected her too much to direct her attention away from his lips. And Jimmy Murphy well, she wasn't his to direct. But then again all is fair in love and war or so they say. I myself feel that while all may be fair, it will not stop you from getting your ass kicked by me if you touch my woman.

I don't necessarily believe that Frankie was spreading around the chocolate over there in Korea, but it is what the Mayor told Lorraine when he was trying to get some figa palosa from her.

Sorry again, I have to stop doing that, but hairy pussy sounds a lot better in Italian. This was the 50's after all and I am absolutely sure that most of them things was hairy, I mean up until the mid to late 80's you could get lost in that jungle and ladies I am sure you will agree that a lot of men did.

My Uncle Frankie has an extensive collection of vintage Playboy magazines in his basement, and while doing intensive almost clinical research, in my early teens, I found that the overall volume, or square footage if you will, of pubic hair rapidly decreased in August of 1987. I didn't want you to think that I just make shit up. I would like to thank Miss August Sherry Konopski for her invaluable contribution to my studies.

When was the Safety razor invented, in 1885? Ladies more than a hundred years? There is no excuse. How about a scissor? Any objections to using a scissor?

Anyway, Lorraine had grown up with both of them and had known in her heart that the stories about Frankie were, only that, stories, but she needed to believe them in order to feel justified in breaching her long standing promise of marriage to Frankie.

I apologize for my earlier remarks. I am not complaining about the current state of a woman's vagina, cover it in cheese, make it wear a hat, whatever you want. It will still look good to me. Maybe even better, I don't know.

Just do what you want, but protect that thing with two hands if you have to. I may be old fashioned but I still think that a bella figa while being useful, commonplace, and tool like on occasion, it is still kind of special.

CHAPTER 2

Growing up around here was hard enough when I was a kid, but you can imagine what it was like in the early part of the last century. Everybody was poor, people were not working, and eating soup made from dandelions, or whatever else they could pull up from between the cracks in the sidewalk.

I don't know about you but I haven't missed a meal since I was nine years old. I tried my hand at cards in the boy's toilet at PS#28 and lost my lunch money to a fat kid with a pair of fours. I still get the shakes over what happened that day and have never gambled before a meal since.

Gamble if you want to, but keep the buffet money separate, expect to lose, as it is not in your favor to do otherwise, and never play cards with fat people before they eat. I find that while jolly for the most part fat people often become aggressive close to feeding time.

Where was I going with this? Fat people, old people? I remember now. I was trying to explain the dynamic behind the relationship between the Mayor, his wife, my mother and Uncle Frankie.

I have to go back in the time machine for this one, but the weather is warm and I feel like talking.

Seventy years ago the neighborhood looked a lot like it does now except that the buildings were new, and the old farts were young.

My uncle Frankie was three years old, eating dandelion soup and shitting a pale green. My mother was close to two years old, and sucking on a wine soaked rag given to her by an inattentive mother with no patience for motherhood, the suffering of a teething young girl, or for the depression which was raging at the time.

A rag soaked in wine, home grown and not afraid of the 18th amendment was the babysitter of choice especially when a kid was cutting teeth.

The Migliori family was poor, and couldn't seem to do nothing about it. There was very little work available to new immigrants, except maybe for the Irish. They were here early enough to dig a foothold for themselves and were not likely to share crumbs.

My grandfather, a chocolate maker by trade worked when he could, didn't make much money at it, but the family was able to eat once in a while, which was better than what most people were doing.

My Grandmother, she drank.

Maria grew up in Sicily, her father, the Don, was an olive farmer, with two sons and one daughter, he was the boss of a village named after his family.

The Don made a good living selling olive oil, and shaking down tenants on his property. His name was Narciso Nazione, which doesn't mean nothing now, but a hundred years ago if you were looking for an ass kicking in the middle of fucking nowhere he was the guy who would tell somebody to kick your ass.

Maria wasn't what you would call easy to handle. She was more boy than girl until not long after she grew out her tits. After that the chase was on. Maria could outrun most boys her age and caught plenty. That was until the Don found out and packed her off to the nuns.

The nuns tried very hard to motivate her, but they didn't do so good.

I have been working on my elocution, trying not to get my tongue in the way of my words too much, but I ain't doing so good. I ain't doing so well, I isn't doing so well, I am not doing so well, that's it.

Anyway Maria ran away from the nuns more than a couple of times, and the last time, they didn't find her quick enough to sidestep what followed one night in a barn, with a guy who turned out to be my grandfather, more or less.

Now the Don, he wasn't as upset as you might think. He was getting tired of the nuns complaining, and It was costing him plenty to almost, keep her there.

Maria could have done worse than a chocolate maker as there was no shortage of pickers, and pig farmers polluting the countryside, so a shotgun, a priest, a baby roasting in the pot, and you got yourself a wedding.

The father of the bride, relieved to have the little bitch off his hands, could think of no better way to hide his embarrassment than to ship it off to America before it swelled up and scared off most of his pickers.

The Don, he didn't want any of them to run off before the olives were picked, and business is business. Plus now he doesn't have to shoot somebody, who could have been anybody, which might be somebody he had a use for.

The ceremony was simple, and to the point. Do you Michael Migliori this. Do you Maria Nazione that. And By the power invested in me by that shotgun over there, I now pronounce you gone to America.

My grandfather Michael was a virgin up until the moment before Maria cold cocked him with her feminine wiles that night in the barn.

Michael, like someone else we know, didn't know nothing about nothing so he can't say yes, or no whether he did, or didn't have sex with Maria. I mean, she was here, and she was there. Her tits were in his face, which he did have to admit was very nice, and then her ass was in his face, also good.

Anyway, Michael, he didn't know the word for it, but he was almost positive that a girl doesn't get pregnant by giving a guy a blow job.

Was it a virgin birth? Not this time pal, and not ever in my book. Controversy? No, an opinion, subject to change upon receipt of further evidence. Not something you want to talk about in polite company, or, with your mother. Or to your priest let us not forget that douche bag.

My mother is up this guy's ass three or four times a week, including Sunday, and just because father big mouth can't keep his mouth shut I had to take one upside my head that I will not forget anytime soon.

I was twelve years old, and still a regular, albeit reluctant, churchgoer when I made a near fatal error. One Sunday I was trying to make change from the collection plate. I had a fifty-cent piece, and wished only to part with half. Twenty-five cents to the house and twenty-five cents for me, seemed equitable.

I made my change, passed the plate and went back to the routine of kneeling and standing too much, and sitting not enough.

My mother, she gets a phone call not two minutes after we went in peace, and came hauling ass down the sidewalk to where I was pitching my shiny quarter against the wall of the rectory, trying to go up a few coins before lunch.

Wielding eleven inches of a brass crucifix that had hung over my bed since I was a baby complete with a holy water reservoir, and a sledgehammer appeal, my mother, in no mood for reformation, seeking redemption only through the letting of blood, mine, did smote the blasphemer, me.

Jesus Christ flashed before my eyes right before he smashed into my head and I couldn't see straight for two days.

If I ever go bald I am not sure how I will explain the scar on my head, INRI, plain as day. And believe me when I tell you, I do not look like the King of the Jews.

Anyway, what do I know about the business of marriage, nothing. I know I'd take a bullet before I let some grease ball farmer shove his little whore up my ass, but that's just me. I'm a romantic.

I do the flower bit, the candy, and the candles. I buy smelly soaps, and fancy towels. I even borrow audio books on disc from the Library to listen to in the car that are supposed to teach me how to satisfy a woman.

I keep looking in the box for a diamond tennis bracelet and a ten inch cock, but I guess some other guy forgot to put them back in the box when he returned the discs to the Librarian.

I do like women, very much, and they tolerate me, for about five minutes, during which time they decide whether or not they could stand to sleep with me, which is all right as I am all for a woman's right to choose, but to pretend that it takes longer than five minutes is bullshit.

I don't believe a woman needs half as much time. I think a woman knows in an instant whether or not she wants to ball you.

Her decision whether or not to kiss you, or whether or not to hold your hand, or whether or not to tell you that you have spinach stuck between your teeth, is a much harder choice to make. As it may or may not suggest a certain intimacy which may or may not lead to another date. Fucking, is easy, relationships are not.

Michael, with a twelve-gauge up his ass didn't have a choice. Get married or get dead. Seemed like a good idea at the time, but a thousand miles away from the gun, Not so much?

While he did enjoy his brief interlude with the beautiful farm girl, its magic has since been replaced by exasperation, and uselessness.

Not being a man of action or great strength, Michael could not see a way out of this mess. While he felt no responsibility for the woman, or the child, he did like the money that her father sewed into his coat.

Fifteen hundred dollars, American, was a lot of green, more than what most people saw in a year, and he only had to marry the daughter of an olive farmer/crime boss to get it. That his mother and father would be fed for the pigs, and his sister would get sold on the street, was a consequence also not to be pissed on.

CHAPTER 3

The Statue of Liberty greeted the newlyweds like it had done for a couple million other orphans looking for a a change of scenery. Her torch up, book in hand, and her ass facing Jersey City.

Nice ass, but so rigid, a pretty girl like her should loosen up a little, get with the times. Fashions change, hairstyles, the sandals are kind of sexy but not after Labor Day though, not in NYC. But then again everything old is new again, so who knows? There May be hope for us yet.

I don't have to explain do I? I was only joking about me and Lady Liberty. There is no place for me in her life. She is married to her job as the mother of exiles and being the new Colossus takes up so much her time. What chance do I have really? Slim at best.

Only a few hundred feet away from Jersey City and where do most people go when they get off the boat at Ellis Island? New York City! Three hundred people get off the boat, two of them board the ferry to Jersey City, and the rest of them go to New York. It's enough to give a place a complex.

So you know what? Forget them. Live like a sardine in a can, obviously they have no idea what it will cost to live in that five story walk-up in a hundred years. So the laugh is on them.

Pasquale Schiavo, cousin by marriage to the olive farmer met the bride and groom at the ferry platform when the ferry boat docked in Jersey City, a Sicilian, with no teeth, a greasy mustache, bad breath, and one wooden leg.

Pasquale, forever grateful that the Don didn't feed both of his legs to the pigs was only too happy to kiss the ass of his daughter.

Pasquale carried Maria's bags, opened doors, stole an orange for her when she got hungry and gave her something to drink when she was thirsty.

Michael, was getting sick to his stomach. All the women he had known were hard working and selfless.

This was not going to be a normal marriage and Michael could tell right away who was going to wear the pants in this family.

Maria did not cook, she would not clean, she could not sew, she did eat, and would drink like a man at every opportunity.

What's a man to do with a woman like that? Let her be, and if he is lucky she will run off with a shoe salesman.

How you going to keep her down on the farm after She's seen, Jersey City? It was unbelievable, improbable, and highly unlikely, but not untrue. That woman split her lips with every guy in town except the one she came in with.

After Frankie was born they came knocking, the coal man, the iceman, Fuller Brush, the milkman. The point I am trying to make, is that while Michael and Maria were legally married, and morally bound by the Holy Roman Catholic church to uphold the sanctity of they're wedding commitment, Maria had her fingers crossed when she said I do, so it didn't count.

After the baby came so did every man in the neighborhood, except one. Michael never touched her after that night in the barn and she never bothered to care.

Three more years and one more virgin birth.

The new baby was nice enough, a girl who Maria named Camellia, My mother. She answers to Camille.

CHAPTER 4

Hoboken had been and may still be a waterfront collection of bars where a person can drink to forget, and factories, where the whistle blew to help you remember.

No café lattes or mocha almond cappuccinos for this bunch. Coffee, black, two days old and burnt until pitch, no half-and-half or steamed milk, no sugar or sweet and Low. Coffee, hot and miserable, much like the factory where Michael made his living.

A Salami sandwich, a pack of smokes, and all the chocolate I can eat, man that's living. A Salami sandwich, a pack of smokes and all the chocolate I can eat, man that's living, a Salami sandwich, a pack of smokes and all the chocolate I can eat, man that's living... day in and day out. It can't be good for you.

You get the short end of the stick and no amount of self-pity is going to help you. Big decisions have to be made and selfishness is the way to go.

Let the farmer feed the pigs, tell your sister she has to suck cock for money, do whatever you have to do, just get the fuck away, or stop jerking off and get yourself laid.

In a year or two a cup of coffee and a doughnut would get your dick sucked. By then the depression would be in full swing and money will play hard to get, but for now if you have a couple of bucks you can rent a girl for a few hours.

Infidelity was not a problem, Indifference was easy enough, neglect, not as simple as there were the children to consider, bills to be paid, the grocer, the milkman, and the iceman...the iceman.

Cheating on a cheating spouse can be therapeutic in a vengeful sort of way but a two dollar Puttana, affordable yet dear, could be just the patent medicine Michael needed.

Snake oil for sure, but even snake oil makes you feel better for a little while. Hell a glass of water with 20% alcohol would do the trick but so might some pussy.

In other words, he liked what she did. Worn out at twenty-two years old, and with two kids in the other room, Michael let Sally make it all better for him.

Sally was the archetypal whore with a heart of gold, and Michael was atypical, not at all accustomed to the ways of the street he easily mistook the faster you come treatment for genuine I feel your pain type concern, and was immediately taken to the land of suckers.

Forty times a night, seven days a week and they don't even have to offer you a hand job for a little side money.

Welcome to your local strip joint, home of the twenty-dollar dry hump. I have seen guys max out their credit cards in an hour and a half, I have seen them pay a seven dollar privilege to an ATM machine in a place where Andrew Jackson gets closer to a pussy than they do.

The coccyx, twenty dollars to be jerked off by the bone in her ass, you didn't think that was her pussy rubbing down your button fly did you?

Seven, eight hundred dollars a night and they never have to touch a cock that isn't wrapped in denim, or khaki.

You own the place maybe you get a little something. You walk in the door without using a key, you get taken.

George she likes stacked up at the end of her shift, Abe she likes a little more than George, Alex and Andrew she loves. You, the general you, are forty years old, bald, fat, and you smell funny. Do you like you? If breaking the ceramic pig for a smile and a peek at a pussy is any indication I say no. But if a walking wallet you must be than you enjoy that stupid grin on your face because it sure cost plenty to put it there.

Frankie has an interest in four skin joints. He, doesn't peddle the fish any more because strip money is easy, and keeping whores was a pain in the ass.

You got to house them, feed them, and you got to walk them all night long. They never stop complaining about their job, it's always too big, too many, too hot, too cold, my ass hurts, my feet hurts, I got this fungus and that fungus, it hurts when I pee. You would think they had real jobs.

You would think they had real jobs? Why do men say things like that, I just said it and I don't know why? It is foolish and desperate to antagonize something so irrepressible as a woman.

Men are just dumb I suppose. And someday we will pay the price for our stupidity. Wait a minute, twenty dollars to get jerked off by the bone in her ass? We are already paying boys, all is lost. Thank god for the internet.

Falling in love with a whore is like visiting the public library, and falling in love with the books.

A library metaphor? Who even goes to the library anymore? Nostalgia, that's what it must be. If I am an ordinary man, and I am sure that I am no better than ordinary I can only surmise by the way I speak and the chauvinistic behavior I display that ordinary men are fast becoming superfluous due to their attachment to a bygone system.

Nostalgia breeds fear, so it has to be fear. Well, that's it then. Ladies stop scaring the shit out of us. Problem solved.

Back to my library metaphor, where I can deny my own redundancy and loll around in my memories.

Falling in love with a whore is like visiting the public library, and falling in love with the books. Doesn't that just make you feel all warm and fuzzy inside? It's just so quaint.

One more time.

Falling in love with a whore is like visiting the public library, and falling in love with the books.

They keep going out, and coming back in and each time they come back to the library they lose some of whatever it was that may have attracted you in the first place.

Maybe the dust jacket has a little tear in the back, or the binding isn't as stiff or as fine as it was. Maybe the book feels dirty in your hands, abused, mishandled. It's just a book though, isn't it? Plenty of books around, clean books, maybe you say the hell with the Library, and buy your own book.

Now it's your book. Nice to own a book, but after you have read a book a couple of times it's not all that interesting is it? It's too familiar, still, plenty of books at the library not all of them in great shape, but most in good condition, and all of them available. Pick one, read it, enjoy it, bring it back and get another.

Michael, he wants to buy a book from the library, but the library doesn't sell a book that runs heavy with the borrowers, unless it gets broke up, old, or too sick to hide behind face paint, and a purple spot light.

CHAPTER 5

One of the jobs I do for Frankie is to collect money from scumbags that owe their livelihood to his generosity.

The Depot, a juice joint in Hoboken, managed by Valentino "Tino" Grasso, a four hundred pound, five foot eight inch, triple chin, fat tub of lard, is one of my regular stops.

Tino gives me an envelope; I feel the weight of it, say something like, "A little fucking light this week Tino, what did you do, eat the fucking money, you fucking toilet." Then I push him around some, which isn't easy since he weighs more than my car.

Tino will, as he always does, promise more than he can deliver. And next week I will have to push him around again, and this will go on until I have to hurt him a little bit.

Tino Grasso has an eating disorder, aside from his inability to waddle past a doughnut shop without stopping in for a dozen or two, he shits where he eats, which makes him a liability.

Too many times he has made like Romeo to a juvenile Juliet.

Runaways, independent types looking to finance a lifestyle, and girls That are not old enough to buy a can of beer, but can show their stuff to old men with flashlights, and middle aged creeps hard for chicken.

Tino has to go away soon. His type of behavior is bad for business.

Let me explain. When I say, go away, I don't necessarily mean whack. I mean he has to go some place where he will not embarrass Frankie with his antics. Kind of like how the catholic church cleans up it's messes.

But instead of sending The pervertito to another parish where he gets to try out a new bunch of adolescents we send our dregs to the Dumpster behind the Burger King, the Pizza Hut, or the Arby's. Waste management is another one of Frankie's interests.

I worked on the garbage trucks when I was coming up. Talk about your lousy jobs. How lousy was it? It was so lousy that in the summer your balls would sweat and hang down halfway to your knees from the heat. And in the winter you had hazelnuts keeping company with your prostate.

Under the New Jersey Turnpike at exit 15 W, on the border between Kearny and Harrison, and not far from Jersey City, there used to be a waste facility, a dump.

Nothing fancy just piles of trash a hundred feet high and a half mile square, nothing recycled or separated.

Thousands of fifty-five gallon drums, stacked up high, and leaking, making puddles of day-glow yellow and green. Cement blocks and assorted construction debris tangled throughout with rusted metal bands and piping. Seagulls and rats fighting over garbage and once in a blue moon a dead and/or mutilated body. It was here where you ended your day.

"Have a good day at work Honey?" Said Wife.

"Great, today I saw a seagull with a human eye in its mouth." Said Husband. Nice job, huh?

The Sandbar, a juice joint, on Gates Avenue, not far from the Liberty Science Center, is known for its clams on the half shell, and fried oyster sandwiches with horseradish and lemon, served on a round roll with a bag of chips on the side.

The Sandbar enjoys a pretty good sized lunch crowd, mostly truckers heading north, and longshoremen taking a break from toting bales and scraping barnacles.

Paul Fratello, Pauley the fish to his friends runs the place as a favor to Frankie. Pauley, an old friend and partner of the boss is trusted implicitly, is still a good earner and had once been the night manager at another dump just off of the 14B extension of the Turnpike not far from the harbor.

From that dump you could see Ellis Island and Battery Park to the left, Brooklyn on the right, and the Statue of liberty in the middle. Picture postcard type view, if you could keep the garbage out of your line of sight.

For twenty years Pauley worked at the dump. His only job there was to see to it that no one came through the gate without first making sure they belonged there, and then allowing them to pay for the privilege.

The price to enter the dump with a full truck and leave with an empty one was set beforehand by Frankie.

The contents of the truck was none of his business. Just match the bill of lading to the copy on his clipboard, blank, except for a four or five digit number, a time of arrival and a dollar amount to be paid in full upon entry. Collect the cash, don't ask any questions, let them in, and let them out, simple.

Twelve years ago Frankie gave The Sandbar to Pauley; the dump was closing due to the skyrocketing real estate value of waterfront property. Easy enough to smooth out, cap off, plant over, and in a couple of years you have forty half-million dollar houses with marina parking, and the best view of the New York City skyline this side of Hoboken.

The dump, old and established as it was, for half of the last century never actually existed. There was never a sign on the gate, or a number in the phone book, no tax identification number at the county registrar's office, no company logo on the side of a truck, or name on the back of a bowling shirt. There was nothing.

Pauley took over the bar, started serving food, and paying girls to dance. The money coming in was respectable so he made a nice return for himself and Frankie. Girls in G-strings, and bikini tops, were good enough then. But tastes, were beginning to change.

Four years later an all-nude juice bar opens up a block or two from the Sandbar. Six dollars a pop for juice or soda, twenty-dollars to get in, no food, no booze as you cannot serve booze and show pussy in New Jersey, and the Sandbar starts losing money.

It was decided that the Sandbar could keep the food because the lunch crowd was still coming in steady, but the G-strings, and bikini tops had to go. The girls were told to get naked or get lost.

The beer taps were disconnected, and the bottles of hard booze were stashed in the basement where friends of the Boss could meet, talk business and socialize with each other.

A week or two later the Sandbar was doing better, but still splitting the local crowd between the two joints. Another week, and a gallon of kerosene later, and the Sandbar is doing great. And Pauley doesn't miss the dump so much.

CHAPTER 6

On the first and third Wednesday of each month the receipts are counted behind the dried pasta, next to the walk in refrigerator, and near the ass end of Frankie's grocery store.

A folding table, big enough for two people, Frankie, and one other person, is set up to accommodate the BI-weekly tally sheet, and a sizable bag of greenbacks. As I do the bulk of the collecting for Frankie it is usually me who sits with him while he counts.

Frankie doesn't use a calculator, or a computer. He doesn't use a ledger to write the numbers in. Frankie rips a piece of brown butcher paper from a roll behind the counter, takes a pencil from behind his right ear, and jots down the numbers as I give them to him.

Did Frankie's people give up the cash easy or hard, did they offer me anything to eat or drink, or inquire as to his health and well being.

Frankie wants us to play nice, be courteous to each other, and keep a civil tongue. We do the best we can.

When the boss runs out of fingers to count on the money is wrapped up in the butcher paper, masking tape is placed across the top, the package is dated, and put in the refrigerator next to the veal chops until it is washed and then wired to a bank in the Cayman Islands, or maybe taken to a safe deposit box on Staten Island, I forget which.

An unremarkable van or truck comes by every first and third Wednesday night for a pickup to the laundry. Ten percent goes to the cleaner, I get two, and the rest goes home with the Boss.

What the Boss does with his money is his business. Frankie doesn't spend a nickel on himself as far as I can see, not on his appearance, his haircuts are free, he shaves his own face. His clothes are impeccable finely tailored but old as I am. Frankie owns one car, a seventy-two Cadillac Fleetwood. He doesn't have any kids and his wife, my Aunt Sophia passed away.

Aunt Sophia died on August the 16th 1977, the same day Elvis passed. All of Frankie's guys were big fans of the King so you can imagine what a day that was.

I don't think Frankie has spent the night with another woman since that day back in '77. I am pretty sure that he hasn't spent more than an hour with one since then, or at least since I started keeping an eye on him. Play-date sure, but no sleepovers.

He has his pick of juice joint pussy any time he wants it. But only once in a while does he ask me to take him to the Sandbar for a taste, and if Pauley knows Frankie is coming, the Pope doesn't get better treatment from the Vatican nuns.

After the war when Frankie came home to find his so-called girlfriend married to his best friend, he was beside himself with anger and grief. He wanted to kill them both and came pretty close to doing it a couple of times, but it just wasn't in him to pull the trigger. He loved them both.

Frankie decided to get away for a while the sight of the two of them together was making him puke. He thought that a week or two at the seashore might do him some good

Long Branch, once a classic New Jersey shore town picturesque and brilliant, is now faded and sepia toned. Ulysses S. Grant, James Garfield and quite a few other Presidents had vacationed there. Abraham Lincoln spent some time there as well.

Time and trends, a lack of capital expenditure, and sour economics have worn down what was once a destination beyond local interest.

Frankie took the train to Long Branch. An hour, sitting soft, not a big deal. A sandwich in the club car, a soda on the verge of being flat, but cold enough to taste good anyway, and enough to look at through the glass to keep his mind off of his troubles.

Not having a car of his own at the time Frankie had rented a nondescript bicycle from a shop across the street from the train station when he hit town.

Frankie rode the bicycle to the boarding house where he had reserved a room over the telephone the day before.

Frankie tied a small canvas drawstring bag which held the few belongings he had brought with him to the rack above the rear fender.

Frankie pushed off shakily at first but was steady after a block or so. He had not ridden a bicycle for some time. And after the train ride it felt good to get some blood flowing through his legs.

Later that day one of the tires on the bike went flat about a mile away from the room he let. Frankie had a full pack of cigarettes rolled up in his shirt sleeve, and about a dollar and sixty cents in his pocket, but no patch for the tire.

Before he decided to take the bike out for a look see Frankie had dropped off his bag at the boarding house but left his wallet on the bedside table in his room not wanting to peddle with it in his back pocket.

Frankie sat down on the sidewalk under the awning of a pasticceria or Italian pastry shop that also sold candy as well as confections such as salt water taffy, chocolates and such, to get himself out of the sun.

Frankie was not much for hats even though most men wore them. His olive colored skin would tan deep and dark, but peeled if he burned it too quick.

The noise from the taffy twister behind the storefront window he had his back against caught his attention. The sweet smell of the candy was bleeding through the glass, or so it seemed to him.

Frankie stood up, dusted himself off, opened the door, and went in smiling.

Behind the cash register was a young woman, her name tag read, "Hi my name is Sophia." Five foot four inches tall. Light brown hair, brown eyes, lips the color of strawberries, tits like cantaloupes and an ass like two melons, a regular fruit salad. Lorraine who?

Five minutes, and eighty-five cents worth of salt water taffy later Sophia agreed to meet Frankie after work for a Coke, root bear, or whatever they had streaming from the taps at the local drug store soda fountain.

Frankie managed to get the bike back to the rental shop where it costs him sixty cents to have the tire fixed and fifteen cents for a patch kit to keep in his pocket just in case.

Frankie had an hour to get cleaned up before meeting Sophia, who would be waiting for him at the Pastry shop.

In one hour he was back at the store smiling that stupid grin that men get when they meet the girl of their dreams. In this case she would be his second one of those, but who's counting.

Frankie leaned the bicycle, now as good as fixed, against the wall of the shop.

Sophia came through the door, smiled, and together they walked close and slow the three blocks to the drug store.

Frankie and Sophia found two vacant seats at the fountain, and ordered two beverages, his a chocolate malted, and hers, an egg cream.

The shape of her mouth, the fullness of her lips and curl of her tongue dumbfounded him as she licked the creamy froth from her lips. Her eyelashes fluttered like butterfly wings when she arched to sip her drink.

Can I stop now before I throw up, butterfly wings? For Pete's sake, Frankie, was staring at this walking wet dream the whole time they were together, and Sophia, didn't call him on it, or slap his face, or do the insulted goddess routine.

Sophia likes Frankie, he was cute, and the attention of boys, and not too few men lately was fast becoming the standard operating procedure since her last birthday, her seventeenth.

Frankie was twenty-one years old, almost twenty-two, a week ago his heart was broken, and his life was turned inside out by a woman who Frankie thought he loved.

The damage was done. But Sophia, she could be his salvation. With her lively eyes, and well meaning mouth, her childlike hopefulness and youthful attention to well, lets call it male optimism.

His experience with women on an emotional level was limited, a woman he had known his whole life, and those women he paid to suck his cock and bend over his jeep in Korea. Frankie had had only one real girlfriend in his life and she picked him.

Frankie was nine years old and playing doctor in the alley behind his house, getting what was his first and only genital examination until he joined the Army some ten years later.

Lorraine, the doctor on duty, finished the examination, and pronounced them engaged to be married and they were together up until the time Frankie went into the army.

Sophia was in Long Branch visiting with her grandmother for the summer, an ancient Italian woman with a mean look in her eye, and a wooden cane to back it up.

Granny put her to work at the pastry shop to get her off of the beach, and out of a bathing suit that was a major distraction to the local men folk.

Frankie decided to play up the returning war hero bit, thinking that most of the young men Sophia knew were still in high school, and it might give him an edge if the world weary warrior could impress the young shop girl with his wartime story.

There were two weeks left until September, Frankie, had enough money saved to last that long then he would have to get back to Jersey City and find a job.

Frankie, a mail clerk in an Army hospital was a good soldier, but had had no use for what he had learned during the eight weeks he had spent at Fort Dix New Jersey but he was good at delivering the mail, and did what he was told.

Frankie did see some things, bad things, the wounded, the dying and the dead, but for the most part his years in the army went by painless and then he came home.

Was he wounded during the war? Sophia noticed a little hitch in his giddy up when Frankie excused himself to go to the rest room. Aside from a paper cut life in uniform was uneventful, and safe.

The hitch she spotted had more to do with the flow of blood, than the loss of it. His dick was hard from staring at her tits, and an adjustment was needed to relieve the discomfort. He told her it was nothing to worry about, and that he had had a doctor take a look at it for him while he was in Korea.

While it was true that Frankie had seen many doctors in Korea, In fact he saw dozens of them everyday when he handed them their mail, but he doesn't recollect any of them looking at his penis. Frankie thought it best to be vague about his recent past, but he didn't want to lie, not too much anyway.

What no comment about "hitch in his giddy up?" I love old movies, westerns especially.

"What do your parents do?" Said Sophia. His mother was a drunk, and a tramp, "A housewife," he said. His father still make chocolate as far as he knew, but Frankie hadn't seen his father in more than six years, and not more than three or four times since he was three years old.

The last he heard his father was living in Hoboken with a washed out street whore named Sally with a bunch of kids some of which might even be his, "A tradesman," he said.

What good would it do Frankie to tell her that his mother was a lush, and his father was a syphilitic, middle-aged, factory worker shacking up with a two dollar whitefish. A two dollar whitefish, I heard that in an old gangster movie from the thirties, don't you love it?

Michael Migliori, Frankie's father had walked away from the family home about the same time that Maria's two older brothers came to America from Sicily to live with them.

There had been some trouble involving the disappearance of a policeman, and the death of a pig. It seems that this pig was having a problem digesting brass buttons and patent leather.

Vomit found near the bloated body of the dead swine not only contained the aforementioned brass buttons amid bits of chewed leather but also a wedding ring attached to a finger recognized by a hysterical woman as belonging to her husband the missing policeman.

The brothers arrived on a Monday and were in jail by Friday. There was some trouble involving the disappearance of a policeman, a coincidence to be sure.

On Saturday, Michael left. He packed all of his belongings into a small, brown leather suitcase, kissed Camellia on the top of her head, gave Frankie a tug on his chin and went out for a pack of cigarettes.

I was going to say, take a powder, but I have already used too many lines from old movies this chapter.

With the brothers locked up for a while, or longer if they found the missing policeman, Michael said fuck the pigs.

Attention to the plumbing was past due. Michael needed his pipes drained on a regular basis and living with the plumber was cheaper than paying for the house calls.

Michael was working steady, and could afford enough liquor to keep the whitefish, the young woman, happy.

Not that he didn't think that Sally was the latest dish, he liked her well enough, maybe he loved her. The braciola was tasty, and he was starving to death.

On a full stomach maybe she was more spoiled beef than a Bromo Seltzer fizz, but who was he to complain. He wasn't no box of chocolates.

CHAPTER 7

Frankie walked Sophia back to the Pastry shop after they had finished their drinks.

Plans were made to meet up again the next day, maybe another egg cream will do some good and Sophia will go warm to the idea of Frankie being part of the scenery.

There would be no giggles under the boardwalk with this girl. Frankie was not going to ruin his chances with Sophia if he could help it.

Frankie had to be a silk purse to the old bag and he knew it. Sophia was too young and too green, to know how loaded her gun was, but the grandmother, she knew.

Get thee to a pasticceria. His mother was sent to the nuns for safe-keeping and Sophia, was sent to the sugar shack to hide behind a hair net. If the olive soaked, aged sentinel was lucky the girl would make it to Labor Day with her cherry intact.

What would impress the old broad, Frankie didn't know? Seventeen may raise an eyebrow these days but back then her price tag was marked down at least one time already.

Frankie owned the clothes on his back and a return ticket to Jersey City.

Frankie possessed a few sundry items I neglected to mention, but for the sake of drama I thought it best not to list them at this time.

Frankie had not yet found the time or propensity to be ambitious. He was a good soldier, but Frankie got paid the same as any other passing time grunt. So why bother to polish the brass.

The money Frankie made shooting crap, and pulling aces when there weren't any, he gave back on days when snake eyes, and short sleeves made winning hard to do.

Michael gave his pay packet to Maria who drank away every penny he had ever given her. The old Don, he gave away everything he had to the war effort. Which meant that one-day he was feeling kind of full of himself and the next day Mussolini had a new summer home that came with a few pigs feeling kind of full of themselves? Not one role model in the bunch.

Frankie was a bastard Sicilian with the bowel movements of swine fertilizing his family tree. He, didn't even look Italian any more.

The only suit Frankie owned was made of khaki, his hair was too short to oil up and slick down, and worst of all years of chipped beef on toast had sucked the calamari right out of him.

He could be complimentary. Women like that sort of attention. I don't care if they squeeze your balls when you come without charging extra, or they cross their legs when Perry Como sings on the radio. Good girl or whore it don't make any difference.

The next day Frankie did his best to look presentable. He combed his hair, and splashed on a handful of Florida water he had found in a cabinet in the bathroom he shared with enough people to make it impossible to shower or take a shit in peace.

A desire Frankie had to spend an extra minute or two on his looks was lost to the irritable bowel of a tenant who kept time with measured tapping on the bathroom door.

Frankie, one step away from being too good looking, knew that with young girls it's all about eyelashes and attitude.

Remember this was when Elvis could still pass a fried bacon and banana sandwich, and didn't have to hide his pot behind a belt buckle the size of Newark.

Sophia liked him, he could tell. She did all of those girl things that are supposed to tip a guy off as to whether it will be yes or no, like twirling her hair, biting her lip, and sucking his dick. She didn't do that last thing, but all the other things she did.

"Will she ever suck his dick?" Frankie thought to himself. "Do nice girls suck cock?" He didn't know. I say yes. Well, I say yes until they realize that the flavor doesn't change no matter how many times they suck on it.

But even if a dick did taste likes cherry cough drops, or lemon pie, sooner or later a woman would go sour on it.

All cock sucking aside he likes her and will do his level best to have her.

CHAPTER 8

The Pastry shop was crowded when Frankie went to pick Sophia up, so he had to wait a few minutes before they could leave.

Sophia smiled when she noticed Frankie standing by the door attracting just enough attention to make her cheeks flush or so he imagined.

When you have been tortured and abandoned by a woman a few times, you realize that there are rules that women abide by. Men in general have no rules. We don't know nothing. We are an open book filled with geometric shapes, race cars, rocket ships and boobs.

Do you Ladies remember peeking into a boys notebook in school when he wasn't looking? It hasn't changed.

The rules say that a woman only wants you when she can't have you, or if she thinks you don't want her, or if somebody else wants you more than she does. That is until she finds out that you are the equivalent of a hot fudge sundae.

Follow me on this. You hang around with a woman for a while and her comfort level goes up, and so does her dress-size. She starts packing it away like Little Debbie just bought page twelve of the Weight Watchers handbook.

She takes notice that He is shooting his eyes left and right as they waddle to and fro with nary a glance going her way. She, irked by the lack of socket time she is getting, goes on a diet and that is when He becomes a hot fudge sundae.

She wants attention. She needs attention like she needs to pay somebody to lie about the size of her ass. So who does she blame for the rear view? That's right she blames the ice cream sundae.

Now He, The ice ream sundae, gets the, "I need a Man who loves me for who I am, not what I look like," speech.

And then the prize pumpkins that She has been growing out of her ass get harvested by a sensitive fat loving, sex deprived rebound fuck that She will keep around just until She can stop sucking off Ben and Jerry.

Frankie made eyes at a very attractive yet forlorn looking twenty-something victim of the war still wondering what the hell happened to her young man, and the cherry he took with him to Korea.

If he wasn't trying to put the lock on Sophia Frankie might have gone for a sit down in the shade with this sad sack of sexual what the fuck.

It would have been a cinch to steal away for a few minutes alone with the winsome widow, and set something up for when the teen dream was tucked in for the night.

Not that Frankie didn't need or desire the kind of intimacy offered by the blue eyed and Raven haired lonely heart with an all day sucker in her mouth, he did. His doubts were building in his mind faster than he could beat them down. What to do?

Three little one piece bathing suits, all of the under ten range, were staring through the plate glass window at the candied apples, and caramel covered pop corn balls on a wooden stick, and couldn't care less if he looked like Elvis or one of Sinatra's toenails.

Frankie waved the girls in. The bell hanging over the door gave a little tinkle as they piled through dressed in their itty bitty red white and green, respectively, bathing suits. I know I wanted it to be blue also, but it was not to be.

Frankie bought them each a candy apple making sure there was plenty of shredded coconut on the bottom.

Three smiles went out the door of the shop, and one stayed inside behind the counter.

Sophia was sufficiently impressed with his philanthropic bent so the thirty cents it cost Frankie to buy the apples was well spent even though it did add to the strain of his almost empty billfold.

If Frankie was lucky the donna asciugata behind the cash register looking at him through slits in its fleshless face would take notice of his good deed, and funnel it back to the matching bag of dried bones of a grandmother.

The Grandmother, and the fossil at the cash box looked to be sisters, sun dried tomatoes both, probably sold off to the first two farmers with a spare cow to trade by a father with eyesight good enough to see that a windfall just wasn't coming.

CHAPTER 9

A cellophane tinted display case filled to full with sweets of assorted varieties, an older than dirt thumb on the scale to give an edge to the house and a few cuties positioned with their youthful perkiness facing front to push it all out the door.

A nice set up seemingly profitable all on the up and up except for the soothsaying sister of Methuselah selling the future from behind the Almond bark and honeyed buns.

For the price of a pound of salt-water Taffy you could have your fortune told. A con for sure but not a bad set-up, if you don't lay too heavy on the melodrama, or drag the line too fast.

Frankie was wondering who the fortune teller, and the cash register hag were and what did they have to do with Sophia, if anything.

This makes three the point. One more and Frankie, might have gone for the door, but the palm reader didn't scare him He enjoyed the second sight gag as much as the next guy, but it is unlikely that winking at the fortune teller would help his position.

Frankie would play it soft. First he would let the chiromante read his palm or feel the bumps on his head or whatever it was she did for the few coins she charged, and after the usual gloom and doom report, he would make with the tear and tissue routine. A couple of minutes of flushing and blushing and a small crack in the shell might show itself as a way in.

Before his thirtieth birthday Frankie will contract syphilis from a toilet seat, lose his will to live, and go mad as a result, so said his left palm. If you should live so long, said his right. Not exactly word for word but the sentiment was dead nuts.

"Woe is me, I am but a child. I have not yet lived!" Frankie shouted to the heavens. "My sins will not die with me as I have used many a public toilet seat and the innocent shall suffer my fate. Thousands upon thousands will perish, What have I done!"

What really happened was Frankie listened patiently as his future was being erased by disease and unclean habits. When the end was near he grabbed and held the hand of the fortune teller, produced a few tears, fluttered his eye lashes several times, added a bee sting pout and pledged to be forever more hygienically responsible.

Frankie did give a fine and low key performance, and he received a favorable response from the audience.

"Such a fuss you are making." Said the old woman. "Would it kill you to put some toilet paper on the seat before you sit down."

No, he thought it wouldn't.

CHAPTER 10

Next to Frankie was a three-pound white paper sack of Swedish fish attached to two hundred pounds of solid, stocky short guy.

"You want one of these fish?" Said short, stocky guy.

"Who are you?" Said Frankie.

"Pauley, Pauley Fratello, who are you?"

"Frankie, Frankie Migliori"

"I seen what you did, not bad." Said Pauley.

"What are you talking about?" Said Frankie.

"The tears were the cherry, so which baby you snatching. The one pushing her tits by the coin box, or the red head selling her ass by the gum drops?" Said Pauley.

"Tits, obvious?" Said Frankie.

"Oh yeah," said Pauley.

"The old broad by the money is the fire door, but she will let you get close to that one if you buy something." Said Pauley looking directly at Sophia.

"Like three pounds of jelly fish?" Said Frankie.

"Swedish fish? I hate them things, but those things, them cheeks was overhanging the display case when she was dishing fish for a guy. I happen to see them all squeezed up and magnified in the glass behind her. The only way I figure I can keep watching them is to buy some of the things myself.

"One minute I'm bucks up by two and the next minute I'm passing my chips." Said Pauley.

"Newark?" Said Frankie.

"Elizabeth, you?" Said Pauley,

"Jersey City," said Frankie.

"Thought so." Said Pauley. "You open the book on the tits yet?"

"A page or two," said Frankie.

"You looking to find out how it ends, or are you setting your lure?" Said Pauley.

"You ask a lot of questions." Said Frankie.

"I got a curious nature, what can I tell you. So?" Said Pauley.

"So? So what?" Said Frankie.

"You and the tits?" Said Pauley.

"She has a name you moron." Said Frankie.

"So what the fuck is it?" Said Pauley.

"What's the matter with your eyes, you stare at her tits through three pounds of candy fish and you don't see a name tag?" Said Frankie.

"I must have missed it. What does it say?" Said Pauley.

"Fuck you. That's what it said. Are you always this stupid, or are you just practicing?" Said Frankie.

"I don't have to practice I'm a natural." Said Pauley.

"Sophia," said Frankie.

"Nice Tits," said Pauley.

"That's the last time I'm going to let you say that without kicking you're ass." Said Frankie.

"Can I say Breasts?" Said Pauley.

"No" said Frankie.

"Boobs?" Said Pauley.

"No!" Said Frankie. "

"Nice name tag?" Said Pauley. "I got to go. Are you going to be around for a while?" Said Pauley.

"A few more days, you?" Said Frankie.

"The same as you," said Pauley.

"You know that bar by the mailbox next to the statue of President John Garfield?" Said Pauley.

"Don't you mean James?" Said Frankie. "John Garfield was a movie star."

"Are you kidding me?" Said Pauley. "We had a movie star for a President?"

"No" said Frankie. James was the president and John was the movie star."

"So they were brothers?" Said Pauley.

"Ugh" Frankie groaned. "I know where it is don't worry." Said Frankie shaking his head in disgust.

"Tomorrow then two o'clock," said Pauley.

"Let me put it on my calendar. Two o'clock at the bar by the mailbox, next to the dead movie star with Pauley the fish. I Got it," said Frankie.

"I told you, I don't even like these fucking things." Said Pauley.

Pauley the fish was not handsome in the classic way, his features were not chiseled or symmetrical even but he was not exactly unattractive not if you have a thing for gargoyles or garden gnomes.

Pauley was Well dressed with pins pointed straight to the laces, a fedora, dusted, and slightly off flush, rakish, but not too much.

A wise guy, low level, but making good with the grunts and the yes boss. He might have a face only a mother mud hen could love, but Pauley knew when to stick and when to blow.

Sophia tapped Frankie's shoulder a moment or two after Pauley departed. The couple went off to the soda fountain for an egg cream, a Coke, or whatever.

CHAPTER 11

With sodas capped and carried to a sandy stretch of beach circled by tall grass, and edged with boardwalk, a short walk Frankie and Sophia managed easily. Sitting with shoulders close, fingers touching and their voices low.

Frankie and Sophia watched as the Sun set through oranges and reds into the boardwalk behind them and the surf crashed in rock piled jetties in front of them. The heat of the day went face down and bloated.

With high school polished and a job working as Daddy's secretary just ahead of the cool breezes, Sophia made with the fat lip end of day's pout.

Crystal clear to Frankie, and damned near invisible to Sophia, was the stuffing in the couch propping her ass when the salt-water deal went cold.

Sophia learned to type and file from the Nuns at an all-girl Catholic high school. Office preparatory courses, on how to outrun your boss until you land a one-knee deal, and a double bed.

Those years with the nuns had to be rough with the black and whites hovering, and no boys around to wear down the nuns thoroughly sermonized, virgin determination.

Frankie went to a public school, where the cracked pots kept their lids on, or got smacked, and virtue was tagged, and put up front until sold as thrift.

The nuns were the guardians of the hymen, it was their collective duty to keep as many of the girls off the stick until they graduated, and it was the devil (teenage boys) who made sport of their good intentions.

The nuns seemed to do well by Sophia, as far as Frankie could tell she knew enough about the real world to fill a pepper shaker and saw life through candy-coated glass.

The father will supplant the nuns as the hymen keeper, and bookkeeping will replace the tits for pastry scam now showing daily at the beach.

The father owned a junkyard in Elizabeth and another one in Linden where they lived. Sophia had two brothers, Peter, and little Sal.

Little Sal was named after his father Salvatore Nasorosso, the Boss of two junk yards that he shares with his brother Jackie Nasorosso better known as Jackie N to his friends, and the cops.

Her Mother was dead.

Salvatore Nasorosso, Big Sal, Sal Nas, Big Sally Nas was a bad guy. Not the worst, but bad enough to have three nicknames, any of which would make you piss your pants if it has a reason to.

If you were stupid enough to do business with him and reneged on the deal in any way or maybe you were coerced into a limited partnership type dealing could not produce to his satisfaction then either way you lose.

Frankie had to admit that if he knew then what he knows now, maybe some things would be different. Frankie was wise for sure, but he was not connected. Would it make a difference? Who knows, but he was certain that each new footstep had better land square.

Peter and Little Sal were both twenty-two years old, twins not identical, and were not married. They were still living at home, worked the yard in Elizabeth doing whatever they wanted to do unless Daddy said different. My guess is they were the pressure valves set in red that made it all go good on the Nasorosso end.

Frankie heard that Big Sal had semi-retired when the twins passed the score mark. Big Sal went to the yard when shit was flying from the fan blades which was often enough to annoy him.

Jackie N was not in favor of this arrangement as he thought it counted backwards. Jackie, with only twin girls to move his pieces for him, did not have the luxury of a semi deal as his girls and their mother Big Ruby, an old Fan Dancer from high hat Manhattan, was a constant drain on his resources.

The girls were pretty and their mother was still worth the price of admission, but his retirement account was more like flushed down the toilet than flush with assets.

Sophia didn't see much of her Uncle Jackie, not since the boys took over the yard, but she did get together occasionally with her cousins, also twenty-two born only two days after Peter and Little Sal, Jr., not married, and living at home as well.

Tiffany and Ruby junior are big time, mid-Jersey man-eaters with a taste for junk and joint. Jackie, very aware that his daughters were smack addicts and cock suckers, did his best to dissuade contact with the low element his daughters found so alluring. But what's a poor junior crime boss to do, a role model he wasn't.

"They were so innocent when they were kids, the nuns, they did their best, but the cock pull was too strong in those two and the drugs? I don't know where the fuck that came from." Said Jackie N, to anybody who cared to listen.

Sal Nasorosso and Jackie N do not sell drugs, gambling, skin, money lending, straight theft, highjack, traditional strong-arm goon shit, yeah, but drugs no.

Jackie used to handle the packets up in Harlem back during the Jazz age. Where from his home in Elizabeth he would drive twenty miles or so to the George Washington Bridge, fairly new at the time, and over to the musicians hoping to find their groove inside of a syringe, but he dropped the route when the Stock market crash of 1929 finally made its way uptown.

Jackie and Sal then established a beer and gin transit operation through a deal worked out with an Ex-Newark beer boss down on his luck. All arrangements made peering through the bars of a Prison cell in Rahway.

Jackie and Sal moved booze, a lot of booze, so much so that they needed help with the heavy lifting.

They began pulling worthy types from their bunks three decks down in Port Elizabeth, Port Newark and even the Sardine eaters anchored at Perth Amboy.

CHAPTER 12

Two o'clock by the stone dead guy, Pauley the Fish stood fast waiting for the Ok to feed.

Frankie walking, sees Pauley and acknowledges him with a jut of his chin and with it points to the door of the bar and grill.

Two seats empty in the backroom, Pauley took the chair facing the entrance easily observed through the open division between the dining room and the tap room.

Frankie sat opposite Pauley partially obscuring his view of the door.

"Why don't you sit over there?" Said Pauley pointing with his index finger to the chair placed diagonal from his own.

"Why?" Said Frankie somewhat confused.

"I like to watch the comings and goings." Said Pauley bemused.

"ok." Said Frankie with a shrug.

Bar and Grill, that's what the sign says, cherry stained plywood walls, cracked linoleum under foot, pictures of half-naked beer pushers on hangers around them, a sawdust sprinkled shuffleboard table, and a free standing jukebox playing too white.

Pauley waved a finger at the waitress busing a table near the bar, she stacked a half-dozen empty glasses on to a tray, wiped her hands on an apron showing too much of what's for lunch, took a couple of steps toward their table leaving the tray and gave them a, "What will you have?" with a wink to Pauley who smiled. "Beer for me," he nods at Frankie, who nods back.

"Two Beers and give me the special."

Frankie, he nods again.

"We'll have Two beers, two specials, and for me sweetheart, you on a plate." Said Pauley, with a wink back. "No substitutions," She said, and turned toward the kitchen, a half-door, left of the jukebox, grabbed the tray stacked with glasses and wiggled her ass away.

"Not much coming, but man she goes, don't she?" Pauley said in a low voice not loud enough for the hair net to hear him.

"Let's get to the point." Said Pauley.

Frankie braces, after his conversation on the beach with Sophia the day before he suspected his chance meeting with Pauley the fish was no accident.

"Sophia," Pauley paused, " is not somebody you want to fuck around with."

"I don't follow you." Frankie said, tipping nothing.

"Sophia," another pause, "is the daughter of somebody you don't want to fuck around with." Said Pauley, a shade darker on the fuck this time.

"Pauley," Frankie pauses, "I still don't follow, are you telling me to blow."

"I guess I am." Said Pauley.

"But why?" Said Frankie, doe eyed.

The waitress, returned with their beers, and a promise to come back soon with the specials.

Frankie wondered for half a second what the special was, but he, didn't ask, the less he knew the better.

"You ever heard of a guy named Salvatore Nasorosso?" Said Pauley.

"Sophia mentioned him to me yesterday, he is her father." Frankie said, trying to sound unimpressed.

"The name, it don't mean nothing to you?" Said Pauley.

"I never met the guy, why should it?" Frankie said.

"You playing it dumb for a reason, or are you just trying to piss me off?" Said Pauley.

"Come on Pauley, I know who he is, but why the heat. I didn't know who she was when I met her, and now that I do, am I supposed to run away?" Said Frankie, with a vinegar tinge in his voice.

The food came, it was some kind of a meat, with a syrupy kind of brown gravy on the top, and mashed potatoes with corn niblets on the side, maybe it was meatloaf, or pot roast. It didn't matter.

They didn't talk while they ate, but after a burp and two more beers, the conversation was resumed.

"You know who Big Sal is, and you are not scared?" Said Pauley.

"I'm no coward, but I have to admit my nerves are running up some." Said Frankie.

"They should be, if Big Sal knew what you was doing with his daughter, he would not be pleased." Said Pauley.

"I have not done anything with her." Said Frankie, slight anger in his voice. "

"You not trying to fuck her?" Said Pauley.

"Jesus, Pauley, why do you have to talk about her like that. I told you once already I don't like that kind of talk, not about Sophia." Said Frankie, his face going tight.

Pauley smiled, "Take it easy, Frankie, I don't mean nothing. I love the kid like a sister, I know her since she was six years old."

"So why are you pushing my buttons." Said Frankie, more composed, the vein in his neck shrinking, and the blood leaving his face.

"I got to find out things." Said Pauley.

"What things?" Said Frankie.

"I got to find out if you just trying to do stuff with her, or if you are really sweet on the kid." Said Pauley.

"Why didn't you just ask me, you jerk?" Said Frankie.

The waitress came back, trying to bump up a few coins.

"Can I get you two bums anything else,

"I go off shift in five minutes." Said the waitress.

"You go off shift now." Said Pauley, rising from his seat, pulling the apron from around her waist, throwing it across the room, and manhandling her, in a familiar way, a step closer to the door.

"What about the check?" Said the waitress.

"The kid will get it, won't you kid?" Said Pauley, ripping the paper scrap from her fingers and tossing it down in front of Frankie.

"Sure Pauley, but, is that it?" Said Frankie.

"For now kid. Don't worry, you did good." Said Pauley, pushing a distended pinstripe into the waitress's ass, which only made her giggle.

"What about my tip?" Said the waitress.

"Forget the tip, I'll give you the whole thing." Said Pauley, with a crooked lip.

"I'd rather have the money." She said.

"She thinks she is funny." Said Pauley, making a fist and holding it up to her face.

She kissed one of his knuckles.

"Tomorrow, we meet here at two o'clock, Ok?" Said Pauley, looking in Frankie's direction.

"Sure thing Pauley." said. Frankie

"Say good-by to Sylvia." Said Pauley.

"Who is Sylvia?" Said Frankie.

"She is." Said Pauley, pointing to the waitress, who smiled, and gave a wave.

"Do you two know each other?" Said Frankie.

"Funny, that makes two of you." Said Pauley, making another fist and holding it near Frankie's face. He kissed it too.

"Jesus Christ," said Pauley crossing himself. "Madonna!"

He pulled Sylvia outside through the door and that was it.

"What the hell?" Said Frankie to himself. "Now what?"

Frankie had planned to meet Sophia at the beach, should he beg off? Frankie will do whatever he has to, if it means spending time with her, he didn't cancel.

CHAPTER 13

Frankie and Sophia planned to meet at six o'clock beneath the Frozen Custard sign on the boardwalk next to the miniature golf course. But Sophia did not show up at six, and she did not show up at six-fifteen, or six-thirty.

Frankie took this to be a bad sign, as he had caught sight of Pauley entering the Pastry shop when he rode by on his bicycle.

Frankie padlocked his rental to the chain links next to the seventh hole, a giant clowns face, and took a seat on the nearest bench and waited. At six-forty five he shrugged, and lifted himself off the slats.

Frankie stared at the blinking red nose of the clowns face for a minute, pulled a single key from his pocket, and turned to the bike.

He was slipping the key into the padlock when he heard, "Frankie," through the sea breeze and steady wash of the waves nearby.

Sophia gave a small wave with her hand when she realized that Frankie had heard her call, and hurried to reach him.

Sophia, suddenly aware Frankie was watching her walk to him, flushed up around the cheeks, but held it together until she reached his side.

Sophia apologized to Frankie for being late, touched his hand, tipped up her toes, and gave him a kiss on the lips.

Frankie put the key in his pocket, and took Sophia by the arm and led her to the beach.

Frankie handed Sophia to the sand, his arm, extended, balanced as they set. Folding, cross-legged, into her, his arm easily found its way around her waist.

Windswept and soft as ash, the sand, bleached white, and grooved deep, made sitting easy and comfortable.

The Sun in full decline would disappear within the hour. The tide, more in than out, traced and erased its path. When the sun set, the water would rise to meet their feet.

"This is nice," Frankie thought, "but, is it smart? Am I just asking for it?" "It," being whatever avvitato e pazzo mob shit, he was walking into.

"Can I ask you something?" Said Frankie into the side of her head.

"Of course anything" Said Sophia, a ginger draw into neutral, looking into his face.

"I noticed Pauley going into the pastry shop when I passed by on the bicycle, but I didn't see him leave."

Frankie hesitated allowing Sophia to pipe up and flutter.

"Do you know Pauley?" "I just met him, but yeah, I know him." Said Frankie.

"It's funny." She said, "Pauley, my Grandmother, my Aunt Sophia, it's her I'm named after, and my Aunt Connie who operates the cash register went into the back room together and closed the door."

"I could hear them talking, but I couldn't make out what they were saying. Half an hour later Aunt Sophia sticks her head out from behind the door, tells me to go have a good time, and to say hello to the nice boy who cried when he had his fortune told." Said Sophia.

"Frankie? Did you really cry when my Aunt Sophia told you your fortune?" Said Sophia.

"No comment," said Frankie, cringing.

"You did, didn't you?" Said Sophia.

Frankie lowered his head, and thought about his shoelaces, but said nothing.

Sophia lifted Frankie's chin with a feather light touch, turned it to her own.

Before him was a warm butter ascent into parted lips a mere breath space away. Frankie, nine clouds away, banging doors and pulling latches, "Open the door Rapture, I know you're in there, you rat bastard!"

Sophia pulled air, paused, called Frankie a, "Pussy," and pushed him to the sand.

Sophia, stilted, stumbling, her bare feet sinking into the sand, made a move toward the water now closer to them then than it was before.

Frankie, with Sophia's wrist in his hand pulled her on top of him; her blush was cherry deep, and her laugh flypaper.

"What did you call me?" Frankie said, assaulting all unobstructed tickle spot, pecking salty tears as they rolled to giggles.

"You heard me, Sissy boy." Said Sophia, upper handed and nearly spent, fell to honey instinct. Catching kisses until her lips, warm, moist, and open pressed hard into Frankie's.

A few moments were lost and later found in the gutter when Sophia's flying elbows reminded Frankie that she, isn't, and probably wouldn't, so he shouldn't even try.

Frankie leaned into Sophia's kiss, and held her to his chest. She weighed less than air, a sock on his foot, a glove on his hand, a fit so snug and comfort filled, his thoughts weighed more. Frankie turned his body and with Sophia still in his arms landed in the sand a paper slice away.

The spell held, until cool late Summer Sea made a play for their toes. Darkness, marked their faces as shadows went long over the sand.

"I should go, it's getting late, and my grandmother will worry if I stay out too long." Sophia didn't move an inch; her words tailed off low to the ground and muffled.

Sophia put her hand to her mouth as if to prevent any new offense from leaving her lips.

Frankie would let her go, he had had about as much joy as a man, not accustomed, can stomach in one day.

"Tomorrow, same time, by the clowns face, and bring some candy with you, it will give me something to look forward to." Said Frankie, waiting to be slapped, he wasn't disappointed.

"My grandmother cooks enough for an army, why don't you come by for lunch? " Sophia offered. Frankie was about to say yes, when he remembered his date with Pauley the Fish for two o'clock eats.

"I am meeting Pauley the Fish at two, so " Said Frankie, before getting cut mid sentence by a snort.

"Pauley the What?" Sophia chortled.

"Fish?" Said Frankie,

"What, how, why do you call him Pauley the Fish?"

"It's a long story." Said Frankie, not wanting to tip out, but willing to dribble.

"Tell me now." Sophia demanded.

"It's late, and you don't want to worry your grandmother, and" Frankie was cut down again, no piggy noise this time, a finger, ramrod stiff and quivering. "Tell me." Said Sophia.

"Tomorrow, it will give you something to look forward to."

CHAPTER 14

Pauley, early, was standing just inside an alley to the right of the Bar and Grill. He stepped from the gap when Frankie stepped down from the curb across the street. Frankie gave a "Hey" to Pauley who tipped his chin, made steps to the door and held it open for Frankie who went in.

In from sun, black was all Frankie could see when he entered the under lit greasy spoon. Blinded and with unsteady feet Frankie accidentally touched the cap of one patron, and the nose of another.

"I saw you going into the Pastry shop yesterday, what gives?" Frankie said rather quickly as he and Pauley took their seats in the dining room. Frankie kicked up some linoleum with the front right leg of his chair.

"So how was your fucking day?" Pauley, adjusting his trousers, and making himself comfortable, said with an unappreciated air, and a tossed up palm.

Frankie, getting the drift and going along, said, "Fine, and yours?" "Peachy" said Pauley.

Pauley, again facing the door, and the bar, sees Sylvia sitting, her great ass making use of every inch of the bar stool, and then some.

"Sylvia, two beers, will you honey." Sylvia, raising ham, hops to her feet, leans over the bar top, a full moon rising, and fills two tall glasses with suds, pockets the receipts she was counting before the summons was served, and carries two beers to the back room.

"Hey Sweetie," Said Sylvia to Pauley, as she put a coaster under each glass, and her ass into his lap.

"Hi" Sylvia said to Frankie, warm and friendly, then turning her face into Pauley, who smacked it, loud, his lips sucking the skin off her face, almost.

Sylvia whispered something into Pauley's ear that made his face turn beet red. Frankie feeling neglected coughed. Pauley, peeking through Sylvia's bouffant, winked at Frankie who raised an eye, and looked at the space on his arm where a watch would be, if he had one. Pauley patted Sylvia on the hip, and sent her to the kitchen.

"Two specials?" Said Frankie.

"Yeah" said Pauley.

"You in a hurry?" Said Pauley not annoyed, but curious.

"No, Not really" said Frankie.

"Good," said Pauley, "because we got things to talk about."

"I figured as much." Said Frankie. "I seen that you saw me yesterday. I waved, but you was gone down the boardwalk, and was parking at the clown face with your back to me, so I went inside." Said Pauley.

"When Sophia didn't show, and you didn't come out, I was hitting the road. Then Sophia hailed me from the shop. What's going on Pauley?"

Sylvia came back with the food, two plates of loose meat on a Kaiser roll, she called it a sloppy Joe.

"Did somebody take an axe to the meatloaf?" Said Pauley. "What is this shit?"

"Try it." Said Sylvia, trying to sound positive.

"Is it too hard to make a fucking meatball, or one of them Salisbury steaks? What did this meat do that was so terrible that you had to whack it?"

Frankie and Sylvia were holding their breaths until Pauley took a bite of his sandwich.

"Not too bad" said Pauley. "Could use some oregano."

Sylvia, relieved. "Italians!" She said.

"Sally Nas wishes to make your acquaintance, tomorrow." Said Pauley, taking another bite from his sandwich.

"He wants to meet me?" Said Frankie.

"Are you deaf? Tomorrow" Said Pauley, his mouth losing its fight to contain the loose meat.

"Where?" Said Frankie. Pauley held up his hand, chewed until he swallowed, and then after wiping his mouth, replied, "Linden."

"New Jersey?" Frankie said.

"No, Linden fucking Idaho, where do you think?"

"How do I get there, all I have a return ticket to Jersey City?" Said Frankie.

"I am going to take you." Said Pauley.

"In your car?" Said Frankie.

"No, I am going to carry you on my back, sei un idiota." Said Pauley, laughing. "Why don't you peddle there, with me on the handle bars?"

"You are too funny, you know that?" Said Frankie, ready to smack him one time in the kisser.

"It's a gift." Said Pauley, now calm enough to finish with the instructions.

Pauley, looking at a notepad lifted from his jacket breast pocket, reads, "Ten o'clock, pick the kid up at his room. Eleven o'clock, the kid sees the boss. Twelve o'clock take the kid's body to the river. Twelve-fifteen throw it in. Twelve-thirty eat lunch."

"Come on Pauley, you're killing me" said Frankie. "Not yet, twelve o'clock tomorrow" said Pauley, looking at his notebook and laughing.

"Shut up, will you? I am nervous enough without you making jokes every two minutes." Said Frankie.

"Who's joking?" Said Pauley, enjoying himself.

"What happens after that, do I come back here, or what?" Said Frankie.

"I take you home." Said Pauley, noticing that Frankie had not touched his food.

"You going to eat that?" Said Pauley, pointing to the greasy mess on Frankie's plate"

"You want it?" Said Frankie, surprised.

"It grows on you, what can I tell you." Said Pauley, reaching across the table, spilling the salt as he lifted the plate to the spot recently vacated by his empty platter, pushed to the side with an elbow.

"Home?" Frankie had to say it twice before Pauley heard him. "To Jersey City?"

"Yeah, so?" Said Pauley, filling his face, round two. "Why can't I come back here?" Said Pauley.

"Because" Said Pauley, lost in the meat.

"Because? " Said Frankie, annoyed, still trying to get a straight answer. "Because why?"

"Because I say so, that's why." Said Pauley.

Frankie finished his beer, called to Sylvia's ass, facing him. The back door was open to the alley, Sylvia stood facing out, her right hand with fingers stretched was poking in and out of her hair as if to somehow make it stand higher on her head which would have been impossible or so Frankie thought.

Sylvia turned and faced Frankie. "He liked it?" Said Sylvia, taking the empty plates into her hands and shaking her head.

"Anything else for you, Sweetie?"

"Two more beers?" Said Frankie. She lined her arms with plates and left.

"I could really go for another beer." Said Pauley, thoughtless, his meat gone, instincts awakened.

"On it's way." Said Frankie.

"That's Good" said Pauley.

The beers came, and Pauley downed his; Frankie sipped, and wondered what was in store for him. Frankie had never met the big time, he never wanted to, he had always been content to deal in small bills.

"Pauley, you know I didn't do nothing to her."

"Who?" Said Pauley.

"Sophia, who else?" "

"I know that. Believe me, if this was your last meal, I would have done better for you than a loose meat sandwich, so Relax."

Pauley his stomach filled turned his attention to the waitress. Sylvia feeling horns, made ready to leave. She removed her apron, and made again with the fluff and flatten, fixed her face and sat, waiting for the call from Pauley.

"What's he like?" Said Frankie.

"Who?" Said Pauley, looking at Sylvia, licking his lips, and leering.

"Salvatore Nasorosso." said Frankie, deadpan serious.

"We got about a forty-five minute ride tomorrow, ask me then, and I will tell you, but now I got business to take care of, if you know what I mean." Said Pauley.

"Sylvia, come over here, will you baby."

Pauley was feeling good, feeling sexy.

"Pauley, pay the man, will you? The check yesterday almost broke me." Said Frankie.

"You paid that thing?" Said Pauley with a chuckle.

"You told me to, didn't you?"

"Kid, this is one of the Sal's joints, we don't pay no check here. You take the thing to the bar and stick on that ice pick." Said Pauley pointing to a spot next to the cash register on the edge of the bar near the kitchen. "It was a figure of speech. I thought you was wise." Said Pauley. "Stay here."

Pauley got up from the table, passing Sylvia on his way to the kitchen, he patted her ass, and then closing both halves of the door, top and bottom, he disappeared into the kitchen.

The sound of pots falling, and dishes breaking, was loud enough to raise heads, and eyebrows.

Pauley left the kitchen, taking the bottom door off the hinges with his foot when it didn't open after he palmed it.

Sylvia tucked an elbow, and latched on to Pauley when he went by with speed. Pauley tossed a buck and change to the tabletop, and said, "Tomorrow, ten o'clock," Pauley shot a finger, and left. Frankie pocketed the dough and walked out.

CHAPTER 15

Frankie got to the clowns face just as Sophia planted her ass onto the bench. He gave her a kiss, a squeeze, and some bottom lip. Frankie pouting, was leaving the next day, and did not like the idea very much. Not hiding his disappointment, he made a Boo face.

Sophia knew that Frankie was going home, but not before he meets with her father. She talked to Pauley a half-hour earlier, was filled in, and brought up to speed.

Sophia didn't envy Frankie, she knew her father, and she knew he could be a tough character, when he wanted to be.

"We don't have much time, in a couple of hours the tide will be in, and I will have to go inside for the night, so let's get to it." Said Sophia.

Frankie startled by her tone, was willing to be led.

They reached the sand, sat quickly, and, got to it.

"When you speak to my father look him straight in the eyes, but don't blink too much, it annoys him. And don't touch your face when you talk, he thinks people who touch their face when they talk are lying." Started Sophia.

"Don't call him anything, except Mr. Nasorosso, don't shuffle your feet, and don't ever look at his feet. You got it!" Sophia rattled off.

The panic in her voice made Frankie squirm, but the mention of Big Sal's feet made him laugh nervously, more to himself, but loud enough for Sophia to hear.

"Are you laughing at me?" Said Sophia, perturbed. "No," Said Frankie, envisioning every possible foot abnormality, but not getting passed corns, and hammer toe, before Sophia tapped him hard on the forehead.

"Hey!" Said Frankie, rubbing his brow.

"His feet?" Said Frankie, "What's wrong with his feet?"

"They are small, very small, size seven, but he wears a size eleven shoe, and stuffs newspaper in the toes." Said Sophia.

"Why are you telling me this? If I didn't know about his feet, I would never think to look at them, but now, how can I not look at them. What are you trying to do to me?"

Frankie grabbed his face with both hands, and shook his head. He was playing with her, going light trying not to work himself up.

"Are you worried about me, or that I might embarrass you?" Said Frankie.

"Yes," said Sophia.

"Which one?" Said Frankie.

"Both," said Sophia.

Sophia was no babe in the woods, and Frankie, was glad.

"You know what your father does for a living?" Said Frankie.

"Do I look stupid to you?" Said Sophia, pistons picking up, steam building. "I wasn't kept in a box you know, I can read a newspaper." Sophia said derisively. "I read what they print about my father, and my brothers." Sophia breathed deep and kept going.

"I know that my Uncle Jackie runs the Elizabeth operation and that my Father oversees the Linden shop." Sophia continued.

"I know my Father, Salvatore Nasorosso, also known as Big Sal, Sal Nas, and Big Sally Nas, is not a very nice person, and far from honest. He makes his living in the gray spaces and I deal with it. But he is good to me, and generous to my brothers, who are no Einstein and Oppenheimer, believe me."

"Ein who, and Oppen what?" Said Frankie.

"Never mind." Said Sophia.

"I don't give a damn what your father does for a living, and I don't care what the newspapers say, but I do care about what he thinks about me." Said Frankie, piping up, ready to stick it out.

"Why do you care what my father thinks about you?" Said Sophia, with her gun loaded, she shoots.

"Because I care about his daughter." Said Frankie, trembling a little bit.

"Do you really care for me Frankie?" Said Sophia, pulling back the hammer for another shot.

"Very much so," said Frankie.

"Do you love me Frankie, or do you just want to have sex with me?" Bang!

"What the, where the, how did we get to this place. Damn their eyes, those fucking nuns, or was it her cock crazy cousins?" Thought Frankie so loud in his head that he was sure that Sophia could hear it.

"I, we only just met a few days ago, but I, well, I would be nuts if, I guess I do." Said Frankie.

"Do you guess that you love me, or do you guess, that you want to fuck me." Said Sophia.

"Don't say fuck." Said Frankie, never having heard that word from the mouth of a woman who didn't come with a price tag.

"So, you don't want to fuck me?" said Sophia.

"Of course I want to fuck you." Said Frankie, falling deeper, unable to stop the tumble, not knowing how to stop talking.

"I knew it, you don't love me at all, you just want to ruin me, make me worthless, take away the only thing I have to offer to any number of good looking, decent, young men that may wish to marry me one day." Sophia cried.

Every time I tell this story I can't help but feel that Sophia's speech sounds a little practiced? Almost as if Sophia was the witness for the prosecution, the day after giving a deposition.

"Sophia, please don't cry, I never meant to hurt your feelings, or give you the wrong idea about my intentions." Said Frankie, trying to soothe Sophia, to ease her suffering. In other words, he was trying to shut her the fuck up.

"What are your intentions then?" Said Sophia.

"I love you." He said, defeated, yet relieved.

"I love you too."

Sophia cried, happy tears, for about two-seconds.

"You still can't fuck me." She said. "Not until you marry me."

"Are we getting married?" Said Frankie.

"We are." Said Sophia.

"But, you don't know who I am, or where I come from, not really." Said Frankie.

"You had better get to it then, we don't have all night." Said Sophia.

Frankie would begin at the beginning.

His Mother, the lush, his Father, the whore loving chocolate maker, his Grandfather, the pig wielding, olive growing Don, his uneventful tour of duty in the Army, he would tell her everything, but not yet.

Frankie paused long enough for the subject to change, thankfully it did.

"What time is Pauley picking you up tomorrow?" Said Sophia.

"Ten o'clock," said Frankie.

"Meet me at the Pastry shop at nine." She said.

"Why?" Said Frankie.

"Just do it, I'll explain in the morning, trust me." Said Sophia,

"Now kiss me, and tell me you love me."

Frankie put his arms around Sophia, her waist was thin, so he pulled up slack, and kissed her, hard at first, then soft.

Frankie was in love with Sophia, he hadn't known that he was, he had suspected that he might be, but he didn't know for sure, until she told him he was.

"I love you." Said Frankie.

"Are you sure that you just don't want to fuck my brains out?" Said Sophia.

"That too," said Frankie, "but not exclusively." He added quickly.

"So, who else do you want to fuck?" She said, squinting, and making a fist.

"I don't mean I want to fuck anyone else, I only meant, shut up." Frankie kissed her again.

"Now, if she can ride a horse half as well as she calls the race." He mused.

CHAPTER 16

Frankie was still tossing and turning in his bed when the sun came up. He had given up trying to sleep, and dragged himself out of the bed.

Frankie took a bath, shaved his face, splashed on some Florida water, packed up his clothes, and pulled the knob long before his neighbors stirred.

He left the key to his room in a box marked keys on the front desk, returned the rental to the bike shop leaving it in the rack near the entrance, cashed in his return ticket at the train station, and still had time to grab a Kaiser roll with butter and a coffee from the lunch counter at the drug store, open early for the men and women that worked on the boardwalk.

At nine o'clock, Frankie was standing at the door to the pastry shop, ready to turn the knob, when the venetian blind went up the door opened.

Sophia, with a pull string in her hand, looked happy enough to see him. She smiled big, and pulled him inside.

Frankie and Sophia were alone, they kissed as soon as she turned the key in the latch.

"Good morning," he tried, with a mouth full of lips. Frankie reluctantly pulled away, He was eager to find out why he was standing there, and not curled up in a fetal position someplace, biting his fingernails.

"Right on time." Said Sophia.

"If nothing else?" Said Frankie.

"Do you see that box," Said Sophia, pointing to a brightly wrapped, red ribbon tied parcel atop the counter beside him.

Frankie nodded.

"Take it with you, and give it to my Father." Said Sophia.

"What's in it?" Said Frankie.

"Candy, you idiot." Said Sophia.

"I guessed as much, but why the sweets?" Frankie said.

"These are his favorite," Said Sophia, picking up the box, and holding it up between them. "My father loves these. They are chocolate, hazelnut, Caramel Clusters."

"They, my Grandmother, and my aunts will not let him have any at home, so here is your invitation. Give him these." Sophia picked up the box, and placed it onto the counter closest to her. "And then we'll see how it goes from there." Said Sophia

"Chocolates? My life hangs in the balance, and you want me to give your Father a cavity." Said Frankie, hopeless, wilted.

"Such drama, you should be on the stage." Said Sophia.

"Give him the box," Sophia was pointing to the counter. "trust me."

"That's two times you told me to trust you, what are you selling, confidence, or used cars?" Said Frankie.

"How old are you?" Sophia wanted to know.

"Twenty-one, Why do you ask?"

"No reason," said Sophia.

"Too old?" Said Frankie.

"No, not at all," Sophia tossed off.

"When will you be twenty-two?"

"February the 13th," said Frankie. "Where are you going with this?"

"Nowhere in particular," said Sophia. "These are things I should know about you." Making a mental note of the date, pursing her lips, and looking up into the corner of her eye.

"What is your Mother's name?" Said Sophia.

"More questions?" Said Frankie.

"Just a few," said Sophia.

"How many is a few?" Said Frankie.

"A couple," said Sophia.

"I forgot the question." Said Frankie.

"What is your Mother's name?" Said Sophia, volume up. "She has had many names, mephistopheles, Satan, the beast," Said Frankie. "But she will answer to anything that ends with, can I buy you a drink?" Said Frankie.

"No, really," Sophia was pleading. "What's her name?" "Well, Baby, was popular for a while, and then Sweetheart, but now I think, Can't you do anything about that smell, is what she answers to." Said Frankie, with a shrug.

"I don't know what that means, but I can tell that it isn't very nice." Said Sophia.

"Frankie, please tell me what your Mother's name is." Said Sophia, weary.

"Maria," said Frankie. "Will that be all, miss?" "No," said Sophia.

Frankie sighed, and looked at his wrist. "Gee, look at the time. I should go."

"Frankie, you are not wearing a watch." Said Sophia.

"I really should go and buy a watch, don't you think?" Said Frankie.

"Frankie?" Said Sophia.

"Yes," Said Frankie, mud stuck, and staring.

"What is your Father's name?"

"My real father, or the guy my Mother came over on the boat with?" Said Frankie.

"Frankie, please no more teasing," Said Sophia, going long on the, please. "The man from the boat, what is his name, did he raise you?"

"His name is Michael Migliori, he lives in Hoboken, makes chocolate, or he did, and has been living with a woman named Sally for as long as I can remember, and no he didn't raise me."

"Your real father, who is he, do you know?" Said Sophia, direct, and wanting.

" No," said Frankie. "A migrant picker, farm worker, I never asked."

"Why didn't you?" Said Sophia, pushing. "I don't know why, maybe it wasn't something I needed to know." Said Frankie. "Maybe it's not something I want to know."

"I would want to know who my Father is." Said Sophia. "Can you, I mean, is there a way that we can find out?"

"Who my real father is?" Said Frankie incredulous.

"Yes," Sophia said. " My Father will need to know."

"Need?" Frankie thought.

"My Mother, Maria, was born in Sicily, her father, Don Gianni Nazione, was the boss of a small farming community, and her Mother, also named Maria died giving birth to her."

"Michael Migliori, the person I know to be my father, also Sicilian, was forced at gunpoint, to marry a woman, carrying another man's baby."

"Maria and Michael were packed up, and shipped off to the land of the free, handcuffed, for the time being, by their marriage pledge." Frankie paused. He realized that it made him uncomfortable to talk about his family.

"Their vows, written on the back of a matchbook cover, went up in flames before the boat left the dock."

"Michael set up house, but never settled. Another child was born, Camellia, again not Michael's. He left to find better, but he found Sally instead. Sally is a whore." Said Frankie.

Surprisingly, Sophia didn't run screaming into the street. She didn't give him the crossed eyes, or yell cooties while scraping her tongue with a sharp rock.

"Is that the best you can do?" She said.

"The Nuns might not approve," said Frankie.

"The Nuns can pray for us, and they will, if they know what's good for them. And if they want the new roof Daddy promised them, and the new tile floor in the rectory, and the new Buick for fat, old, Sister Mary Margaret," Sophia paused for a breath.

Sophia suddenly realized that having to list the many ways her father pays, and will keep on paying for his sins had become tiresome and felt hypocritical.

"I get the idea." Frankie cut, "Your Father is a heavy supporter of Catholic charities."

"If you mean paying off the church to look the other way at his many indiscretions then you are not kidding." Sophia sighed and was finished.

Frankie kissed Sophia on the mouth, and went for the door handle, but it didn't move, he forgot about the latch.

"Let me do that." Said Sophia, putting one hand on his arm, and the other to the latch.

"These ought to do the trick." Sophia had taken the chocolates from the counter, and held them up to Frankie.

He took the box from her hand, closed his fingers around it, careful not to damage the look, and shook it lightly, listening with his ear close to the sound of the candy moving around inside.

"If these were dice instead of chocolates I might have a shot at this thing." Said Frankie with a mournful tone in his voice.

"Don't look so sad it's not the end of the world." Said Sophia smiling.

"Thats what you think." Said Frankie.

"Buona fortuna amore mio" Said Sophia.

"Grazie bella." Said Frankie in return.

CHAPTER 17

Frankie ran back to the hotel, sat on the front steps, two up from the sidewalk flatfooted. He had time to pose for a moment before all hell broke loose from the horn of Pauley the Fish's blue Cadillac.

Frankie jumped to his feet, and Pauley reached across the bench, flipped up the handle, the door opened, and Frankie got in.

"Nice car Pauley, is it yours?" Said Frankie.

"Sure its mine, what do you think."

"Like I said, nice." Said Frankie.

"What do you drive, besides the young girls crazy?" Said Pauley, laughing at his joke.

"Sei pazzo Pauley." Said Frankie.

" Crazy Me? I don't have a pussy. I'm safe from your charms." Said Pauley still laughing.

"So Are you ready to meet the boss?" Said Pauley, suddenly serious.

"Ready?" Said Frankie.

"Yeah, didn't Sophia tell you things, like the whats and not whats." Said Pauley.

"The do's and don'ts?" Said Frankie.

"That's what I said." Said Pauley.

"She told me." Said Frankie.

"The foot thing?" Pauley whispered.

"What?" Said Frankie whispering back at Pauley.

"The foot thing, did she tell you about the foot thing." Said Pauley, louder this time, agitated.

"She did, but I don't get it, what's the big deal, so he stuffs his shoes, so what. Some guys roll a sock, other guys lift, more of them comb over then what should, so who cares if the Boss wears his feet long." Said Frankie.

"You ever seen a clown, with the big feet, well the boss looks like that, only he don't wear the fake nose, believe me he don't have to." Said Pauley.

"What's wrong with his nose, Sophia didn't say anything about his nose?" Said Frankie.

"Too many glasses of the grape," said Pauley.

"What does that mean, he drinks too much?" Said Frankie.

"Like a trout." Said Pauley.

"And the nose?" Said Frankie.

"Like a tomato." Said Pauley.

"Good to know." Said Frankie.

"Yeah," said Pauley.

The drive from Long Branch to Linden was about an hour, give or take, depending on the traffic, moving, or not moving up Route 9 north.

On the way Frankie and Pauley were delayed by a stalled car and a fender bender, so they decided to stop for coffee and a cruller at a roadside joint near Perth Amboy.

A 40's style dining car with a row of spinners, the grill up front, table top nickel juke boxes, and booths lining the windows.

Pauley parked the Cadillac facing up road, and almost tripped himself up getting out of the car trying to avoid a puddle of muddy water on the driver's side

"Fuck," Said Pauley. "Fuck." Said Pauley again.

Pauley got out of the Cadillac tip toeing around the puddle. Frankie followed close to Pauley until the handle to the diner was pulled.

Pauley held the door open for Frankie, who went through first. "Are we going to be late Pauley?" Said Frankie, taking a seat at the counter, and turning to Pauley, who had taken a booth facing the door, and the pie rack.

"Nah, the Boss, he never wakes up before noon, unless he has to, and you don't rate, so we would be waiting anyway." Said Pauley.

"Get off of that ledge and sit down, like a civilized person." Said Pauley, motioning to the seat opposite his.

Frankie stepped down from the ledge and slid into the seat opposite Pauley.

Ten minutes passed and Pauley was going down for the third crueler, and licking his finger tips.

"You going to finish that?" Said Pauley, pointing to the half-eaten pastry in front of Frankie.

"No, you go ahead, knock yourself out." Said Frankie.

"You want me to order you another crueler, maybe they have some hidden somewhere, you know, for everybody else?" Said Frankie, with a smile.

"I only had three, yours don't count. The thing had a piece missing from where you took a bite." Said Pauley.

Pauley finished what was left of his coffee, tossed a fin to the counter top and left.

Pauley, sucking a toothpick, and sliding in from the passenger side, skipping the mud altogether, hit the gas, and with a whiplash snap slammed the pedal down.

Twenty-five minutes later they pulled into a driveway, fenced up, and barbed, and long maybe a hundred feet or more bordering a three door garage.

The door to the far right went up slow, and Pauley pulled in, stopping short of a wall stacked high with tires to the left of a door with its blind pulled down, and a doorbell showing.

Pauley shut down the Cadillac, flipped the keys onto the seat between them, and got out, fixing his pants, and pulling at wrinkles, before slipping on his jacket.

Frankie stepped around the car and followed Pauley to the door, Pauley rang the doorbell two times, and pushed. The door opened easy, no lock, or buzzer.

Twenty-six steps split between two flights of stairs to the top level, a narrow hallway, three doors with a half glass and a transom above each. There were no names painted on the glass, no numbers, or plates. The third door on the left was open,

Frankie and Pauley went inside by the open door.

Pauley pointed to a chair, wooden, no cushion, no style. "sit," said Pauley. And Sit, Frankie, he did, and waited.

Pauley went into an inner office, shutting the door behind him. Frankie could hear voices, but no words.

Five minutes of knocking knees before the door opens and Pauley stepped back into the anteroom.

"Lets go." Said Pauley, tugging at Frankie's elbow.

The room, an office, a desk, two stools, and a folding chair.

Frankie was pointed to the folding chair. Pauley sat on one stool, and a tall, slim, olive skinned gentleman, well dressed in a sharkskin suit sat on the other.

"Frankie?" Said Pauley, "Joey Spoons." "Joey Spoons?" Said Pauley, "Frankie Migliori from Jersey City."

"Glad to know you." Said Joey Spoons.

"The same here," said Frankie.

Joey Spoons was Joseph Cucchiaio, a driver, knuckle man, and stick-pin for Salvatore Nasorosso.

Frankie had heard the name one time before.

The Jew, a dealer in coin, jewels, and buyer of items lost or found, a fixture down neck, Newark. Long before the Portugueses took it away from the Immigrati who were there before them, got stuck by Joey Spoons for not holding without a deposit a gold and ruby ring in lieu of coin. Not yet returned, but soon to be ill gotten.

The Jew sold the ring, and lost a quart of blood to the gutter before the ambulance came to get him. They applied direct pressure to the wound, but the heel of the boot they pressed it with, didn't do it any good.

The white coats were partial to Joey, and Jesus, so they let the Jew bleed a little extra, before they took him to Saint Mary's hospital, where it was suggested that they keep going north, Beth Israel Jewish being six blocks up on the right hand side.

The Jew did not die, and two weeks after he was released from the hospital the boys downtown escorted Joey Spoons to the State Correctional facility at Rahway.

So while Joey sat idly by in his cell the Jew was buying, selling, and making dough.

The Jew sold Joey's ring four more times, before he sent it to Joey, as a sort of peace offering. Unfortunately for the Jew, Joey mistook the olive branch for a slap in the face, and vowed to serve it up cold, but he didn't, the Jew, he came in handy once in a while.

Frankie said nothing, Pauley said nothing, and Joey said, "Thanks for the fish," to Pauley, who said, "Don't mention it."

Joey Spoons was chewing on one of the Swedish fish Pauley had procured from the fat ass at the pastry shop, some three days earlier.

"I got six pounds of the things." Said Pauley, winking at Frankie.

"Was they on sale, or something?" Said Joey Spoons, taking another fish from a sack lying open in his lap.

"You want one of these, Frankie?" Lifting the sack, gash open, red spilling.

"No thanks." Said Frankie.

"Suit yourself." Said Joey Spoons, looking at Pauley, waiting for an answer to his previous question.

"Do you like them?" Said Pauley, turning stiff.

"Yeah I do so what" Said Joey, facing.

"So, why the fuck do you give a fuck what I fucking paid for them." Solid punch to the, fuck, each time he said it. "I gave them to you, that's all you got to know." Said Pauley.

Joey Spoons turned square to Pauley. "Because I know you, you cheap fuck." Said Joey.

Pauley went round in the shoulders. "What the fuck is that supposed to mean?" Said Pauley, not exactly insulted, more annoyed.

"The Cadillac, you buy it, or lift it?" Said Joey.

"Lift" Said Pauley. "So?"

"That suit you wearing, you buy it, or did it fall off a truck somewhere?" Said Joey.

"Truck." Said Pauley, shy like.

"That watch you got on your wrist, you pay a good penny for that fine piece of jewelry, no?" Said Joey, fish in the net, flopping.

"No," Said Pauley, too low for Frankie to hear the first time Pauley said it.

"What was that, I didn't get you?" Said Joey, cupping his ear.

"No," said Pauley. Long on the O, and louder this time.

"How did you come by such a thing, as that timepiece, without having to pay for it," Said Joey, rolling his hands.

"I found it?"

"Is that a question, or you stabbing?" Said Joey.

"I found it." Said Pauley, satisfied.

"You stupid fuck, I was with you when you, found that watch," Joey, making a double scratch in the air with his fingers, when he said, found. "You found that watch on the arm of that guy we put underground two months ago."

"I forgot about that." Said Pauley, laughing small.

"You are not only a cheap fuck, sei Un muto fanculo." Said Joey.

"What the fuck is that supposed to mean?" Said Pauley, Laughing, loud now.

"Whats the matter did you forget how to speak Italian too?" Said Spoons Laughing so hard that he starts choking on a Swedish fish.

Soon Spoons was turning red in the face as the fish was caught in his throat. Luckily Spoons was able to hack up the fish which sent it flying across the room just missing Pauley's face which was beet red from laughing. The red fish hit the floor in front of the door just as it was swinging in.

"What the hell?" The door was laboring. The fish was stuck underneath, and skidding. "What the hell?" The door was shoved in, with enough force to move a cow's ass out of your face, overkill.

"What the fuck is wrong with the door? And what is all the noise about?" Said the bulled nose coming through the entryway.

"Nothing Sally, just a fish what got stuck." Said Joey Spoons.

"What the fuck you mean, a fish, like a sardine or something?" Said Salvatore Nasorosso.

"No Sal, not a real fish, a candy fish, like the ones you eat sometimes, them red ones." Said Joey Spoons.

"Swedish Fish?" Said Salvatore.

"Thats them, you want I should give you some, I got a whole bag what Pauley, he give me." Said Joey, holding open the bag.

"Pauley gave you the fish, thats nice. Pauley, you give Spoons the fish?"

"I did." Said Pauley.

"Thats nice," said Sal. The door was pushed closed, the fish was still stuck.

"This the kid?" Said Sal, pointing to Frankie, who had not said anything in a while.

"Yeah," Said Pauley, getting up from his stool, pulling Frankie up by the armpit.

"Salvatore Nasorosso? Meet Frankie Migliori, from Jersey City." "Sit." Said Sal. Frankie sat, but Pauley stayed upright.

Sal made one revolution, put his hands on his hips, fished his lips, and waited.

Pauley went through to the front room, opened the door to a closet, that Frankie did not remember seeing, with a key, and squeaked his way back into the office.

"Why do them casters still squeak, didn't I tell both of you, one time each, to get some oil on them?" Said Sal to Joey Spoons and Pauley.

Pauley wheeled into the office an old, cordovan dyed leather, executive chair, shiny in spots, cracked in places, and installed it behind the desk.

"I put oil on them things three days ago, but it don't do nothing for the noise, I guess." Said Joey.

"Do you think?" Said Sal, disgusted.

"I don't know why it don't work, I rubbed the oil in real good." Said Joey convinced that he had done good.

Sal sat in the big chair, it made him look small, not a good chair for him. Salvatore Nasorosso was short, five foot nothing, a fireplug in shoes, big shoes, Frankie can't help but look at them, they are freaking longboats.

"What kind of oil did you use?" Said Sal. He leaned back in the chair, and put his feet on the desk, which made the top of his body, the whole upper torso, disappear from sight, leaving those big shoes moving around all by themselves, very creepy.

71

"I put a lot of oil on them, Sal." Said Joey.

"I believe you, but what kind of oil did you use, what type of oil, 3 in one oil, gear oil, what?" Said Sal, with his shoes, making gestures, points, and gaps.

"Olive," Said Joey, mumble, mumble.

"Olive?" Said Sal, his shoes confused, unable to find their place, at a loss, perplexed.

"Yeah," Said Joey, his eyes fixated on the shoes.

"You put fucking olive oil on my chair?"

"The wheels yeah," said Spoons.

A man of few words, Sal Nasorosso let the oil problem go with a, "Fix it," to Pauley, who said, "sure thing."

"Joey, get the fuck out, and Pauley, you shut the door and sit the fuck down." Said Sal.

"I should get the fuck out of the office, or I should get the fuck out of the building?" Said Joey.

"Go sit the fuck outside, and make sure nobody comes in here until I tell you." Said Sal, blood pressure blush in the cheeks.

"Outside the building, or in the other room?" Said Joey.

"Go sit on the fucking Moon you fucking moron." Sal, his shoes pointing like arrows at Joey's face, his voice raised and his small hands, balled tight.

"Get the fuck out of here before I gives you something to make it unnecessary for you to leave at all, you stupid fuck."

Joey Spoons hauled ass, two stepping down the stairs, and slamming out.

Sal sat in his big chair, feet up, and then down, looking across the desk at Frankie, who looked back.

"You got something to say to me?" Said Sal, shooting straight.

Frankie put his hands to his pants, and lifted with both of them the aforementioned gift-wrapped, and ribbon bowed box. The chocolates were in good shape, Frankie took good care of them.

Frankie, box up, a level view, held it out, leaning in to reach middle desk.

"What is this?" Said Sal, softening.

Frankie touched the box down on the desk, and pushed the box, two-finger style to Sal, who took it up into his hands.

"Is this what I think it is?" Said Sal smiling, sly.

Frankie, he made a hush sign.

"I get you." Sal, pulling the ribbon, snapping tape, and flinging paper to the floor.

With the top of the box now open, Sal could easily see the hazelnut clusters there were four good size chunks.

"Sophia, she gives you these to give to me?" Said Sal. "Yes, Mr. Nasorosso Sir, she did." Said Frankie, sitting straight, hands back at his side, and keeping eye contact. "She's a good girl." Said Sal.

"I haven't seen Sophia since before the beginning os summer, how is she doing, how does she look." Said Sal, not to Frankie, but to Pauley.

"The kid is Doing good, looking good, and missing you. She said to make sure that I told you how much." Said Pauley with his arms open wide across his chest.

Sal was choking up, sniffling a couple of times before he could get a hold of himself.

"She's something, that one, not like her brothers who give me the fits." Said Sal looking up. "From Sophia, I get candy, from those two, I get indigestione. I think their brains stopped growing when they were twelve."

"You?" With eyes at Frankie, "You going to give me the fits too?" Said Sal.

"No Sir, not if I can help it." Said Frankie, meaning it.

"So, Frankie Migliori, from Jersey City, what will I do for you, and what are you going to do for me?" Said Sal, suddenly weary.

"Sir?" Said Frankie.

"Why is it that I'm sitting here with you, when I could be home, drinking wine, watching the television, or eating a sandwich? Tell me this." Said Sal.

"I would like to keep company with your daughter, Sir." Said Frankie.

"Keep company?" Said Sal, his lapels ruffled. "How the fuck old are you, Keep Company? You want to fuck around with my little girl, but you say it nice, like I don't know what you mean." Sal was getting hot.

"Do you think I am stupid, do you think I don't know you? I know you, because I was you. You want to fuck my daughter, don't you, Frankie Migliori, from Jersey fucking City? You want to fuck my baby, which I raised alone, her mother dead from the minute she was born. You fuck, you fucking punk." Pauley came between them, he put two hands on Sal, holding him steady.

Frankie, not sure what to do, but staying back, kept it calm. "No Sir, I do not want to have sex your daughter, I want to marry your daughter."

Sal, flat footed again, shoulders his own, Pauley backing away.

"Then why didn't you fucking say that, keeping company, what the fuck does that mean. Non Capisco. Azienda di mantenimento? Do you love Sophia?" Said Sal calming down and his face going soft.

"I do," Said Frankie, now standing to face Sal.

"Do you love her more than fucking life itself, because that is what it will cost you if you hurt my Sophia, you understand what I am saying to you, Capisci?" Said Sal, not blinking once.

"I think I do." Said Frankie. Sal went face to chin with Frankie, about forty degrees, in tight. "You had better." Said Sal.

"Pauley?" Said Sal, backing his ass into the chair. "Go start the Caddie, mine, not yours, and let's go to Mr. Chin's for some Chinese food. See if Spoons is out there somewhere, if he isn't, then fuck him, no Egg Foo Young for him. Five minutes, let me talk to the kid alone, go ahead."

"Five minutes, Spoons, Chinese, good," Pauley gave Frankie a wink, and left the room. Frankie heard the outside door open, then close, Sal's Caddie fire up and then go idle, waiting.

"Frankie?" Said Sal. "How long you know my daughter, a week, maybe less?" "Four days," said Frankie.

Sal put his arm around Frankie's shoulder, dipping sideways his stance.

"My Sophia is a pretty girl?" Said Sal, soft. "Very pretty, beautiful really." Said Frankie, trying to balance, without tripping into Sal.

"I can understand the attraction, I see the way guys look at her when they think I'm not looking. She is built good like her Mother was, God Rest her soul." Said Sal crossing himself and kissing up.

"You can't help what you're feeling, I know that, but," Sal paused, and let go of Frankie's shoulder, Frankie raised, relieved to be standing straight up.

Sal was rubbing his eyebrows, outside in, slow and steady.

"I think we better step it back, do this thing the right way, and see where it goes." Said Sal.

"I don't follow." Said Frankie.

"Starting Monday you will work for me. Pauley will come get you at your house, every day, and take you with him to do things for me." Said Sal.

Frankie, a little boy lost, and showing it through the eyes. "You got a place?" Said Sal, recognizing the look. "Not really," said Frankie.

"You will stay at Pauley's until you get settled, if you don't mind sharing digs." Said Sal.

"No, that will be fine, if Pauley doesn't mind." Said Frankie.

"Pauley does what I tell him, and after Monday so will you. You got a problem with that?"

"No Sir," Said Frankie, not sure if he did or not.

"It's Sal, for now, maybe something else later, we'll see how it goes." Sal smiled at Frankie.

"You and Sophia can see each other, but no more than once or twice a week, and not without me knowing where you taking her, and not without Pauley being with you.

You guys can double up for a few months, and then we'll see. Good?" Said Sal.

"Good," said Frankie.

"Sunday, you eat at my house, macaroni, okay?" Said Sal.

Frankie nodded.

"Every Sunday," Said Sal with a firmness that led Frankie to believe that this was important to him.

Frankie nodded.

"Good," Said Sal satisfied.

Pauley honked the horn. "Pauley is hungry." Said Sal.

"So what else is new." Said Frankie.

"So, you know Pauley already?" Said Sal, laughing. "I guess I do." Said Frankie.

CHAPTER 18

Pauley drove Frankie to his Mother's house in Jersey City. Frankie had left what few things he owned there, until he figured out what to do with them.

His Mother, wasn't home, no surprise, bars being open at the crack of dawn, and bartenders yelling "cocktails and toddies for you!" at first light, so he took his stuff, threw it into the back seat of Pauley's Cadillac, and went to his new place.

Pauley's apartment, in Elizabeth, was neater, and tidier than Frankie expected. Frankie said as much, asked where his room was, and made his way there.

A small room, cozy, with a window, and a closet, empty except for an extra pillow, a blanket, and a few towels, folded square and shelved.

The room was painted blue, powder like, and trimmed in white. The woodwork is old style, deeply grooved, tasteful. The floor was wood, stained, varnished, and topped with an area rug, Navy. A nice room, comfortable, and more room than Frankie ever had.

"You like the room?" Pauley had followed Frankie and stood behind him, holding a vase, two flowers in it, and a doily to put underneath. "I like it." Said Frankie. "That's good," said Pauley.

"You like flowers?" Said Pauley.

"I guess so, I never thought about it, but Yeah, I do, thanks." Said Frankie.

Pauley took the vase, and doily, and set them onto a nightstand, cherry colored, next to a same colored bedstead.

The bed was a double, and covered in a pale yellow bedspread, matching pillow shams, and a white lace dust ruffle.

"This used to be my Mother's room when she came to visit, but she don't come no more since she's dead." Said Pauley.

"I'm sorry." Said Frankie. "You sure you want me to sleep here, I can hit the couch, no problem." Said Frankie.

"Don't be stupid, this isn't a shrine, stay in it as long as you want to, I appreciate the company. It's a good room, the broads like it, must be the lace."

"It's too bad you and me, will not be chasing tail together, that bed is good and strong, even though it don't look the part." Said Pauley, ribbing.

"Don't rub it in, Pauley." Said Frankie.

"You are not making a mistake, so don't sweat it. Sophia is the good stuff you can't do no better, believe me." Said Pauley, sticking up.

"But still, it is a nice bed, and the flower arrangement alone should get me a little something." Said Frankie, giving back the business and laughing low.

"It's not getting you nothing, maybe I better take them daisies out of here, before they get me whacked." Said Pauley, with mock terror in his voice.

"Don't worry about it Pauley, I will take nothing from those posies except maybe a smell." Said Frankie.

" They are Daisies." Said Pauley.

"Daisies, sorry," said Frankie.

"The bathroom is in the hallway," Said Pauley, pointing to the right of the doorway. "Three doors down, on your left."

"Fresh towels, in the closet behind you. If you need hangers I got some in my room, two doors down and to the left."

"I have my own toilet, so, read War and Peace, or the Sunday comics in it I don't care. Keep it clean, I'm not your mother, same goes for the room. In the kitchen, which you don't see yet, pick up after yourself, you cook you clean".

"I sleep like a rock, so don't worry about noise. I don't keep regular hours, and neither will you, so sleep when you can." Said Pauley.

"You like bagpipe music, Pauley?" Said Frankie. "You better be kidding me." Said Pauley, making a fist.

"The kazoo?" Said Frankie.

"Better, not good, but better." Said Pauley.

"What are we going to be doing? What's my job Pauley?" Said Frankie, changing the subject.

"We are going to do things, like what the boss tells us to do, whatever that might be." Said Pauley, casually, turning to leave the room.

"But what does that mean, Pauley, whatever?" Said Frankie.

"Whatever, is whatever." Pauley left the room and Frankie followed him.

The hallway was filled with photographs, framed, nice, not cheap.

Frankie recognized a few of the heads, some famous, from movies, and music.

Salvatore Nasorosso and Sinatra of course, Nasorosso, and Sammy Davis, Rosemary Clooney.

"How come you are not in any of these pictures, Pauley?" Said Frankie.

"I take them." Said Pauley.

"They came out good." Said Frankie, looking at a photo of Sal, with a drink in one hand, a cigar in the other and a woman who looked to be Anna Magnani on his lap.

"I like this one." Said Frankie, fingering a tits outline. "Yeah, that one come out nice. I forget who the broad is, but the boss, he likes her." Said Pauley.

"I can tell." Said Frankie.

"Who is Mr. Nasorosso with in this one, the other guy doesn't look very happy." Said Frankie pointing.

"Which one, oh, that's Jimmy Roselli, another one of them Hoboken singers? He has a beautiful voice, a crooner, Torno Surento, wonderful. Only he doesn't like wise guys?" Said Pauley.

"Wise guys?" Said Frankie.

" Hoods, you know, us." Said Pauley, leaning against the wall.

"I'm a wise guy?" Said Frankie.

"Starting Monday," said Pauley.

"And what is it again that I will be doing?" Said Frankie.

"Wise guy stuff." Said Pauley, moving to the kitchen, just passed the living room at the end of the hallway.

The living room had a modern look to it, thick carpeting, solid brown, two tables right and left of the couch, overstuffed, beige, with three pillows, brown, and a coffee table to match the side tables, all mahogany.

Lamps, on each end of the couch, beige, with white shades, doilies under each, and coasters in front.

There was a television off to the side, an afterthought, a record player, 33 rpm and 78's in a cabinet underneath, and 45's on a stem to the side.

A chair, winged back, a color to match the couch, a standing lamp for reading, extending hat like, and a magazine rack, floor level, some photos, portrait style, and a painting, big, lots of flowers, centered on the wall behind the couch.

The kitchen was spotless with all the amenities. There was a toaster, a mixer, a rotisserie, pots and pans hanging from a copper rack above the counter to the right of the stove, a four burner nothing fancy, white with the oven in the front and a broiler underneath.

Cabinets, plain wood, painted white above a sink, free standing, old style, claw and paw leg, with more cabinets below the counter top, butcher block. Tables with chrome trim, four chairs with steel frames and cushioned red and a refrigerator with the freezer inside.

"Do you cook?" Said Pauley, pulling a chair, making himself comfortable.

"I eat." Said Frankie. "What about your mother, does she cook?" Said Pauley.

"She drinks." Said Frankie, pulling a chair.

"When you was a kid, what then? You are not dead, she must have fed you once in a while." Said Pauley, making moves up, and over, to the counter where a coffee press sits empty on avocado ceramic tile.

"You want some of this," Said Pauley, while holding at shoulder height, a wooden box, with the word coffee spelled out on the side. There was a mechanism on the top of the box that when cranked coffee beans placed inside were ground into an almost fine powder.

"I'm making for me, do you want a cup?" Said Pauley, first setting the coffee box onto the counter, and then pouring water, distilled, from a jug stand in the corner of the kitchen, into a clear glass kettle placed onto a match lit gas burner set to high heat.

Pauley pulled up the lid on the coffeepot, and spooned in a generous amount of the freshly ground coffee.

Pauley took a cylinder, flat ended and with a stem from the drain board next to the sink, and put it down next to the pot. And from the cupboard he took out two cups, a saucer for each, a matching sugar bowl, two spoons, silver in color and delicately etched, and placed them on the table.

The water boiled quickly. Pauley filled the coffeepot with the bumbling liquid from the kettle until it had risen to the line marked (2) two, waited several minutes and then inserted the cylinder stem flat into the water, and pressed it down slowly. The snug fit of the of the cylinder offered resistance as The grounds were pushed to the bottom.

While the liquid left behind was not as dark as the grounds when dry they were now separated from the liquid.

"A good thing," thought Frankie.

The smell of the coffee was strong and appetizing.

"I take mine straight, the corredi is there," Said Pauley, pointing to a sugar and cream set up.

Pauley poured the steaming hot coffee into the two cups leaving some room for cream in one and then placed the press, now empty, onto a tile.

"Put the cream back into the fridge when you are finished. By the way there are cookies in the cabinet if you want some, so help yourself." Said Pauley, taking his seat.

"The cookies?" Said Frankie, raising up.

"The cabinet, over the press, two kinds, Anisette toast, and Uneeda biscuits." Said Pauley.

"Uneeda biscuits? They are not cookies, they are crackers." Said Frankie, opening the box and looking in.

"Cookies, crackers, what the fuck is the difference, give them here, unless you want to study the things." Said Pauley, holding out his hand.

Frankie took two biscuits from the box, handed over the rest to Pauley and took a bite from one, and coughed.

"A little dry, don't you think." Said Frankie.

"You got to dunk them in the coffee, stupid." Said Pauley, demonstrating.

"It's a cracker Pauley, you are not supposed to dunk crackers." Said Frankie.

"You read that in a book, or something? Show me where it says you can't dunk a cracker in your coffee." Said Pauley, getting excited. "I'll dunk a horseshoe in my coffee if I want to."

"The horseshoe would taste better than these things." Said Frankie with a smile, throwing down easy in mock disgust, the half-eaten cracker.

"Maybe so, but I love the things." Said Pauley. "Try one of the other ones."

CHAPTER 19

Monday morning, eleven o'clock, Pauley pulled the Cadillac up to the garage doors, their desire to reach their full height was less than Pauley's desire to get the fuck in there.

"A passo di lumaca!" Said Pauley loud enough to scare the hell out of the poor snail that must have been pulling up the thing.

As soon as the height of the door exceeded that of the car Pauley hit the gas with a desire to kill that fucking mollusk and then slammed his foot on the brakes a half of a second later when the front bumper hit the wall.

"That will leave a mark," Said Pauley giggling. "Exhilarating, no?"

"Exhilarating, Yes," Said Frankie, not amused.

The doorbell was rung two times. Frankie and Pauley passed through the door and climbed up the twenty-six steps to the office level and walked down the hall, the same as they had done the last time they were there.

Only the office was not empty this time in fact the place was topped off. A motley bunch as you have never seen, a real collection of oddballs.

"The Mutter museum doesn't have mugs like these in their glass jars, but I am sure that they would like to." Said Frankie to no one.

Four heads were showing in the front room, and two more snaking their way through the door to the outer office.

They were all different yet all the same, flashy, overdressed in pinstripes and sharkskins with wingspan shirt collars, patent leather two-toned shoes and transparent silk hose.

These men wore Gold teeth, gold chains, gold watches and a wonderful assortment of precious and semi-precious stones adorning their gold and mostly pinkie style rings.

"This must be where car salesman go to die." Thought Frankie.

Pauley went up through the middle, blocking, while Frankie followed one length behind.

Pauley cleared his throat.

"Everybody shut the fuck up for a minute so I can tell you something." Said Pauley.

Joey Spoons, acknowledging Frankie, is the first to clam up, followed by the others in succession.

The inner office duo, came through, one going left, and the other one going right both stopping at the far end of the room like a couple sparkly bookends.

"This here is Frankie Migliori from Jersey City." Said Pauley, as he turned his head to Frankie. "He rides with me, starting today." Said Pauley.

"Pauley has a new girlfriend." Sing song from the back corner left side. "From hand lotion to Vaseline, Pauley, you are moving up." Said Joey Spoons, getting in on the chuckle.

"Fuck you Spoons." Said Pauley. "Not no more, I've been replaced." Said Joey Spoons.

"Go fuck yourself then." Said Pauley.

"Frankie, you know Spoons," Pauley was going through, clockwise. "That over there is Tony One Ton, next to him is Charlie Chili dogs, one more over is Sammy Tombe, or Sammy Graves, Philly Cheese from Philadelphia, and his cousin, um, Philly's cousin, I forget his name, but it will come to me." Pauley thought for a minute, holding his head, squeezing.

"Hey Philly's cousin, what the fuck is your name again, I forget?"

Philly's cousin was one of the office guys Frankie had seen through the door, Philly Cheese was the other. "Jimmy." Said Philly's cousin.

"That's right, Jimmy the cousin, and that's it, resume."

Pauley walked out of the room from the outer into the inner office and shut the door.

Frankie, at a loss, drifted to Spoons, who was making conversation with Charlie Chili dogs. "Hey" said Frankie to Joey Spoons.

"Hey" Said Joey Spoons. " How goes it, I hear you and Pauley is playing house together."

"Yeah" said Frankie.

"Tidy son of a bitch." Said Joey.

"Yeah" said Frankie.

Charlie Chili dogs, five foot ten and a half, black hair, jet and curled, bad skin, medium color, an olive blend, a nicely tailored black suit, warm weather wool, his pants were pressed to a single edged sharpness, his two toned black and gray shoes were polished up shiny. No socks though, but we will get to that a little later.

Pennsauken born, Charlie had once sparred with Jersey Joe Walcott back in the day, or maybe he just sparred with a fist in his face by the look of his kisser.

I mean to say that Charlie was a fair puncher but he had a catcher's mitt for a face. Charlie was hard to miss.

Charlie was Big headed with an ever-present five o'clock shadow that was sharp like sandpaper. That stubble attracted fists to it like flypaper, and when a fist made contact with it, which was often, the fist would seem to stick to it like velcro. Luckily for Charlie he soon found better things to do with his face, but not right away.

The story goes that one night many years ago Charlie was fighting all comers for a couple of bucks and all of the beer and bratwurst he can stomach at a shuttered warehouse/social club in the old German section of Newark.

Salvatore Nasorosso, a distributor, who was selling beer and spirits to any below ground jazz club, tea house tavern, or cash flush speak easy willing to pay for it walks in to the joint. Nothing unusual about that as this was one of his regular stops.

While Sal was eager to get home, this being his last drop of the day, he stopped pushing his hand truck setting the wheels flat to the concrete. It was heavy, strapped with two full kegs and a case of whiskey, it was a long day, so why not stop for a minute and catch your breath.

Hearing a loud cheer coming from the back of the warehouse Sal, tired and in no mood for entertainment, stood still and listened.

Sal had been to the this place a dozen times before that day, never hearing more than a low murmur from the immigrants that frequent places like this.

Bone tired and ill used by their employers the Men who find themselves in a place like this after a fourteen hour shift at the slaughterhouse are generally held upright by sheer will and no small repellant urge to go home to their ungrateful and unsympathetic brood before knocking back enough beer to numb their pain.

During his respite with his chin carefully balanced on the handle of his hand truck and his weary arms stretched at his sides Sal through bleary and half open eyes sees Charlie surrounded by a ring of fat german men with their arms locked and their faces flushed to a deep almost crimson red. They were screaming.

Charlie was flailing away he was six bums in, and three more bums to go before the house was cleared of palooka.

Sal could see it, Sal could smell it, not the fat sweaty Germans, he could smell them too, who couldn't they stink but opportunity. The concession, the gate, taking bets from swells and mugs alike.

There was money, maybe big money, he didn't know, not yet anyway, but there was money to be made by the man who could sell it.

Feeling energized Sal hung around until the end of the fight.

"First I should talk to the fighter." Thought Sal. "Let's see if this bum is manageable."

Charlie stupefied, winded, but still able to chew his brats could taste the spiel side dish and doesn't spit up.

Charlie agreed to work the game for Sal, for a percentage, (hypothetical) and meals, (considerable) provided free of charge.

Things were going well, swell even, the beer was flowing, the Germans, Italians, Puerto Ricans, Portuguese, the Jews, they were all buying in.

Charlie walks into a drinking establishment, one that Sal has already scoped out and happens to be in at the time, has a few beers then hops on the bar and starts yelling,

"I can lick any one of you fucking whops," spics, micks, polaks, pork chops, whatever the main ingredient was at the moment.

"You assholes are nothing, but pussies," Charlie will yell until somebody calls him out, it usually didn't take more than a minute or two.

Sal, or his brother Jackie, would interject, "A hundred bucks says the bastard can do it." And from there the money starts changing hands, always finding its way back to the bank.

Sal, or Jackie, whoever, would bet, that hundred bucks ten times before the first fist is thrown.

Charlie would razz and howl until all the bets were down and then proceed to beat senseless every neighborhood thug, n'er do well or wife beater within earshot. And when the kegs were empty, the beer was gone and Sal had given the Go ahead to get ahead of the sore losers they departed.

Charlie mopped up in Newark, cleaned house in Jersey City, took out the trash in Trenton, but lost his lunch in Atlantic City. Eight months, forty stitches, three teeth, and a loss of appetite made the game harder to sell.

Charlie has had his fill, but kept it up to please Sal, who he had become attached to. One more fight, and Charlie was begging his release, one more saloon, one more night.

Atlantic City during the twenties, and thirties was called Vacationland, USA, or vaccination land Use a rubber, either way, a hot spot for night crawlers, was the perfect spot for the end game.

Sal picked The Club Forty-one a notorious gambling joint and wet bar. Off the beaten track and filled with ricchi de pazzi. These rich fools were ferried from Manhattan and points north of the little red lighthouse free of charge.

The Club Forty-one offered it's patrons a fine selection of games of chance. Craps, blackjack, roulette, slot machines, poker and the occasional boxing match.

It would be a real fight, regulation canvas, stools, spit buckets, corner men, a bell with a hammer, a referee to call it fair and square, and a two grand purse for the winner.

He may have been a street fighter, a barroom brawler, a roadhouse ruffian, yeah he was all of them things, but Charlie was no boxer. He had never even fought in a ring. Flat footed on wood slats, balancing on beer slick oil cloth, sure but never raised up and roped.

Sal figured a fight was a fight, and Charlie had never lost him a dime. The odds on Charlie were good, nobody ever heard of him except for a few bartenders, and half drunk losers, north of Manasquan.

A fight wasn't just a fight, and Charlie Chili dogs, was not the Marquis of Queensbury. Charlie thought the dough would kiss the Boo Boo and make it all better went into this thing with his chin out, all bliss and ignorance.

"This guy is no bum." Said Sal to Charlie who was having his hands taped up and wondering why, if he had to wear these gloves, did they have to put tape on his knuckles?

"This guy, Phil Chesbro, he wants to be the champ. A middleweight out of the South side of Philadelphia, Phil got beat once already this year, so he needs to win this fight, and a few more before his shot for the title can be arranged. I offered you up, but you don't have to do nothing except your best. This is no dive, you don't have to go down, you just got to make a fight of it, if you can." Said Sal shrugging his shoulders with his palms open.

Charlie, not one to get his nerves up wasn't worried about the fight, he would do his best, and try to finish standing.

Ten rounds, three minutes each, a half-hour or so until the last bell rings. This being a big deal and all, Charlie, who had somehow regained his appetite, figured the buffet would more than make up for the beating he was going to get.

"Sal, they got chicken here, I could go for one. A nice place like this I bet they got good chicken, what do you think Sally?" Said Charlie, thinking more about his stomach than his teeth, which within the hour, he may, or may not have to eat his chicken with.

"Sure they got chicken, they got all kinds of chicken, fried, broiled, roasted. Whatever you want, don't worry." Said Sal.

"Sal, you think we can bag up a few roasters for the ride home?" Said Charlie.

"Sure Charlie sure, whatever you want." Said Sal.

Phil Chesbro was a good puncher and a fine dancer known for his footwork, but he had a jaw made of glass. Nailed only one time, in a three round, under card tryout for the Camden boys, who were willing to finance a bout and tentatively offering to manage him, but were not yet ready to give up the farm for Phil's signature on a contract.

The Camden boys had put him up against a buzz saw in a jock strap whose name was Smith, or Jones, depending on the city, and the age of consent, but fought under the moniker Kid Portugal.

Philly hit the Kid with everything but a toilet seat as soon as the hammer hit that first bell, and was doing good, until round three, when a nod came from the ringside topcoats.

A brick through the window, a foot through the ice, a glass blowers misfortune, ding-dong, fight over. Phil's jaw iwas pulverized.

When he woke up a day later his durability was in question, as was his ability to eat solid food, so at the X he signed, but not with the Camden boys.

Sal was at the fight. Twenty-two kegs of beer and seventeen cases of almost Crown Royal, but not quite Cutty Sark, made the eighty-five miles to Camden worth the wear and tear to the treads. Sal made the delivery by himself.

The beer and whiskey go through the side door, with Sal slipping in through the front door passing through the tap room on his way to a rear pavilion where the regular fights were held.

A smoke filled padiglione with a small ring set up in the center, a couple hundred chairs positioned fifty to a side, Standing room to the back.

The first fight was over, and the second bout on a three fight card was about to start. Phil Chesbro, nicknamed the Philly Cheese, verses Kid Portugal.

"An even match by the look of things."

"This Phil Chesbro character had a few pounds on the Kid, but no advantage in height, or reach." Said Sal under his breath.

After Round one was finished Sal thought that maybe Phil Chesbro could be the next great middleweight pretender, and heavyweight meal ticket.

After Round two Sal thinks Philly could hit with the best of them, during Round three Sal watches the Philly Cheese go to sleep. Count to hundred if you want to this guy is slab meat.

Sal, undaunted, gets the idea that if for no other reason then to sell suds, Phil, not today, not tomorrow, not next month, but eventually, could fight Charlie.

Sal hung around after the fight, made a few inquiries, and learned about the Camden boy's interest in Phil Chesbro, no longer an issue, and then followed the ambulance to the scrap heap.

Philly got his jaw wired shut. For the next eight weeks there would be no solid food, and no boxing for three months after that. So with no money to be made until then Philly made a deal with Sal, who paid the sawbones, bought the aspirin and consommé, and kept Philly from going under.

Charlie would be singing "O solo Mio" until Sal could figure out what to do with two fighters. In the meantime Philly Cheese would be kept safe and snug in a single room only flea circus in Hoboken.

Sal who offloads his whiskey from rail cars running through the Lackawanna Station in Hoboken, could easily look in on Philly when he was down there supervising the operation.

About twice a month Sal would mule his cart up Route 9, to the rail yards. The ride was an easy one, and the return was generous.

Eighty cases of Canadian made whiskey at twenty dollars a case with a tip to the brakeman for slowing down out of the gate and a buck a case to the guys who did the heavy lifting.

CHAPTER 20

The Hotel Victor was, and maybe still is a narrow, four-story SRO, with gray painted bricks. I have seen the old sign on the building. Who knows maybe the bed bugs are still biting down at the end of Hudson Street, oh wait a minute I think they only sell booze these days. Well, anyway, I will give you the particulars as told to me by my Uncle Frank when I was a snot nosed kid of around ten or so.

One flight up from the ground was the lobby which had a front desk with a bell, and a sign that reminded you not to spit on the floor. There was a pay phone at the end of a hallway next to a staircase, a cigarette machine and a please knock before you enter, crapper.

The pay phone with its cord stretched out to the limit had a chain link governor going from the mouthpiece to the base and was bolted to the wall at the bottom near the slug return to hold it together.

Sitting beside the phone was a naugahyde and nickel chair dyed canary yellow with a duct tape pattern and connect the dots burn holes.

To the front and slight right of the phone was a space, ten by twenty, with two tattered and faded red easy chairs, a failing at the seams sofa in a reddish brown, and a rattan and glass coffee table.

The sitting room, or day room was painted a flat gray with white gloss enamel painted woodwork. Aside from the second handed furniture it had a radio, a rubber plant made of plastic, twenty-seven ashtrays, and the smell of cigarettes and too many unwashed pits. Phil pain addled and hungry most of the time, didn't notice the smell.

Phil was wired up and sipping water, milk or clear broth through a straw. He was Losing weight, miserable, and wishing he had signed with the Camden Boys when they first asked him to, a month to the day before the fight with Kid Portugal.

Phil was scheduled to fight Tipo Tosto, a middleweight from Cherry Hill, with a light punch, and soft gut, when the Camden Boys came to visit.

The Gym where Philly had been working out belonged to a Philadelphia splinter group operated in association with the Camden Boys.

Gus Bologna, an ancient lightweight knuckle fighter from before the turn of the century, ran the gym, gave out lockers, swept the floor, set up fights for local pugs and was a cousin to Camden tough guy, Marco Bologna.

Marco Bologna who was Philadelphia born and raised relocated to Camden when crossing the river was the same as leaving the country to the Philadelphia cops, who were glad to get rid of him. Marco quickly set up his book, and made himself at home.

Marco Bologna stood five feet seven on two inches of wood and shoe leather was handsome had black wavy hair, thick brows, a fine nose, strong chin, and a trim waist.

He was Well-dressed, silk double breast, three-piece pinstripes, tweeds, all Jew tailored. Marco wore a fedora, brushed, and dyed to match exactly the topcoat he favored. Marco Bologna was always dressed to the nine's, when eight would do fine.

Marco Bologna made most of his money on the Philadelphia waterfront, but when they kicked his behind over to Jersey, he made the rest of it in Camden.

The money didn't come easy in Camden but It was obtainable, if you didn't mind working dark, which he did not.

The Blacks were most prevalent, with the browns, mostly Puerto Ricans and Cubans, sharing space with whites, mostly gutter Irish, and Italians.

Camden was nickel low and wishing for dimes. Harder to come by in Camden than mayonnaise on white bread. But Marco, he made his nickels, his Pennsylvania connections held up, and on the first anniversary of his being deported to New Jersey his operation was flush.

Gus Bologna, his skin wax paper thin and sallow, his teeth stained a deep yellow from a decades long nicotine bath. Gus's body was shrunken and his back was hunched, his knurled and twisted knuckles were broken, and arthritic.

Gus was Baldheaded, with cauliflower ears, a permanently swollen brow, and beady black marbles poking through vegetation.

His costume was surely an afterthought with it's oversized khaki trousers piss stained and too big for a gorilla, a heather sweatshirt, and laced at the calf red boxing shoes cracked and faded and dying of thirst.

Twenty or thirty pugs a year fought their way up from nothing, one, maybe two, saw the middle and the rest hit bricks on the fly. Gus, he picked through those rags looking for silk, pulling mostly corduroy. Corduroy may be inexpensive, and durable, but it, don't hold up against a high thread count.

Once in a while a fighter would come across with the stuff, quick hands, balance, good eyes, the instincts to defend, and a desire to inflict.

Gus decided that the Philly Cheese was one of them once in a while guys and made the play.

Philly Cheese verses Tipo Tosto, one for the win column, a test, a showcase for the boys. Only Phil didn't sign on the dotted line, he didn't like the arrangement, he thought the percentages were too low on the side of the meat.

Phil said no dice to the ink, but agreed to fight Tosto for his share of the purse, offering a look see to the Boys, hoping he could bump up his going rate.

Knowing how to read, not a plus in the fight game. Understanding that net is not gross, and that their expenses are paid from the gross and your expenses are paid by you, information best left in the small print.

Might be enough money left in the purse to buy the house a drink, make a few payments on an apartment, or a late model used car. You might even have the dough left to impress a dame for a few minutes, but lets not get carried away remember the meat either rots on the plate or gets eaten either way it's never good for the cow.

Fight after fight the same thing happens. You are making a living it's not so bad really, until you get a little tipsy, eventually you get so drunk from the punch that you don't remember where you left your power of attorney.

Suddenly you realize or maybe you don't realize that you have been cheated but it's too late Pal. You are broke and have been managed into the ground and left for dead. Taxes, what taxes?

Phil Chesbro, not one to fall, and stay fell. Dusted himself off and made plans. Another chance to make a noise on the canvas will have to happen, but not before the wires are clipped, and not before he can shed the beer runner.

Sal, not wise to the impending brush off, makes plans of his own. He puts up the money, sets the match, and keeps the game going. The game pays, and the overhead doesn't pinch and the pugs belly aching will fall on deaf ears until he decides otherwise.

A contract is a contract whether signed by a handshake or paper drawn. Sal will hold on tight until the money dries up.

Charlie Chili Dogs never intended to live off his fists. To subsidize, yeah, to free up some booze money, fill his stomach, and quiet down his aggressive urges, sure, but mostly as a counter punch to his day job and to bring home the bacon. Charlie had no wife, but did have a dependent mother who was sickly and in need. Somebody had to pay the druggist.

Charlie made his living on the Port Newark docks, lifting bales and toting whatever needs toting, he had a strong back and was a hard worker, but he was never good with the cow tow. Charlie was a trouble maker and an agitator who because of his attitude didn't get picked up very often at the Union Hall unless a job was too heavy, or too dirty for the seniors.

Charlie was middling hoping to scrape through until he could get his act together and learn to shut the fuck up. Working the game for Sal was tough going, but the extra dough filled gaps between union gigs, and got him out of the house and away from his mother.

The destructive nature of the job, the late hours, the traveling, the short-term memory loss, a severely deviated septum were all good reasons to quit the game.

Charlie made a list, a mental note, something a lot harder to do since he took a beer mug to the skull in Piscataway, all of the reasons why he should quit brawling, go back to the docks and make a go of it. Charlie was sure that he could keep it civil and do what the dock foremen and union stewards told him to do.

The lights were going out, the fight in him was gone, and the middle of the road seemed the right way to go. Charlie would fight Phil Chesbro, for Sal, collect his percentage eat some chicken, and get his ass to the Union Hall first thing that Monday morning.

Sal split his time between The Philly Cheese and Charlie Chili Dogs. With Philly mending and holed up in Hoboken, and Charlie working his day job when he could and fighting for Sal most nights it would be easy enough to keep them apart, and unaware.

CHAPTER 21

The wires came off a week early, sore, sensitive, but working, the jaw felt solid. Philly wolfed down his first meal, swallowing most of it whole, not tasting and barely chewing, three hamburgers, fried potatoes, and a beer to get the blood going.

Philly vomited.

A two mile run slow at first, and then faster, his heart racing, the roads in and around Hoboken, the steps, some two hundred or so, a pedestrian incline to Jersey City, cut into the cliffs, almost ladder straight, no problem two days in. Philly was in training.

Sal was relieved to find Philly had regained his strength, and the desire to pummel, but the upkeep was costing him plenty.

Sal set a fight, the venue, modest, a three hundred-gate limit, with no head charge and the bar would be open. There would be no bottle percentage, or keg returns, but the betting would run hot, and the payoff, would follow the book.

Sal went to bed with the house on this deal in return for supplying the booze to the patrons receiving a small but generous percentage of the take on all elicit activities would be his. A win, win since both fighters were his to deal, the purse was minimal, and the addicts were bringing cash.

Charlie had fought in beer gardens, and social clubs, at company clam bakes, political fundraisers, anywhere Sal left a keg, or dropped a bottle.

Charlie floored bums in two strokes, but took one in between, his face was telling tales. He was never what you would call handsome, but now he was plug ugly.

Sal stopped the game three weeks shy of the match between Charlie and Phill, gave Charlie a fifty to hold him, and told him to take it easy until fight night. Maybe a few weeks without knuckles pelting him would heal his broken face.

Charlie would not be Charlie on fight night since Charlie, who did not wish for his Mother to get wind, did not carry a license to box in the state of New Jersey, and chose not to apply.

A minor technicality since fight cards were bought and sold like used cars, the more cash you were willing to spend, the better the mileage, or record. If Philly had been an amateur, no hitch, but now the state boys had to be paid.

All done the commissioner approved. Phil Chesbro, The Philly Cheese, Zero wins against one loss, would fight Sailor Tony Jones, a middleweight from Chicago, the South side. A record of nine wins against two losses.

With a much better record, Sailor Tony Jones will be the heavy favorite to win the bout. Early odds of five to one were floating around before the fight, and would settle at seven to one when the betting starts.

The place was packed like matchsticks in a box with big winners seeded throughout the crowd to keep morale up.

There were half naked cigarette girls sucking cock in the cloak room, high kickers showing their pussies to the heavy rollers upstage, and making appointments for after the fight, and Band members selling smack and weed from their trumpet cases.

The Cigarette girls, the high kickers and the jazz boys were all sacrificing a percentage to the house. It was of course the price of doing business. As stated gin, bourbon, beer and bubbles, were free of charge and on the house.

Charlie was ready to go. Philly was ready to go. Sal was anxious, but ready, the corner crews, cut men, were ready. The water bottles were filled, the towels and spit buckets were ready.

Philly owned a robe, but Charlie, he had never needed one, so Sal had Sailor Tony Jones embroidered on satin for the occasion, and patched onto a terry cotton shell for Charlie.

Betting held at seven to one, as predicted Sailor Tony Jones was favored. The fighters were called to the ring, and announced to the crowd. Philly was first, and then Sailor Tony. The two men met center ring, they were barely able to see each other through the smoke made worse by a low ceiling and poor ventilation.

The referee wanted a clean fight, Blah, Blah, Blah, bell rings, come out fighting. Sailor Tony and The Philly Cheese touch gloves, back away, and commence to fighting.

Philly moves in first, as Charlie stood flat-footed with his hands up, determined. Charlie tucked in his chin, and threw a left hand which was blocked by Philly who countered with a left of his own that caught Charlie mid cheek, no damage.

Charlie started moving to his right side, while jabbing with his left hand, and covering up when he could afford to. Philly, footloose and moving, shoots a left, right, left, left combination, connecting with two lefts and missing with the right.

Charlie felt that first left, it hit him square. he avoided the right, got tagged by the second left, and took the last one on the elbow.

Charlie, defensive, but jabbing, moving, jabbing, took some punches, one to the head, another to the chest, and too many to remember on the arms.

Philly on the offensive tries to stay in, but backs away from the jab, forcing Charlie to follow him.

Charlie throws a right hand, misses a glancing blow to Phil's head, only to take one himself. Charlie was stunned, but all right, and pelts Philly with three quick jabs into the face, only one hits square to the nose, blood drips.

Charlie tried another jab, aiming, but Philly backs out throwing from the left, one, two, three jabs, and Charlie, he stopped two of them with his chin before he got his gloves up. Ding, ding, the bell rings.

Round two, more of the same, the edge again to Philly. Charlie, was seeing stars from one too many head connectors, backed away when he could, but otherwise stood in close, throwing body shots, and chin poppers.

Philly was surprised, shocked even, as he had hit Charlie with some good shots, square to the head brain rattlers, rib crackers, lip splitters, but Charlie wouldn't go down.

Rounds three through ten, a wash, even up, and getting monotonous. Philly, not dancing, was sucking it deep, and gasping. After forty shots to the cage, and as many to his egg, he had forgotten how to pull a breath, and couldn't seem to catch a breeze.

Charlie, faring no better, and feeling like shit, poor conditioning taking it's cut, waited, the bell seemed far off, and was taunting him.

Round eleven of twelve, the turning point, Philly went up in this one, he somehow found some spare change in the ashtray and paid his toll. Charlie was tapped out, unable to put up the fare, he lost his feet two minutes in, and took his bones to the yard.

Eight, nine, ten, Charlie was still seeing bluebirds. The referee called for the bell, the corners came in, and Charlie, was dragged, to a corner stool.

Philly Cheese, was the winner by a knockout, two minutes and twenty into the eleventh round.

With the big money riding on the back of Sailor Tony Jones the house made a killing. A few Granny's who put their bingo money on the Cheese, left the joint smiling, but the majority of players took it high, bet the favorite, and lost.

In the dressing room, buckets filled with ice provided relief for knuckles, swollen, and stiff.

Charlie came back to life with the help of smelling salts, ice, and a slap to his cheek.

"Where the fuck am I?" Said Charlie, rising from the dead space between his ears. "Is that chicken I smell?" Sal will spring heavy for the fowl, and Charlie will eat his fill deservingly.

Sal called it right, but sat on the edge from the fourth round until the final bell. Sal didn't fix the fight and hindsight proved him right, but not by much.

CHAPTER 22

Sailor Tony Jones, fought his last fight, in the body of Charlie Chili Dogs. Charlie broke the news over a chicken leg, and a bottle of beer. Sal took it smiling, he was bucks up, and sated. Sal saw no reason to push the issue, and would let it heal.

Sal reintroduced Sailor Tony Jones to the Philly Cheese two days after the fight at a Hoboken string and balls joint, serving it up hearty with a jug of Chianti on the side. Linguine and clam sauce for Sal, The Cheese labored, his jaw sore, Penne Ala Vodka, and Charlie made love to the Veal, stuffed with garlic and escarole with spaghetti on the side.

Mario's Trattoria was in the basement of a Brownstone four-story walk up on the south end of Washington street. It was low lit and sleepy eyed, with gaslights converted to Edison bulbs. The tables were made of wood, battered, checkered, and bolstered, with matchbooks propping them up.

On a buffet top stained dark and deep a crank turned phonograph with a prominent plated steel and brass horn was spinning a Caruso record. Next to the record player was an open bottle of Anisette liqueur, a finger bowl of coffee beans and lemon rind and a Milanese Bezzara espresso machine.

The atmosphere at Mario's was speak easy lively with a regard for low tones and polite conversation. Also the food was very good and enough.

Philly fought three more times before his jaw got busted again, and kept him off the mat for good.

Phil Chesbro held to a handshake, humbled, and looking to hide from the leather, and stay off the canvas, took his place, alongside Charlie Chili

Dogs, who decided to forego the Union Hall altogether. And with Sal, and his brother Jackie N, chartered the Elizabeth crew.

Tony One Ton, Sammy Graves, Pauley The Fish, and Joey Spoons came later, and except for Spoons they all started out pulling kegs, and driving routes.

The Philly Cheese became Philly, Philly Cheese, or Philly Cheese steaks, and Charlie became, Charlie dogs, chili dogs, Charlie Chili Dogs, after one particularly memorable pit stop.

Snappy Nappy's, the home of the happy nappy, just up the road from Secaucus, on the Patterson Plank road, in Jersey City, was a truck stop dog house, known for its boiled dogs with chili downed with a bismuth chaser.

Six dogs for a dollar, and thirteen, if you pay for twelve dogs.

Charlie, and the Cheese, fresh from a keg drop in West New York, would occasionally stop in at Snappy Nappy's for a bite, to take a piss, or use the phone, etc. Philly, not a big fan of hot dogs wants one, plain, no chili, and a Coca Cola on the side.

Charlie slapped two bills and two bits on the counter top, demanded a dozen dogs, loaded, one plain for Philly, and four Coca Colas in hobble skirt glass bottles. There was a nickel left over so Charlie flipped it to the kid at the cash box.

A tray filled, six dogs across the top row, six along the bottom, and one dog, naked, on a separate plate was carried side arm to a barrel top set off to the side.

Philly sipped at his Coke, and took a few bites of the plain Jane before abandoning the dog. Charlie, was two dogs down by the time Philly surrendered his one to the barrel, another dog down, and another. Philly took another sip of Coke, two more dogs gone, six so far.

"What the fuck?" Said Philly. The top row was gone. "Huh?" Said Philly. Charlie with Gillespie pouches was slobbering.

"A trophy, your picture in the papers, a pat on the head? What's the fucking prize for making a pig of yourself?

Take a breath, a sip of cola, a look around, just put the fucking dogs down, for a minute." Said Philly.

"I'm hungry." Said Charlie, giving pause, but champing at the bit, there were six dogs left, and they was getting cold.

Six more dogs, swallowed whole, or so it seemed to Philly. Farcito come un maiale e soddisfatto, in other words Charlie was stuffed like a pig and happy with himself. It was awe inspiring gluttony, a sickening display,

"Do you always eat like that?" Said Philly. "Like what?" Said Charlie. "Like a man eating his last meal." Said Philly. Charlie shrugged his shoulders and made no comment. "It can't be good for you." Said Philly.

"Philly Cheese Steaks, and Charlie Chili dogs?" Said Charlie, smiling.

CHAPTER 23

Frankie and Pauley had an early pickup in Elizabeth on Monday morning. The load was going to be heavy in weight but small in size. Not nearly enough to fill out a trailer so after the merchandise, airplane part this time around, had been secured in place empty barrels would be used to fill out the truck.

The barrels while relatively lightweight are a good filler, not only do they prohibit clear sight to the head from the tail, they help to keep still whatever is strapped to the floor.

Frankie and Pauley delivered the merchandise to the Linden shop, had the truck unloaded and the barrels put into the warehouse to be used at a later date.

The hangar measured 40,000 square feet and was used primarily as a transfer hub, a temporary resting place for all things coming in and going out. The rest of the space was used for storage of items not yet placed.

The Hangar was situated within the perimeter of what was called the Linden Airfield. The salvage yard lay against the Southwest corner of the airfield.

For a long time the Linden Airfield accommodated single engine propeller planes, duel engine cargo planes, some BI-plane antiques, air show favorites, and trainers, small time. The Linden Airfield now called The Linden Municipal Airport holds dear no memories of those heady days all on the up end up as they say. The goods come in on the wing, or down the highway, Route 9, and leave the same way.

"Airplane parts, engines, electronics both cutting edge experimental, and commercial. Jewelry, precious gems, bulk first quality costume and semi precious stones, high end timepieces, objects d'art, exotic animals, all manner of illegal imports, and exports.

Linden Airfield, and its sister operation in Elizabeth, bordered on one side by the Newark airport, where a supplemental hangar was leased, and on the other side by Route 9, offering transit options, storage solutions, and a central hub, ideal for the many problems associated with the distribution of stolen goods." Said Pauley.

Pauley was in the driver's seat, with Frankie riding shotgun. The yard of the Linden shop was empty, except for Pauley's Cadillac, which is parked.

Pauley only has to drop the empty truck beside the loading dock. His truck would be number five in a row of empties sitting side by side. Pauley and Frankie can call this day dead and buried. It was their first as a duo.

"Why the speech?" Said Frankie. "This is how the boss explains it to the potentials, and I won't do it no different." Said Pauley. "Potentials?" Said Frankie. "Potential buyers, subscribers, regular deliveries of hard to get diesel engines, airplane parts, hijacked fuel oil selling below market, blanket orders, sales." Said Pauley.

"What's a blanket order, Pauley?" Said Frankie.

" A blanket order is an agreement to deliver, say once a month, a week, whenever, with no purchase order after the initial handshake. No need to meet, just payment on delivery, no paper, less risk, more routine. The Coppers can't tell us from the legal." Said Pauley.

"I get it. We don't manufacture we don't build, or buy, but, then how do we keep it going, how do we supply the demand and keep to a schedule. Who supplies us?" Said Frankie was interested, but very much confused. "We do." Said Pauley. "Huh." Said Frankie. "You lost me."

"Take fuel oil for instance, the blanket set up, we deliver, fill the tanks, do some free maintenance, upgrade the usage meter at no cost to the consumer, and leave. The fuel meter is ours, installed on first delivery, and maintained by our own people, it will say whatever we want it to.

It's like kiting a check we withdraw, and deposit, withdraw, and deposit, always moving from one tank to the other. We make sure the tanks don't go dry, but rarely are they ever full.

If, by accident, one does go dry, we diagnose a fuel leak, charge for repairs, clean up, which means we dig a hole, remove the, "contaminated," soil, drive it around the block, and then put it back in the hole, all at great expense to the consumer. We do have to trade for, or steal a full tanker once in a while, but the overhead is in the labor, not in raw materials. A sizable profit, everybody gets a cut." Said Pauley.

"What about all the other stuff, the jewels, engines, animals?" Said Frankie. "Where do we get those things?" "We consign most, and steal the rest. Money up front if you buying, cash on the sale if you're selling." Said Pauley.

"The liquor, where does it come from, the beer, the whiskey?" Said Frankie. "All on the level. Sal does own a distribution company, and while he don't pay much for the hooch, he does bottle, and deliver." Said Pauley.

"Where does it all come from?" Said Frankie. Pauley paused and took a breath. "Breweries on both sides of the airport in Newark, Gordon's gin mill not a quarter mile from the yard in Linden, where do you think?" Said Pauley.

Frankie's turn to take a breath. "We rob the breweries?" Said Frankie.

Pauley who doesn't necessarily like to talk all that much almost wishes that he never started this conversation as he was tired from a long day of dishonesty.

"Not exactly. I never said all our stuff was first quality, maybe the bathtub was dirty, or the hops took a turn, these are old arrangements, prohibition shit.

We pull the tanker, number four, the clean one, up to the hose behind the loading dock at the Gordon plant, or one of the other joints, clamp it on, turn the spigot, and in goes the gin, scotch, beer, whatever.

We drive the truck to the bottling operation, disguised as a Newark laundry service, empty the spirits into their oil tank, which ain't held oil since January 16th 1920, stupido divieto. Oh, and then we take off." Said

Pauley sliding his ass along the bench seat away from Frankie believing that he had explained well enough for any reasonably smart and not retarded person.

"And then what happens?" Said Frankie.

Pauley took an even deeper breath and sighed one time. "Questo ragazzo non e molto intelligente." Pauley said shaking his head. "Two days after that we pick it up, bottled, labeled, this time in a laundry truck, and then it goes back to the hangar, the crates are marked, meted out, and made ready for delivery." Said Pauley now resigned to the idea that this may take some time and that Frankie would not let up with the questions until he exhausts himself.

"Jewelry, gemstones, art, where does it come from?" Said Frankie."And by the way I am smart, and maybe you just don't explain it very well." "Per favore scusami' Said Pauly mostly with his eyebrows.

"So where does the fancy stuff come from. Said Frankie. "The fancy crap used to go through Queens, or the East River cargo piers, but the New York crews was cleaning them out, so the cooperatives, they decided to send it through Port Newark, or the airport, and drive it through the tunnel, into the city. Naturally, we take our cut.

The diamonds, precious stones, and bulk gold go Antwerp, Paris, Newark, or they ship from Liverpool to New York, but not before we catch up with them. We offload in the harbor if we have to, take a percentage, and then guarantee delivery.

The Jews working the lower east side of Manhattan and down neck Newark get the stones, most of them anyway, and we get a sideline." said Pauley.

"Sideline?" Said Frankie.

"The stones, ours, is taken to Newark, set for a fraction, and sold wholesale to the dealers, some whom are the original owners." Said Pauley. " The art shit, just happens, if it's there we take it."

"Animals, you mentioned animals, where do they fit in?" Said Frankie.

"The order comes in, maybe a roadside zoo needs a billboard pull, the receipts is counting quick, and the T-shirts ain't selling. With any luck, in six to eight weeks, cars is lining up to see, "The Dragon," twenty feet high on the boards, and breathing fire. Only to find, after shelling out a buck to the house, and two more for the all cotton misrepresentation, they find a big lizard in a wash tub.

Big money in exotics, cats, birds, monkeys lizards and shit. Bat shit, mostly, from Mexico, guano it's called, tons of it. Brooklyn Botanical pays through the nose they it's good for the plants, or something.

We pull the wildlife in on the run, if we hang on too long it will drop dead. The birds ain't too bad, they flop, we pluck, the feathers sell big to the needles and thread in the garment district, but the gorillas, they croak and you got to dispose of them. You don't want fucking Mighty Joe Young washing up in Keansburg, or finding his way into the morning papers.

The saw, and grind, it takes too long and even the house cat won't eat a dead gorilla. If you burn them up it smells too much like a barbecue and people start showing up uninvited. So we bury them under the Pulaski Skyway. The big cats too, in the old cemetery just off the traffic circle, near the Holland tunnel access chute.

A week and three days ago we planted an albino tiger that went paws up four days after it crossed the pacific. We packaged him with an orangutan that didn't make it two weeks outside of Borneo." Said Pauley.

"Seems like a lot of trouble to go through for a dead cat." Said Frankie.

"You might think so, but." Said Pauley, then cut off.

"Dig a pit somewhere, tie a rock to a leg, ferry the thing out with the garbage, Ok, but box and bury? Sounds excessive to me, a lot of fuss and bother." Said Frankie. "Why don't you put flowers on their graves too while you are at it."

"Sometimes we do. Listen all I can tell you is that bodies get found. I don't care where you stash them, maybe not today, tomorrow, or next year, but one day, some kid finds a shoe, or a goddamned dog digs up a fucking shinbone, and carries it home, wagging it's tail, and licking chops.

Bodies, they don't stay buried, they don't stay sunk, and once they surface the little piggy starts wagging his curly. And unless you shot the guy with a pearl handled heart attack, or drowned him in natural causes, the cops get curious. Believe me, it's better this way." Said Pauley.

"I thought we was talking about cats, and monkeys, Pauley. Who said anything about bodies, what bodies Pauley?"

"The old slabs they come up easy with a crowbar, and shovels are handy. Bury two, sometimes three, throw in a baboon, or a ocelot always plenty of room." Said Pauley.

"What fucking bodies?" Said Frankie.

"Shit happens, people die, mostly on their own, but once in a while they need a boost." Said Pauley.

"A boost?" Said Frankie.

"A nudge." Said Pauley.

"A nudge?" Said Frankie, still unable to digest.

"Do I have to draw you a picture, or do you got some kind of brain damage?" Pauley agitated, uncomfortable with this line of questioning. "People die because somebody kills them." Said Pauley put on the spot, losing his composure.

"You Pauley? You kill people?" Said Frankie, staring hard into Pauley's eyes. Frankie, not a killer, no intention, looking for definition, expectations.

"I'm no trigger man, but I will shovel, and so will you. So you had better find the stomach for this shit Frankie. I thought you was a big war hero, went to Korea, carried a fucking gun didn't you, what's the difference?" Said Pauley.

"I was a mail clerk in a hospital Pauley, I hung my hat on my gun, when I could remember where I left it." Said Frankie. "Grab a shovel then." Said Pauley. And another thing, It ain't never pretty, and it don't never smell good." Said Pauley.

"So how will I tell which one is dead, and which one is you?" Said Frankie. "

I will be the one with his foot up your ass." Said Pauley. Pauley turned the key in the ignition and pulled it out after the mother died. "Look at me, now I'm killing engines too." Said Pauley laughing and throwing his hands in the air.

CHAPTER 24

Taking your cut and getting a piece, is not the same as punching a clock, pay me, or counting piecemeal, pay me. It don't equal twenty after ten pair of Mary Jane's are sold at five percent, or what's left after you throw in a free set of snow tires.

Acquisition is only the breach, moving the goods, converting it into paper, plays like Chinese checkers. A half dozen moves, maybe more, if the goods, are low end, chintz, or made in Japan, no AA battery addicts, not yet.

The consumer end, the blanket side, it goes straight to the top, very little trickle down, mostly grunt work for the entry level privilege to work the outside angle, or the side job.

For every great ape, and cashmere goat, there is eight hundred pair of Levi's pulled to the shoulder, offloaded in Carteret, and swapped for cold storage furs and held until sold well below wholesale to your local fur and fancy dress shop. The cash that comes from that deal, it goes a few steps up the ladder, and then splits, payday.

The prime cuts come butchered, and wrapped. A driver in need of green, a dispatcher looking to supplement his forty hour steady paycheck, a tip from the scales clerk at the weigh station, a blow job confession to the highway honey working the truck stop and begging a nickel for the phone call that bleeds her Johnny dry, and pays crack shut.

Always on call, a midnight baby to deliver, a truck load of pinball machines getting a coffee to go at the Diner, get to it in ten minutes, or we got to go chase it. "Where the fuck is my truck." a piece of Cake, Sugar coated. "Pull over, pull over, pull over, pull the fuck over!" Niggling.

An orthodox diamonds mule, carrying yellow, and flawed, in an insurance mock theatrical, heads North to the tunnel pulls to the side, goes hands up, and hands it over.

The stones are reported to the adjusters up in Hartford as a stick up, the assailant who gets drawn with a brown pencil is described to the coppers, the insurance claims are filed, and the payoff is forthcoming.

The diamonds are set up cheap, sold to youngsters looking to tie the knot on a shoestring. And as a last ditch, white trash, "I can't believe you slept with my sister," escape hatch.

CHAPTER 25

Frankie, Sophia, Peter, Sals Jr. and Senior, Pauley the Fish for Sunday dinner at the Nasorosso house. Sharp at three. The soup, escarole and navy bean in an oiled chicken stock. Salad, hearts of romaine, ripped, not cut, in a lightly salted balsamic vinegar, and lemon zest.

A meat course, stuffed breast of veal, broiled and layered with a sharp cheese, hot ham sliced thin and topped with a basil paste and crushed garlic.

A pasta course, semolina gnocchi in a light cream sauce made with butter, light cream and Parmesan cheese, grated fresh.

Seasonal fruits, an assortment of nuts, gelato, and coffee, a demitasse.

The house from the street, was a pale brick, almost pinkish. The ground level doorway was an arch with two marble posts one right and one left with the door between them.

The first level windows were decoratively barred and set well into the frame, and the second Story windows were not barred but as the outer walls went up flat and mortared tight they were made inaccessible unless maybe you were carrying a ladder or some rope. not that you could get close enough to the house to use either.

The rooftop was level with no pitch, and sunken about five feet a design reminiscent of an ancient Sicilian castle with a parapet.

The lot, an acre, maybe, was planted green and cut low to the ground with unobstructed views of the road and of the tree line front sides and back.

The backyard was walled in solid at twelve feet high and forty feet square, bounded by fig trees and floored with plum red and cherry small tomato plants.

The brick used to build the wall was the same brick used to build the house. The shade was a little too pink if you ask me, but who am I to criticize. Me living with my mother and all.

There was a table, and six chairs, enameled white, and weathered, an iron worked lack of comfort made better with a cushion.

A citronella candle placed center to ward off the pests, and light softly the faces of those who choose to sit.

A bowl of figs, pulled fresh, rinsed clean, and wiped dry, and a basket of tomatoes, red, ripe and ready to eat, were placed to the right, and to the left of the light, respectively.

A house just like any other house, albeit safely kept, and with a tight-ass disregard for pretension. A comfortable place fit for the man with big shoes to almost fill, or fill out with newspaper in this case.

Sunday dinner with the Nasorosso family was not something to look forward to, not for a half scared son of a whore, trying to impress the Boss with little on the good side of Emily Post.

They, the Nasorosso's are crooks from the low end, but with more practice at caulking the cracks then Frankie had. He had to move it smooth, keep his mouth shut, and try not to put a foot to his tonsils.

The food was glorious, Soup to nuts with a cherry for a topper. Sophia made eyes at her fork, but didn't use it much. Pauley on the other hand made like the sky opened up and heaven slid bare-ass down his throat. Frankie was amused, but remained silent. He kept his eyes to his own plate and his thoughts on the inside of his head.

Sophia smiled when she looked at him but didn't say much. She listened intently when Daddy stoped packing his jaw long enough to say something.

Serving, but not sitting, was another aunt, or relative who looked to be wrung from the same olive soaked rag as the rest of them. Frankie would ask Sophia who she was the next time he was alone with her which might just be on they wedding night if the rules were to be followed, or if Pauley could be persuaded somehow to take a nap or something when they doubled up.

The meal over, and the demitasse sipped, the party moved fat and slow to the clear plastic covered blood red couch and matching chairs in the parlor.

Not a television in sight, and seeing as how televisions just fell off the back of a truck it just didn't seem right that there wasn't one, or twelve of them.

Parlor speak, spoken as it was, through the ass hole and the throat came through loud and clear with no actual words, but still saying too much. The urge to let one rip weighed heavy on the belt loop of Frankie's waistband. But being as he was new to the game Frankie held his breath and kept his sphincter clenched.

Respectful is how I will describe the Half-assed kiss that Frankie gave to Sophia at the door when he and Pauley were leaving.

Sideways and off balance, thank you so much for inviting me, thanks again, a quick peck, maybe one lip, trying not to hit any, and aiming for a cheek.

Sophia on the other hand tilts and goes in for the full splat, luckily Frankie was a moving target, and avoids any damage caused by unintentional, inflated or misdirected testosterone.

"What a fucking Mary." Said Pauley, making with the limp gesture. "Was that supposed to be a kiss, or was you thinking about your grandmother's hairy chin at the time." Said Pauley, after the door was closed behind them.

"I was nervous, her father was standing right there opposite me, giving me the eyes." Said Frankie.

"Are you or are you not engaged to the girl?" Said Pauley. "Am I?" Said Frankie, looking confused and stupid at the same time. "You better believe It."

"But Sal, Mr. Nasorosso said that this was just the beginning, and that we would have to see how it goes, and." Said Frankie.

"And fucking nothing. You are engaged to the girl. Don't you think you deserve to kiss the girl you are engaged to." Said Pauley, with a, you silly ninny, look on his face.

That's not exactly what Pauley said but I was getting tired of all the bad words that Pauley used to say. I want to tell it like it was but, well, I will try to keep the cheese sharp without it stinking up the place.

"But what about Sal?" Said Frankie. "If you are in love with the girl like you say you are, you might want to show her, and her father. Love is good, let it flow baby.

These are emotional people, but very suspicious. It's better if Sal thinks he got your balls in his pocket. He would rather squeeze them a little when he thinks you are getting out of hand, then to think that you are after something other than his daughter." Said Pauley.

"Yeah?" Said Frankie, incredulous.

"Just don't let none of your love flow to your dick, Mary. Said Pauley.

CHAPTER 26

Three weeks into the job, and Frankie still ain't found his rhythm. The hours suck, and the pay so far is still in bulk and not yet converted to folding money.

Frankie and Pauley had appropriated four trailers from pot bellied long haulers. They also delivered two high-end jet fuel injection systems somewhere up the interstate.

The cash for those jobs was to be forthcoming upon the completion of another such type delivery that Philly Cheese was orchestrating out of Pennsauken. The dough will be coming through on Philly's end. Frankie was counting chickens.

Philly Cheese pulled into the garage two days later with a suitcase full of Rolex watches and assorted trinkets and started handing them out to Sal, Pauley, and Frankie as if here we go around the mulberry bush was the number one song and we were all singing along.

"Pauley." Said Frankie. "Yeah." Said Pauley, watching the Cheese as he is doling, counting diamonds, and separating the stainless from the platinum, the solid from the plated. "I thought we were getting paid today." Said Frankie. "What do you think this pile of Swiss is." Said Pauley, still watching the division of boodle.

"I thought we were getting some cash money out of this deal, not more shit I still don't know how to convert." Said Frankie.

"You need dough, why don't you just cop some petty cash if you are low on green?" Said Pauley, now counting on his fingers as the piles are almost topped.

"What petty cash Pauley?" Said Frankie. "Didn't I tell you about the petty cash that I keep in the false bottom of the steamer trunk in the hall closet?" Said Pauley offhanded. "No Pauley you must have forgot to tell me about the petty cash that you keep in the false bottom of the steamer trunk in the hall closet." Said Frankie, rolling his eyes.

"I'll show you where it is later when we get home, now chiudi la bocca so I can make sure Philly Cheese don't try to fuck us over." Said Pauley, now counting on his toes.

" Ok Pauley I will shut up." Said Frankie.

"What the fuck is that supposed to mean?" Said Philly Cheese to Pauley. "Not now, I'll call you a crook later, when I'm finished tabulating." Said Pauley.

"Maybe you should let the Kid count them watches for you, I don't think you got enough fingers and toes, and since you got only one dick you may need some help when I start pulling out the rings I got in my pocket." Said Philly Cheese.

"You got rings too? Philly you done good, now shut the up so I can finish my figuring." Said Pauley.

By all accounts...fingers, toes, etc it was a good take. Ten, twelve watches apiece, five or six rings, all gold or better, most precious only one or two that will not cut glass, and a share of the swag on racks in the van parked downstairs. Coats, some carrying fur, high frill evening gowns, some on the low end of fabulous, but most sitting elevated.

Sal got a cut, equal to their own, and another equal share went in the pot to be used in exchange for two full tanks of heating oil for the supply side deal going on like clockwork, and paying back continuous. Every once in a while oil has to be purchased, must have been a blue moon that night.

"Tell me about this petty cash, Pauley." Said Frankie when Pauley pulled the Cadillac from the garage and made way. "I keep some dough around for when my pockets go empty." Said Pauley. "How much you talking about, a few hundred?' Said Frankie. "Five, maybe six." Said Pauley. "Hundred?" Said Frankie. "Thousand." Said Pauley. That's a lot of money Pauley." "Not so much." Said Pauley.

Frankie tried to digest, but it kept coming up acid. Five, six grand, in a steamer trunk, and Frankie was wearing the same suit for three weeks, and counting toes through his socks.

"Pauley, can you spare a few bucks until we unload some of the watches and rings we got today?." Said Frankie. "Take what you need, measure up, and put it back when you are flush." Said Pauley.

"Measure up?" Said Frankie, "Yeah, you take an inch, you put back an inch and a quarter. You take two inches, you put back two and a, two and, you put back more than two inches. You got it?" Said Pauley. "I got it." Said Frankie.

"What do you need the cash for anyway?" Said Pauley, trying to skirt around a thirty-eight Ford with a hairnet going blue tinge behind the wheel, doing twenty and swaying.

"I can use a few things." Said Frankie his arms stretched to the dashboard and bracing himself for the impact as Pauley goes around the history lesson mowing down the center stripe in front of the Cadillac.

"Like what?" Said Pauley, casually curbing two wheels, and landing flat after the pass. "Clothes." Said Frankie, happy to be ahead of the Ford and alive. "What, like pants, shoes, socks and shit?" Said Pauley, easing the Cadillac down to forty and cruising.

"A new suit would be nice, some shirts, and maybe a hat." "A hat, what do you need a hat for, you got a good head of hair." Said Pauley, wishing he had half the head that Frankie has.

"I want a hat, why I can't have a hat if I want a hat." Said Frankie, indignant. "You need a hat like I need a...a fucking, a fucking," "A fucking what?" Said Frankie. "I got nothing." Said Pauley, his mind still racing, but losing. "I didn't think so." Said Frankie, smiling.

"Where we going Pauley?" Said Frankie, not recognizing the here, and thereabouts they, were passing. "To the warehouse." Said Pauley. "The hangar?" Said Frankie, wondering. "The warehouse." Said Pauley. "Pauley, what warehouse? The gin stack, the cages, the tanker shack, which?" Said Frankie, getting annoyed. "The warehouse where we keep the dry goods and sundries." Said Pauley. "The what, and the which?" Said Frankie. "Suits and shoes and whatnot." "Oh." Said Frankie.

The warehouse was the third building behind a front faced chop and shop auto parts and such. The building was a street level graffiti covered red brick shell with a keep the fuck out attitude.

Pauley worked his way through a Buick and two Fords, both on blocks and missing most of what it is that made them what they was. Pauley pulled the car up to a locked steel plated black door.

Frankie and Pauley got out of the Cadillac, Pauley produced a key, popped the lock and led the way through a maze of cotton, silk, and wool, pausing only when he reached midway. Pauley cut left and stopped in front of a rack of sharkskin suits.

"Take your pick." Said Pauley, pointing to the rack, arranged up from small to big. "I don't know Pauley." Said Frankie. "I'll look like a gangster in one of those things." "You are a gangster." Said Pauley, pulling a 42 regular from the rack and handing it to Frankie.

"Try this on, and shut up." "But." Said Frankie, hesitating. "But your ass, try it on, it's a nice suit and it don't cost nothing." Said Pauley, getting agitated.

"Alright I'll try it on, but I don't see why I got to look like Al Capone when I see a blue blazer hanging on a rack over there." Said Frankie, nodding to the rack of sport coats not ten feet from where they standing.

"You can't wear no blue fucking blazer and Al never wore nothing that wasn't wool." Said Pauley. "Take this shark and put it on before I get mad at you."

"What is wrong with a blue blazer." Said Frankie, refusing to take the sharkskin from Pauley. "It's stupid." Said Pauley, still holding. "How can a sport coat be stupid, it doesn't have a brain, it can't think for itself, it doesn't talk." Said Frankie.

"Oh it talks" Said Pauley. "Oh yeah, what does it say?" Said Frankie. "It says I'm a stupid fucking blue blazer, and any stupid fuck who wears me is too fucking stupid to know how fucking stupid he looks when he wears me." Said Pauley.

"Give me the suit." Said Frankie, yanking the shark from Pauley's hand and disappearing behind a rack of green dresses.

Frankie stepped from behind the rack wearing the suit it fit well, and didn't look bad at all. "You look good, now let's get out of here, I'm tired and I want to go to bed." Said Pauley, moving away from Frankie and turning to the way out.

"It feels good, but it doesn't do much for me." Said Frankie, trying to see himself in a cracked, but still in one piece mirror hanging from a rope on one brick column holding up it's part of the roof.

"Here's two more, now let's get out of this place before I have to kill you." Said Pauley, handing Frankie two more suits and double timing his steps to the exit. "What about shoes, I need some shoes Pauley, and shirts, and socks, I don't have any socks that match the suits you gave me." Said Frankie louder now as Pauley had disappeared behind a rack of trench coats.

"I'll go wait in the car. I got no more patience for you. Find what you need and then wake me up when you get behind the wheel, you are driving home. Take the keys, and lock the door on your way out. Pauley appeared from behind a rack of ladies house coats and threw a ring of keys at Frankie landing on the floor by his feet.

Twenty minutes later Frankie found Pauley sleeping in the back seat of the Cadillac, curled up like a baby.

Into the trunk Frankie put two pair of shoes, both black, one wing, one cap toe, five shirts, three white, and two blue, wide open collars on the white, button down on the blue, six pair of black socks, a dozen handkerchiefs, and one blue blazer.

CHAPTER 27

Frankie feeling more like one of the bunch than a rotten banana checked the crease in his new pants. Nice material, not cheap, and not Khaki which Frankie thinks is good, not having much of anything to wear since he returned to the states.

Frankie didn't look like a gangster, even though he was wearing standard issue sharkskin. "French cuffs." Said Frankie to the mirror. "Who wears French cuffs when a button works just fine.

Frankie doesn't have cufflinks. He has twelve watches, half a dozen rings and one and three quarter inches of petty cash, but not one cufflink. Not that one cufflink does anybody any good.

Frankie rolled his sleeves up one time and put on his jacket, he would find a way around the cufflink problem later when he and Pauley were out doing whatever it is they would be doing that day.

Twenty minutes passed in front of the mirror before Frankie decided that no amount of fussing was going to change the fact that he was a gangster and that to the two eyes staring him down from the inside of his face he looked like one too.

"Are You done making Goo Goo eyes at yourself, or do I have to go back to the kitchen and drink another fucking cup of coffee. I can do that if you want me to. Maybe you want me to jerk myself off in front of you. You being so pretty and all." Said Pauley. Pauley had come down the hall from the kitchen a moment before Frankie realized he was standing next to the door. "Cazzo a Pauley." Said Frankie before taking one more look in the mirror. "Sure thing beautiful." Laughed Pauley.

120

Pauley was a freak about things being kept clean, and Frankie didn't want to screw it up by not towing the line. So he started giving his room the once over, once a day.

The lace Frankie got used to, the doilies and such remind him of nothing since his mother was no kind of fancy pants.

So the doilies and lace would be fine just as long as they did not affect his sexuality or his perception of his sexuality. This being before it was decided that homosexuality wasn't something that could be fixed with a shot of penicillin or by a good ass kicking.

"Where are we going today Pauley." Said Frankie when he closed the door to Pauley's apartment.

"I don't know yet. We got some animals coming in on a train sometime today. That's all I know. Why you asking, you got something you have to do. Maybe you want to go to the beauty parlor, or maybe have your nails done. The way you was admiring your profile in the glass I thought maybe you was going sweet on yourself." Said Pauley.

"I have never had a suit like this before Pauley. Not one without safety pins holding up the hems, or at least one hole in the pocket.

This is kind of a new thing for me so please stop giving me the business. Give me time to get used to the high life." Said Frankie, maybe half-serious.

"No problem just don't wear out the fucking mirrors in the house before I find one what makes me look as good as you think the one in your bedroom makes you look." Said Pauley. "I got plenty of time then," said Frankie. "Fuck you," said Pauley.

CHAPTER 28

When they arrived at the office, or the garage if you will, Frankie stayed in the car while Pauley went in to find out what kind of nonsense they would be getting into that day.

Frankie was slowly getting used to the idea that maybe time wasn't so much his own anymore.

Ten minutes later Pauley came through the door with not so much a smile on his face as a shit-eating grin. "Why am I seeing every tooth in your head. What's going on." Said Frankie, still not ready for whatever or what not.

"You like animals don't you?" Said Pauley still with his teeth showing too much. "I guess so." Said Frankie. "Why? We got to do something with an animal today." "You could say that." Said Pauley. "What do we got to do with it?" "Don't worry about it." Said Pauley. "Why? Should I worry?" Said Frankie.

"It's nothing." Said Pauley. "Pauley what do we have to do with an animal that I don't have to be worried about doing with it." Said Frankie. "Can I start the car so we can get to the thing." Pauley put the key into the ignition turned the key and eased the Cadillac into gear.

"The thing. You said the thing. Its only one thing then?" Said Frankie. "Yeah, one." Said Pauley. "That's good." Said Frankie. "Yeah, good." Said Pauley with no teeth showing this time.

The traffic was heavy up the ramp to the Pulaski Skyway but neither Pauley or Frankie seemed to care. Pauley knowing why, and Frankie not asking any more questions.

The Pulaski Skyway is a long, black, bridge-like structure that arches itself over the junkyards and marshlands between Newark and Jersey City. An architectural marvel when it was built in the 1920's.

A narrow tightrope of a ribbon, that scares the crap out of whoever drives whatever puts its wheels onto it.

The lanes on the Pulaski Skyway are only two and a half feet wide with a double line down the middle so you have to balance on two wheels just to get over the thing.

The skyway isn't that bad but there is nothing wide and luxurious about what amounts to a very tight fit for any vehicle built in America.

Thirty minutes of dead stop traffic for what turned out to be a flat tire on a Good Humor ice cream truck.

After Pauley handed a dollar to the ice cream vendor for a creamsicle he aimed the Cadillac down the ramp working his way into the Holland tunnel lane.

In a mile or two the road forks. Going left will take you to lower Jersey City, and going right will drop you on your head in Hoboken. Straight will put you under the water.

Pauley went right at the fork and veered off onto a side road which guides you into the Erie Lackawanna rail yards if you stay on it for a mile or so which he did. This particular yard is where the freight trains come in from the eastern spur of the rail line.

The eastern spur of the Erie Lackawanna line is not supposed to be a place where freight gets unloaded, or loaded, but it does happen from time to time.

The eastern yard, where they landed was mostly a switch stop and turntable operation that didn't see much of what was inside the two thousand boxcars that passed through it each day.

A greasy, gunmetal gray expanse of iron, wood and assorted railroad incidentals that wouldn't make much sense to me but seem to get the job done without having to be more then it ever was. The rail yard was not fancy it was workmanlike and nothing else.

Pauley pulled the car beside a shack where a soot faced grease monkey was sitting on a barrel eating a sandwich.

Pauley got out of the car leaving the door open and the engine running and took a few steps toward the shack. After a few words passed between the two men. The grease monkey pointed his sandwich in the direction of a brown boxcar parked on a sidetrack.

The boxcar had a refrigeration set up on the roof and a very large lock on the sliders.

"We got to go over this way." Said Pauley not so much pointing the way as leaning in the direction of the brown boxcar.

Frankie followed behind Pauley. They reached the brown box and Pauley took a set of keys from his right pants pocket. He fumbled with the padlock for a minute until he heard the pins click and pulled down the case to free the shackle from the drain hole.

"Pauley maybe you should wait a minute before you open the door to that thing. What if whatever is in there tries to run off when you pull the latch." Said Frankie. "Don't worry it ain't going no where." Said Pauley.

"Is it in a cage Pauley, because we don't have a truck or anything to put it in." Said Frankie just then realizing that if the thing what's in the box has to be taken out of the box then it would have to go in the car.

"We ain't taking it nowhere." Said Pauley. Pauley lifted the padlock from the latch eye and dropped it to the ground. "Damn thing weighs about three pounds. Remind me where I dropped it later. We got to use it after we transfer the thing." Said Pauley.

"I thought you said it wasn't going anywhere Pauley." Said Frankie. "It ain't going but from this box to that box." Said Pauley pointing to another boxcar being pulled by a switcher engine into place beside the brown refrigerator box. This new box, also brown, with a similar cooler setup was slowly sliding up door to door and parallel.

"So all we got to do is move the thing from one brown box to another brown box." Said Frankie. Feeling better but not good.

"That's it. That's all we got to do. Move the thing from here to there." Said Pauley pointing to the new brown box.

"Pauley, why do these boxes got refrigeration units on them. There isn't a polar bear in one of them boxes is there?" Said Frankie getting nervous again. "No, there ain't no polar bear in there." Said Pauley. "Then what is in there, that we have to keep from sweating too much Pauley?" Said Frankie.

"A giraffe." Said Pauley. "A giraffe?" Said Frankie. "Yeah, a giraffe, you heard of them. They are like a telephone pole, but with legs." "I know what a giraffe is but a giraffe doesn't have to be kept cold and it is not going to fit in a brown box." Said Frankie.

"Well, it ain't exactly living no more, so I guess they put it in sideways." Said Pauley.

"We got to move a dead giraffe from one box to the other?" Said Frankie. "Sure seems that way, don't it." Said Pauley.

"Why don't they just leave it in the box that it's in?" Said Frankie. "How should I know. The Boss says we got to move the giraffe, so we move the giraffe." Said Pauley, getting agitated.

"Help me get this door open will you." Said Pauley trying to pull the latch handle down and track the door at the same time.

Frankie put his one hand on the handle and the other hand on a piece of wood sticking out from the side of the boxcar for leverage.

Once the door was worked loose it began to slide easily. "What the fuck." Said Pauley. "What the fuck." Said Frankie. A giraffe was in the box.

"I don't know about this Pauley. How are we supposed to move this thing. It's got to weigh a ton and it's frozen solid." Said Frankie. "I can see that." Said Pauley scratching the space behind his ear where maybe they put some brains he could activate.

"Maybe we can slide it out of there." Said Frankie, being helpful. " Get up there and see what you can do." Said Pauley. "Get up where and do what to which." Said Frankie. "Get up there," Pauley, pointing in the direction of the fog now rising up from the giraffe Popsicle. "And see if you can shimmy it over to the door so we can slide it out of there, maybe." Said Pauley.

"That thing is too heavy for me to do anything with except maybe sit on it. You want I should sit on it Pauley?

Maybe we should get up there and we could try to shimmy the thing over to the door so we can slide it out of there." Said Frankie thrice putting the accent on, we.

"What's a matter with you, you can't move a fucking giraffe by yourself." Said Pauley. " Pauley I don't know anything about moving a giraffe, but if this thing is going anywhere it isn't going to get there on my back. So either you get your ass up there with me or nothing is going to happen to this thing except melt." Said Frankie.

Frankie got up into the box first and gave a hand up to Pauley.

The giraffe was lying there on the frozen floor stiff as a piss hard-on.

"Grab it by the neck and pull it to me." Said Pauley. Frankie was positioned further up the neck than Pauley was.

"Where on the neck do you want me to grab? The part in Jersey City or the part in Hoboken." Said Frankie.

"Grab it up by the head. It's not so thick around at that end. You should be able to get both your arms around it." Said Pauley.

"What are you going to be doing while I'm whispering in it's ear." Said Frankie. "I'll be giving it a hand job. What do you think I will be doing? I'm going to push it from this side, where the legs are. Maybe it'll swing around easier that way." Said Pauley.

"Pauley." Said Frankie. "The things tongue is sticking out." "I didn't ask you to French it. Just grab the neck and pull, Ok, on three. One, two, and." Said Pauley.

"Pauley, my hands keep slipping from the neck. I can't get a good grip." Said Frankie, just before Pauley said three. "Grab it by the ears they are sticking way the fuck out there." Said Pauley.

Frankie grabbed the giraffe by the ears and made ready to pull. "One, two, and three." Said Pauley. Frankie pulled and Pauley pushed.

"What was that noise, and why are you sitting on the floor." Said Pauley.

"The noise was the giraffe's fucking ears snapping off in my hands, and I'm sitting on the floor because that's where I landed after they snapped." Said Frankie from his spot next to the giraffe head.

"Then you got to grab the neck. " Said Pauley.

"I can't get a grip on it. I'll be on my ass again before the thing moves an inch." Said Frankie.

"Try pushing it from the other side of the neck." Said Pauley. On his knees between the giraffe's legs with his two hands on the stomach. "On three. One, two, and three."

This time, they both pushed and the giraffe, it moved. "Keep pushing, the thing is turning good now." Said Pauley. Sweating through his jacket even though the box was well below freezing.

"Pauley, we can't push no more." Said Frankie. Not sweating as much because his end is a lot lighter than Pauley's. "Why not." Said Pauley. Not wanting to lose momentum. "Because the head just banged against the side of the box."

The giraffe was frozen then but it was not frozen when they put it in the box. When it went in it could bend. Now it was Frozen and it could not.

"Pauley, we got to slide the thing down to the end of the box so we can get the head clear to swing it out of the door. Once we get the head through then we can get the rest of the body out with it." Said Frankie.

"Then get down here with me and see if we can't slide this thing to the wall behind me." Said Pauley.

Frankie put his hands on the giraffe's back while Pauley grabbed two of its legs. "One, two, and three. Frankie pushed and Pauley pulled. Four, maybe five feet was all they could travel before the wall came up on them.

The top of the giraffe's head was still behind the doorframe, but was closer to the outside then it would have been before its unfortunate ear extraction. So Pauley being as he is a bull in a china shop gave the giraffe three good kicks to the back of its head allowing sunlight to shine on the poor beast for the first time since it went cold.

"The head is out, now we go back to the push and pull neck and balls style." Said Pauley. Happy that he had been able to kick something.

Frankie took a pull position at the head, not as pretty as it used to be. Pauley was in the push spot, his shoulders going hoof to hoof. "Just push when you ready I'm tired of counting." Said Pauley. They both grunted one time and commenced with the pushing and pulling.

The giraffe neck was now up and out of the box. Extended like a plank hanging over the side of a ship, but not reaching far enough. The other box was seven or eight feet from the door on a parallel track and the body of the giraffe was now wedged into the doorframe.

"The thing is not going out this way Pauley." Said Frankie frustrated.

"The body is too big to push straight out, and we can't turn it because of the neck." Said Frankie.

"Frankie, you remember how them ears came off when you pulled them." Said Pauley.

"Yeah, So." Said Frankie. "Get up on that neck and jump up and down a little and lets see what happens." Said Pauley.

"Get up where? And do what?" Said Frankie.

"Get up on the freaking neck and jump the fuck up and then jump the fuck down. And keep doing it until something happens. Capisci?" Said Pauley.

Frankie shrugged his shoulders and put a shoe up on the animal's stomach and then left footprints halfway up the neck. Frankie didn't have anything to hold on to. His pelvis was shaking front to back while he used his arms to balance himself.

When the earth stopped shaking, Frankie bent his legs at the knees with his arms waving in a circular motion in an attempt to maintain his position on the frozen neck.

Frankie then jumped up, not very high, about an inch or two. He seemed to hover for a moment just above the neck but since Frankie, he don't hover so good there wasn't no where to go but down.

When Frankie's feet landed onto the giraffe's neck his new shoes still slick on the bottom from not having had time to scuff up slipped speedily passed the neck as if attempting to straddle it somehow. Alas failure. Although Frankie did manage with great success to slam his nuts into the frozen neck.

The noise he made was not a good noise. It probably wasn't a real noise at all. Maybe some dogs heard it but nobody else did.

"Frankie spun like a hula hoop on the hips of a skinny eight year old girl. First his head was up and then his head was lying faced to the ground.

If he hurt his face when it slammed into the gravel he did not mention it until after his balls dropped out of his open mouth.

"You alright Frankie. You don't look so good. I think the blood went out of your face for a few seconds. You was white as a ghost." Said Pauley. Frankie didn't answer.

"So what do you think. Did the neck do something when you hit it with your nuts." Said Pauley. Frankie gargled and spit, but didn't produce words that Pauley could understand.

"Frankie why didn't you hold on to the side of the box when you was almost jumping up and down on the neck." Said Pauley. Making perfect sense. Only an idiot would jump up and down on a frozen giraffe's neck without holding on to something.

Frankie lay on the ground with his eyes closed for fifteen minutes before he got up. Pauley was leaning with his elbow on the frozen neck eating a sandwich. "You hungry Frankie? The grease monkey by the shack will sell you one of these things for four bits if you want one. Tuna fish on white bread. The crust is cut off the way you like it.

You sure you don't want one these things. I can get you one, let me get you one..." "Shut up. Please shut up." Said Frankie with tears running.

"So you found your voice. Did you see where your balls went I think I seen them roll under the wheel there." Said Pauley pointing to the wheel of the boxcar.

"This time when you jump up and down on the neck hold on to something will you please." Said Pauley.

"There is no way I'm getting back on that neck." Said Frankie.

"Don't you know when you fall off a frozen giraffe neck you got to get right back on otherwise you lose your nerve. The longer you wait the harder its going to get." Said Pauley.

"I think the longer we wait the softer this thing is going to get." Said Frankie.

"What do you mean." Said Pauley.

"Pauley the thing is frozen now but it ain't going to stay that way forever." Said Frankie.

That frozen giraffe wasn't going to melt inside of a week. But what did they know. This was the first frozen giraffe they ever had to deal with.

"Give me that thing on the wall inside the box." Said Pauley pointing to the inside of the boxcar. "The thing with the red handle, the axe."

Frankie went back into the box. Slow. In his delicate condition slow was as fast as he could go without getting nauseous.

"What are you going to do with the axe Pauley." Frankie was wondering to himself why they kept a fire axe in a frozen box.

Pauley took the axe from Frankie and was about to strike the frozen neck with the business end of the axe. when Frankie yells. "What the fuck are you doing."

"What does it look like I'm doing. I'm going to chop at this fucking thing until it falls on the ground." Said Pauley.

"Oh." Said Frankie.

Pauley lifted the red handled axe over his head, his legs akimbo. The first whack, didn't do much damage. A small dent maybe, and the second whack did the same, mostly nothing. The third strike broke through the skin leaving a wedged shape where the axe made a home for itself.

Twenty-two swings and Pauley grew a blister the size of a silver dollar, and sweat right through his shirt and jacket but didn't get a quarter of the way through the frozen neck.

"You got to do some of this. I think I'm having a stroke." Said Pauley. With his face red like a tomato, his hair plastered to his skull, and puddles forming in his shoes from the runoff.

Pauley sat down. There wasn't anything to sit on, so Pauley just sat down, or fell down. One way or the other he was on the ground.

Frankie took the axe from Pauley and stood perpendicular to the cut wedges. Hitting a frozen giraffe neck with an axe is like cutting a pepperoni with a butter knife.

One hour after the axe made its debut the curtain was coming down on the neck. The giraffe head was almost touching the ground but it still wasn't detached.

Frankie now has a blister of his own, and a tomato face. He sat down, or fell down, he don't remember which.

Pauley, in turn took the axe by the handle, which seemed a lot heavier now than it did an hour earlier. His muscles, were screaming bloody murder while his head was doing the mambo behind his eyeballs.

Pauley lifted the axe above his head then put it back down. It hung beside his leg for a minute then dropped to the ground. Pauley was finished playing lumberjack with the giraffe.

From the leather wrapped around his shoulder Pauley pulled his Smith and Wesson 38 special. With a look in his eyes that made Frankie uncomfortable and a motherfucker on his lips he shot the shit out of that fucking giraffe neck until it fell to pieces in front of the frozen box.

Frankie and Pauley lifted the giraffe neck and slid it into the opposite box. Without the neck, the body, albeit without a couple of its legs (some additional alterations was needed) went through the door unleaded.

A bridge between the boxes was fashioned with a couple planks and the job was completed.

An engine came along a few minutes later and took away the empty box, the one carrying the giraffe was getting picked up later.

"What happens to the giraffe now Pauley? Do we have to bury it?" Said Frankie. "Not this time. Anything that comes in frozen is processed into cat food." Said Pauley.

CHAPTER 29

"Cat food Pauley?" Said Frankie as if no time had passed since they had last opened their mouths.

The Cadillac was out of Jersey City by then and three blocks into Bayonne when the thought occurred to him some twenty-five minutes later. "Yeah. So what. Better they do that with it then we got to give it a funeral. Ain't it?" Said Pauley.

"I guess so, but." Said Frankie.

"But nothing. This is part of what we do. A fucked up part, ma quale scelta abbiamo?" Said Pauley, throwing one hand up in the air, still driving with the other.

"I guess we made our choice already" Said Frankie

"That's right so forget about it. Just some shipping and handling." Said Pauley.

"Where we going now?" Said Frankie, realizing the way back to the office is not the way they were going.

"We got to make a stop in Newark." Said Pauley.

"What's in Newark" Said Frankie.

"I got to go see somebody." Said Pauley.

"This is not the way to the airport, the beer maker or the gin mill. What else do we have in Newark I don't know about yet. It ain't frozen is it?" Said Frankie.

"They don't got nothing in Newark. I got something in Newark." Said Pauley.

"You got a broad in Newark Pauley?" Said Frankie.

"She ain't no broad." Said Pauley.

By now the Cadillac was easing into Newark through one of it's many back doors. Newark is New Jersey's largest city, it has plenty of ways of getting in or out, unless if you live there. Then there doesn't seem to be any way of getting out.

"This isn't a part of Newark that I have ever been to. The woman doesn't live in one of those does she?" Frankie is pointing to one of a dozen or so run down tenement buildings lining the roadway.

The Cadillac continued on through the tenement houses. Frankie was relieved.

A left down a dead end street a mile or so past the project houses on the right hand side. Sunrise Court named long before the sun set on this place and the poor people that live there.

Pauley pulled up in front of a lovely little house, with off white aluminum siding, a newer roof and what looked to be recently installed double pane windows.

Twenty-six Sunrise Court, flowers, deep green grass out front cut clean, and an Italian style fountain adorned with two pissing baby angels, and a couple of fish with water shooting out of their mouths in the back. The fountain was barely visible from the street, or nearly invisible as it should be. The fountain was a horror show.

As soon at the Cadillac hits the curb in front of the house a little black kid came running over to the car. Seven, maybe eight years old, short, stocky, built like a little fireplug.

The kid came barreling up to the driver side door and opened it up. Pauley didn't have time to get up from the seat before the kid had him in a headlock and was kissing him on the cheek.

The kid said something like "Mom is going to kick your butt if you forgot her doody." Pauley told him to watch his mouth and lifted him up in a bear hug and kissed him back.

Frankie is like, "What the hell!" But he doesn't say anything. The situation being what it was until he knew better. A little black kid that looked an awful lot like Pauley was squeezing him around the neck, using almost bad language and kissing him on the face.

Pauley with the kid holding firm to his neck, moved away from the car, pausing at the front end he told Frankie to "come on".

Frankie got out of the car and followed Pauley up the tiled walk, twenty steps and they were in the house.

The foyer, painted pale yellow with whitewash on the woodwork, was small with three coat hooks hammered into the wall on one side, and an elephant foot umbrella stand behind the door on the other. I don't want to know what happened to the elephant what gave up his toenails for a chance to hold upright an umbrella and Frankie, he didn't ask.

Alas, there was no umbrella in the stand. There was a Louisville slugger with a nail sticking out of the fat end, and There was what looked like a fire poker thing made nice and sharp, but there is not one thing in that elephant foot that will keep the rain off of you. Unless maybe your plan was to scare the rain away.

A good looking woman, light skinned, hazel eyes, nice figure, big round bottom, about twenty-five years old, maybe a couple more, came out from what looked like a kitchen, and pulled the kid off of Pauley.

At least I hope it's the kitchen seeing as she is carrying a cleaver, and a wooden mallet.

The kid took off running into a family type room to the left of where they were standing. The television was on in the room.

The kid planted himself like a Buddha in front of the screen, close enough to lick the radiation off of it. The kid didn't move an inch while they were there except to say goodbye when they left.

The woman turned her very pretty face to Frankie and said, "Who are you?"

Naomi." Said Pauley. "Frankie Migliori. Frankie, Naomi Jones."

Frankie said, "Hey." And smiled.

Naomi said, "Hey yourself." And smiled also.

"Good looking kid." Frankie said, turning his face to the lump sitting cross eyed in front of the TV.

" Like his Daddy." Said Naomi. Squeezing Pauley one time around the waist when she said it. Pauley, also a lump though not cross-eyed, was the spitting image though somewhat faded.

"You chopping down a tree or did you finally grow the balls to take me out. What's with the cleaver, who or what are you damaging in that kitchen." Said Pauley.

"Pig knuckles, you want some?" Said Naomi.

"Frankie you hungry?" Said Pauley

"I could eat something." Said Frankie.

Frankie learned in the Army that if you hungry enough you can eat anything.

"You and Frankie go into the kitchen and sit down. I'll be there in a minute. There ain't no more beer in the refrigerator, but we got some in the basement. I'll Be right back." Naomi handed off the knife and mallet to Pauley, backed up a step, turned and slipped through a right side situated doorway.

Naomi went down loud on the steps leading to the basement. "Well she seems nice." Said Frankie trying to crack the iceberg.

"She is." Said Pauley giving nothing away. "The kid. He got a name, or do I just call him Junior." Said Frankie. Taking a deep breath and diving.

"His name is Paul." Said Pauley.

"Junior for short then?" Said Frankie egging.

"The kid is mine. So what. You got a problem with my kid, Frankie? Or do you want me to make this a problem for you." The look in Pauley's eyes and the glint from the still palmed blade told Frankie that he did not want to push that button again.

Frankie didn't have a problem with the kid. "I don't have a problem with the kid. He's your kid. I get it." Said Frankie.

Frankie wanted to say something nice, but the crap between his brain and his mouth didn't let anything come through.

Pauley tabled the knife.

Naomi came up quiet from the basement perhaps listening to the conversation between Frankie and Pauley. She was carrying three beers and a box of Uneeda biscuits.

I guess Pauley eats his pig knuckles with them dry bones. "Not them fucking things." Frankie slips in a "fucking" before he gets the ok to sing from the gutter in front of Naomi. "Pardon my French." Said Frankie, quickly.

"I don't like them either." Said Naomi. "I keep them around for him." Pointing a dead eye at Pauley, already reaching for the box.

"Entrambi sono pazzo. Them cookies is great." Said Pauley.

"Crackers!" Said Frankie and Naomi as if they were co-joined. "They are crackers Pauley." Said Frankie revisiting. Pauley, he shrugged and took two to the throat with a beer tagging.

"Every time I make a noise about them crackers he tells me I'm crazy." Said Naomi."

"Yeah, me too." Said Frankie

"The knuckles look good." Said Pauley after he choked down two more Uneeda Biscuits.

"The knuckles, are raw." Said Naomi. She was splitting joints when they came in.

Naomi made up a plate of knuckles she had prepared earlier with some bitter greens, and another kind of meat, pickled, from a jar sitting on the bottom shelf in the pantry closet, just before the basement door.

"You bring me my shit?" Said Naomi. Another dead eye aimed at Pauley's head. "In the car. I forgot to bring them in. You keep company with Frankie for a minute and let me go out to the trunk and get you your shit." Said Pauley.

"He always forgetting my shit. I need my shit." Said Naomi after the door slammed behind Pauley.

"He tell you about me?" Naomi said. She was looking at Frankie, dead eye gone, smiling. Naomi was more white than black. Her facial characteristics, were narrow. Her lips were full but not swollen. Light eyes and hair more auburn than coal.

"No." Said Frankie.

"I'm not surprised." Said Naomi.

"I am." Said Frankie.

Not surprised that Pauley did not tell him about Naomi. Frankie was surprised more like, like jumping out from behind a tree and yelling, "Boo!" Surprised.

"We are a lot like Romeo and Juliet ain't we, me and Pauley." Said Naomi.

Frankie had heard of Romeo and Juliet, he didn't exactly remember how the story went, but he did know that it did not go well for either of them.

"More like Beauty and the Beast if you are asking." Said Frankie changing shades.

"You blushing? I guess I still got it. The legs, is still good, but my ass got a mind of its own. And all it wants to do is grow." Said Naomi teetering on one cheek to emphasize her point.

"There are worse things that can happen to a person." Said Frankie emphatically.

Pauley came crashing into the house like the bull he is and fell into his seat at the table's head.

Pauley gave Naomi a box wrapped with twine. Taking the cleaver blade to the string Naomi easily cut through the fibers. She lifted the top of the box and reached in with two hands and pulled out a paper tray with six cannoli on it. The pastries were beautiful. Thin, crisp and toasted shells, crème filled and swelled up like a body two weeks in the water.

"I need my shit." Said Naomi going down on one of the confections.

"I created a Monster." Said Pauley. "No wonder your ass is getting so frigging big."

"We were just talking about that." Said Frankie.

"You was just talking about her ass." Said Pauley mocked up mean.

"It came up in conversation." Said Frankie dim-witted. "That must have been some conversation." Said Pauley.

"It was good. Was it good for you too Naomi." Said Frankie laughing.

"Fuck you." Said Pauley.

The socializing was done and the cannoli had been eaten. Pauley got up from the table. Naomi, she got up too.

"Frankie give us a couple of minutes will you. Go and sit with the kid, watch the TV, do whatever you want. I need to speak with Naomi." Said Pauley.

"Sure thing." Said Frankie.

Frankie pushed away from his half-eaten cannoli siting mutilated on a plate and walked to the room where the kid was sitting. The kid was not a fan of cannoli and begged off when asked if he wanted one preferring to stay seated in front of the box.

Frankie sat down on the corduroy brown, high back couch that faced the Television. The kid didn't acknowledge Frankie he just sat there transfixed.

Forty minutes after his behind touched the corduroy Pauley came out of whatever room him and Naomi were in and walked into the living room adjusting the buckle on his trousers. A minute after that Naomi came in wearing a pale blue button down shirt that looked to be too big for her but just big enough to fit Pauley.

From mid thigh down Naomi was showing some of what she got. Frankie was staring at her legs

"First you was talking to Naomi about her ass, and now you are going beady eyes on her gams. Naomi, I think Frankie got a thing for you. What do you think about that." Said Pauley leering knee level.

"Maybe Frankie likes his chicken dark. Frankie you like your chicken dark?" Said Naomi, teasing.

Frankie, he turned colors and went mute for a second. "Pussy is pussy." Said Frankie.

"Speaking of Pussy. Frankie when was the last time you got some?"

"The last time I could pay for it with Hershey bars." Said Frankie. Gritting his teeth.

"You ain't had nothing since you was in the army?" Said Pauley.

"It's not that long ago." Said Franking defending his right to keep his testicles.

"Three days is too long." Said Pauley.

"You know the situation Pauley. Why you breaking my balls." Said Frankie. "Because it's fun. That's why." Said Pauley. "Don't worry things are going to change for you real soon." Said Pauley.

"Why. You going to let me sleep with the Boss's daughter?" Said Frankie. "Sei pazzo! No, I was going to buy you a bottle of hand lotion and a couple of nudie books." Said Pauley.

"Right now a piece of sandpaper and a box of pancakes would do it for me." Said Frankie.

"Aunt Jemima get you all worked up then?" Said Pauley.

"Today she does." Said Frankie, noticing how sexy Naomi looked in her pale blue button down shirt.

"Naomi you better get out of here before Frankie starts chasing you around the coffee table." Said Pauley,

"Maybe he don't have to run so fast to catch me." Said Naomi. "He is kind of nice looking." "Maybe you two want I should leave." Said Pauley.

"Do you have to leave so soon? Well, it's been swell seeing you. Come back again real soon." Said Frankie, with his arm around Pauley's neck ushering.

"You'd like that wouldn't you, you fucking horn bag." Said Pauley.

"Yes. Yes I would. Now leave." Said Frankie smiling dirty.

"We got to go." Said Pauley.

Naomi was pressing herself up against Pauley telling him with her tits not to go.

"When you coming back? You know the baby got a birthday this weekend. He is going to be seven on Sunday and maybe he wants his Daddy to wish him luck.

You want I should tell him his Daddy is going to be here when we cutting his cake. Or do I do like I had to do last year when you didn't show up and I had to rub his back when he was crying because his Daddy, didn't come to see him on his birthday. Which one is it going to be?" Said Naomi.

She was speaking low so the boy didn't hear what she was saying about him. The kid had his eyes glued to the screen but just in case the picture tube blew up while she was talking to Pauley Naomi was trying to keep it down.

"Breakfast Sunday morning is the best I can't do. Sunday night I got to be at Sal's. You know that. So why you giving me shit about what you know already?" Said Pauley rehashing what seems to be old news.

"Saturday night?" Said Naomi, softening.

"No good. We got things we got to do. Sunday morning, I'll be here when he wakes up." Said Pauley.

"The Baby want skates." Said Naomi, almost smiling. "No problem." Said Pauley. "Now kiss me so I can get the fuck out of here."

Naomi kissed Pauley hard on the mouth and then pushed him away like yesterdays egg salad.

Naomi went to the refrigerator and pulled out the pig knuckles she had been working on when they came in.

Pauley, he leaned down by the boy and patted his head to get his attention. When the kid turned his face to see who was patting him Pauley gave him a kiss on the forehead.

The kid grabbed Pauley by the neck, and put his face up against his cheek.

Pauley raised up lifting to full height, the kid with him still attached.

"You be a good boy for your Mommy, and I will see you Sunday morning when you wake up. Daddy will have something nice for you." Said Pauley. "

Skates?" Said Paul Junior.

"We'll see." Said Pauley.

CHAPTER 30

"You got a kid. That's nice." Said Frankie. The Cadillac now short one box of cannoli and motoring it's way out of Newark. Passing once again the projects, neighborhoods on life support, and others dead or near dead from neglect, malnutrition, and malfeasance.

The main streets were thriving at that time with Macy's, and Gimbal's holding forth downtown. The high rise Insurance vendors were still selling big on the top floors, the brewers were busy and there was no shortage of industry within the city limits, oil, gas, and manufacturing to name a few. Yet on the outskirts, people were suffering from a lack of wherewithal. Services to the poorer areas of the city were almost non-existent.

"Do I got to explain the rules to you, or do you think you get it without me having to spell it out for you?" Said Pauley, giving one eye to Frankie.

"What rules?" Said Frankie. "Rule number one you don't never mention Naomi to nobody. You want to say something about her or the kid you wait until we are out of earshot. You got that so far." Said Pauley, serious as a heart attack.

"Rule number two. You don't never talk bad about black people when Naomi or the boy is close enough to hear you. You may think this is a given, but let me tell you something. The things what come out of a mouth when it ain't thinking about what it ought to be saying is exactly the shit it ain't supposed to say. You got it?" Said Pauley.

"Huh." Said Frankie. "Play the music in your head before you start singing." Said Pauley.

"I don't think I'm going to have a problem. I like Naomi. I don't know her or the kid very well, but I think they are good eggs." Said Frankie.

"Just be careful with your words believe me they slip out easy. Before you know it the air is lousy with them and you can't apologize enough to make them go away too quick." Said Pauley relating.

And you know what else? For every, "Black bastard," there are two " Rotten Jews," and three, "Fucking dumb Polaks" And you know something I don't think my Mother raised me too good. Does my tolerance level seem a little low to you?" Said Pauley.

"How should I know? I wasn't raised any better than you were." Said Frankie.

"Was it love at first sight, or what?" Said Frankie. "Not even close. The first time she sees me I was trying to pull a parking meter out of the ground in front the Jew's gem joint.

They don't know me too good over there and I don't want to get a parking ticket. You get too many of them things and the cops, is pulling you over every time you get in the car.

I had a sledge in the trunk so I was hitting it side to side trying to loosen the stem so I can pull it up out of the ground. I figure like this. No meter, no ticket and I would just put it back into the ground when I leave. Smart right?

Naomi was inside the shop getting her watch fixed or her ears pierced something like that. Anyway, she came through the front door posing with crossed arms and looking at me. So right away I feel like an idiot, but I don't stop beating the thing to death. I'm a man right? And real men, they hit things with hammers right? I think maybe she likes to see a man working with his hands and maybe I'm getting to her.

She says, "Excuse me," like three times before I came down from Mount Olympics, or wherever them Greece balls are from. I say, "Yeah?" And she, don't say a thing. She hands me a nickel and walks away, a fucking nickel? Fucking genius. Don't you get it? I'm beating the shit out of a defenseless nickel slot machine just so I don't get a parking ticket. Put a nickel in the slot and you don't got to worry about no parking ticket. I'm thinking, what a dope I am.

I can't let her get away her thinking I don't got no brains in my head, so I went after her. And I catch her before she gets on the cross-town bus, and I tell her, nothing. I don't know what to tell her because I think whatever it is that comes out of my mouth is going to be stupid. So I don't say nothing. My mind goes blank and I just stand there like a dunce.

After what seemed like three days. I say, "Thanks for the nickel." She smiled at me nice, not like I got a penguin on my head, but, nice. Then before I can say something that ain't ridiculous she gets on the bus and takes off without me knowing who she is, where do she live, who do she belong to, nothing.

Now, usually a dame don't never mean more to me than a few laughs, but this one, she hit me like a ton of bricks. I go back to the Jew and I ask him who the woman what just left before I come in. The Jew he says he don't know who she is, but she comes in once in a while for adjustments on an old flap top watch maybe belongs to her father, an old railroad ticker. He says she left the watch with him and is going to pick it up the following Tuesday. The watch been round-trip a few times before so he, don't write anything on the ticket. Except "Tuesday, afternoon, cleaning."

So what do I do? Instead of smiling to myself and moving on to something less complicated, I go back to the Jew the following Tuesday. Four hours I wait for her to show up. Every half-hour after I get there I'm ready to go. Forget this shit, I don't need this shit, what am I stupid? I'm saying all these things to myself, but I don't go no-where.

One hour, two hours, three hours, four-fucking hours. Then she steps off the bus at the same corner opposite where she got on the last time I see her. She looks good kind of made up like she works in an office or a bank or someplace like that. Tweed skirt, white blouse, sensible type shoes, hot.

I went up to her when she was reaching for the Jew doorknob. Before I can say, hey good looking, or what's shaking, or hello even, she says, "You need another nickel?" I tell her no thanks, but I ask her if maybe she is hungry or thirsty and would she maybe like to get something to eat or whatever.

She says to me that she don't think it's is a very good idea, and I says, why not? She smiles at me again, like she did the week before, and she turns the knob and goes inside. I don't follow her in, the Jew, he don't need to know nothing. So I wait outside, leaning on a lamp post, until she come out. Only she, don't come out.

Twenty minutes after she went into the Jews he comes out and starts pulling down the metal grate so as to lock the place up.

I ask the Jew where the woman who came in to pick up her father's watch after you cleaned went to, and he tells me she run out the back door after she pays the bill.

Back door? What fucking back door, I don't know the Jew has got a back door in his joint.

All that time I was leaning I don't think to look any other way but straight ahead, seeing as I was posing. Naomi, she got away again.

The Jew asks me why I'm so interested in the woman seeing as this is two times already I asked him about her.

I tell him to mind his own fucking business and he tells me ok by him. I say, all right then. And I go to slump behind the wheel of the Cadillac for a few minutes until I feel better which don't happen right away.

I got to tell you I wasn't feeling too good sitting there in the car like that, all dejected and depressed.

I know she must have seen me standing outside. So I am thinking that she was trying to avoid me. I don't want to ask myself why she done that because maybe the answer don't make no sense to me, or hurts my feelings more than they were already.

First I got mad, and then I'm thinking maybe she don't want to know nothing about a stupid white guy what beats up parking meters with a sledge hammer.

Now this makes sense to me. But I don't want this to be the punch line. So the next day I wait for the bus like I know she done the day before, and I follow the freaking thing. All the while keeping my eyes peeled.

I done this every fucking day for two weeks, and I don't see nothing. Except a lot of nervous eyeballs looking at me driving too close behind a city bus and watching them who gets on and off.

After two weeks I am finished with this passion play and go belly up on the plan and decide to go and get my dick into something more reasonable." Said Pauley.

"I can't believe you followed a city bus for two weeks for a woman because she gave you a nickel." Said Frankie.

"Are you kidding me. Did you see that ass on her? Imagine it seven years younger and then tell me the nickel had anything to do with it. I went sappy over her." Pauley shrugged.

"And look at the kid he's beautiful. Do you think it's easy having a son you can't talk about or show pictures of?

How about having a wonderful woman who loves you and that you love more than anything in the world and you can't tell nobody about her. You got to keep her holed up someplace out of the way.

I don't got papers on her but I got a kid with her." Said Pauley, getting all red in the face and wet under the eyebrows.

"You told me about them and I am glad that you did." Said Frankie, not knowing what else to say. And waiting for chapter two of the bus scenario.

"Thanks it felt good to show them to you." Said Pauley who coughed up some phlegm and then went on with the show.

"Two weeks of chasing rainbows and not one pot of gold showing. I wasn't getting anywhere except where I had been every day over and over again for two weeks and the scene don't never change. People get on the bus, and people get off the bus and none of them was her.

The city bus don't carry no surprises and the people that ride it ain't looking for any either. A yo-yo moves about the same as that bus and is about as interesting after two weeks." Said Pauley.

"If she doesn't get on the bus then how is it that you two come together." Said Frankie trying to move the story along a little bit. "I decided that I ain't going to chase that bus no more. So I quit.

I pulled the blinker handle two times so I'm going back the way I came, but I don't go no further than the corner coffee shop, which I know from experience, got some nice crullers.

I pulled the Cadillac to the curb in front of the place, which isn't much more than a good smell. All pane glass and peeling paint and giving no indication as to the goodness what lies under a plastic lid sitting counter top and to the right of the ketchup bottle.

Nice crullers, toasted brown with a little powdered sugar. "Said Pauley.

"Enough with the crullers what happened next." Said Frankie, agitated.

"That's the sad part of the story. I don't never get no crullers." Said Pauley, feeling bad still.

"Why not?" Said Frankie, now a little curious as to why Pauley didn't get any crullers.

"Outside the place they got one of them parking meters like the one they got by the Jew. This time I don't go for the toolbox. I go hands deep looking for a spare coin, only I don't got one. All of my pockets is empty. Not one stinking nickel do I got, Benjamin Franklin I got kissing my ass but a five cent piece I don't got.

By this time I can't take it no more. I got to get the hell away from this place real quick or I'm going to do something. Maybe I'm going to punch somebody in the face or maybe I'm going to shoot a hole in one of them parking meters, I don't know which, but something is going to get broke.

I take a step to the car, maybe I'm getting the sledge, maybe I'm getting my piece, I don't know, I don't know." Pauley was holding his head in his hands. "Then I hear click, click, click, click, click, and click coming from behind me. My ears, they can't make out where the sound is coming from. So I turn my face to see what is making that noise." Said Pauley pausing for no reason.

"What was it?" Said Frankie.

"For a second I think it's a rattlesnake or something but this being Newark New Jersey I let that one get away from me.

I turn my face like I was saying and what do I see." Said Pauley milking.

"What?" Said Frankie.

"Naomi putting a nickel in the parking meter, she was turning the knob on the thing." Said Pauley.

"Nah." Said Frankie.

"Yeah." Said Pauley.

"What a nice person she is Pauley." Said Frankie.

"You don't think I know this." Said Pauley.

"So?" Said Frankie waiting for the knot to be tied.

"So?" Said Pauley, not adding more to the conversation.

"So then what happened?" Said Frankie ready to pull teeth.

"What do you got to know everything?" Said Pauley.

"I got to know more than this." Said Frankie.

"What else do you need to know. We had a kid and here we are." Said Pauley like he just finished tying his shoe and is ready to go for a walk.

"What about the seven years in between the cruller and the cannoli?" Said Frankie.

"I never got that cruller." Said Pauley, Smiling too big.

"What happened after you didn't get the cruller?" Said Frankie.

"Another time pre haps. Said Pauley. "It's per-haps you moron. And why not now?" Said Frankie digging a little.

"We got things." Said Pauley.

"What things we got?" Said Frankie.

"Things." Now shut up and let me drive. We got things."

CHAPTER 31

"Hey Pauley." Said Frankie. "Everything go Ok with the giraffe." Frankie had gotten out of bed when he smelled coffee brewing.

He put on his pants because Pauley doesn't like anybody walking around in their drawers and slippers, because Pauley, doesn't want to see bare feet flapping around on his varnish, and socks because Frankie doesn't wear shoes without socks.

Pauley had been on the telephone earlier so Frankie assumed he had been discussing what they had done the day before.

Frankie heard Pauley say, "That fucking thing," about twelve times before he pulled himself up from the bed and Pauley had hung up the receiver.

Frankie had gotten used to Pauley being on the phone when he woke up in the morning as it had become his ad hoc alarm clock, and the smell of coffee.

"That thing is melting away as we speak. The boys in Secaucus are waiting until it does so they can chop the thing up" Said Pauley, Still not dressed beyond his deep maroon silk robe, slippers of the same ilk and duck pattern pajama bottoms.

Frankie sleeps in his boxer shorts. He tried to wear pajamas a couple of times but he could never get used to the cuffs creeping up his legs during the night.

"So what do we do now?" Said Frankie taking his first sip of the coffee. "Good coffee Pauley,"

"I pressed it about ten minutes ago. You might want to warm it up." Said Pauley.

Pauley was sitting at the kitchen table. His robe matching perfectly with the faux leather under his ass. "I guess we drink coffee and wait until I get a call back from the guy that we got to go see down on the docks in Bayonne." Said Pauley dunking a Uneeda biscuit daintily into his coffee.

"Something coming in or going out." Said Frankie putting butter to crisp crusted bread bought fresh from a Portuguese bakery in Newark.

"Put a napkin down, or plate that bread. I don't want to see crumbs on that counter. You want ants or cockroaches moving in?" Said Pauley. Living with you is bad enough." Said Frankie. "Gee, thanks." Said Pauley.

Frankie put a plate under the bread and used a wet thumb to collect the crumbs that fell onto the table's top during the transfer.

"You didn't answer my question Pauley. Coming in or going out?" Said Frankie taking the chair opposite Pauley and moving a vase from the middle space between them so he can see Pauley when his lips move.

"Watch the flower it's delicate and hard to get." Said Pauley.

"I didn't even know it was real." Said Frankie. "It doesn't look like any flower I have ever seen. What do you call the thing?"

"It is called an orchid and it ain't no usual one neither. It came on the same boat what the giraffe went dead on. Pretty, even though it don't smell worth a damn." Said Pauley.

"How did you get it. Do we sell them things too?" Said Frankie.

"Aside from being nice to look at this flower is some kind of anal, anal, analgesiac." Said Pauley.

"What is an analgesiac?" Said Frankie getting nothing from what came out of Pauley's mouth.

"The Japanese, they get a hard on from smelling them.

They dry them, grind them up real fine, mix them up with dried Rhinoceros dick or elephant asshole I don't know which and then they snort it up through their nose.

They go nuts for the stuff. Makes them want to go to town on the misses if you get me." Said Pauley smirking sideways.

" You mean an aphrodisiac" Said Frankie. "Does it work?"

"You are a kid what do you need with a boost. This aff, affro afrody, this stuff is for middle age guys what lost a step or graybeards what makes promises with they wallet." Said Pauley.

"Yeah, yeah, but does it work?" Said Frankie.

"No more than wishing it did." Said Pauley.

"What does that mean?" Said Frankie.

"It's a mind game. The Japanese think it works, so it works." Said Pauley.

"So it doesn't work." Said Frankie.

"It might work if." Said Pauley.

"If what?" Said Frankie.

"If maybe we used real orchids and not ground up daffodils, or maybe we used rhino dick instead of the dried horse cock" Said Pauley.

"The Japanese can't tell the difference?" Said Frankie.

"No, they don't seem to. By the time they get to it, it don't look like nothing no more."

"So Pauley what do we do with the orchids and Elephant cock if we don't do magic with it." Said Frankie.

"The orchids they go to collectors mostly who pay through the nose, and to high end flower shops in Manhattan.

The botanical garden while they pay us for the bat shit don't want flowers what can't sit on the right side of a balance sheet. I guess nobody ever asks where they get the bat shit from.

Elephant asshole and rhinoceros cock? We almost never get that stuff because the Japanese get first dibs on whatever comes out of the jungle, which don't leave much." Said Pauley with a little extra schmaltz on the asshole and cock.

"What do we charge for this love potion?" Said Frankie.

"Two hundred dollars" Said Pauley firm.

"Two hundred a pop A pound?" Said Frankie.

"An ounce" said Pauley.

"Two hundred dollars an ounce Are you kidding?" Said Frankie his tongue hanging.

"Sometimes more when we can clip the real shit before it goes behind a counter someplace." Said Pauley.

"Two hundred dollars an ounce for daffodils and horse cock, unbelievable." Said Frankie.

"What's the matter, a hard dick ain't worth that much to you? Wait thirty years and I'll ask you again." Said Pauley.

"It is not even real Pauley." Said Frankie.

"Real enough for some peoples" Said Pauley.

"You thinking about anyone in particular Pauley?" Said Frankie.

"The boss he uses it. Only he doesn't know it don't come from the jungle, and I'm not telling him that it comes from the funeral parlor and the glue factory." Said Pauley.

"The funeral parlor?" Said Frankie.

"Yeah, where do you think we get them daffodils from, or carnations, or whatever flowers is going dead when a stiff goes underground." Said Pauley.

"Is the boss having problems with hydraulics Pauley?" Said Frankie.

"Nothing a little horse cock can't fix. He wants the stuff as soon as it comes in from the boat, only sometimes, most times it's coming from the trunk of my car.

I keep the shit we get from the boat as long as I can before I got to start cutting with the homemade. He mixes a teaspoon into a glass of prune juice every morning, the boss, don't put it up his nose, he says it makes him sneeze. So as long as I can get the color right he don't notice.

The dried plums probably do more for him than the dried horse cock does. But like I was telling you. It's a mind game. The Boss thinks it works, so it works. And as long as it gets his pecker hard I'll keep making it for him." Said Pauley.

"The stuff ain't bad for him, is it?" Said Frankie.

"It ain't killed him yet has it." Said Pauley.

"Hey maybe it'll make is feet grow too." Said Frankie. "Don't go there." Said Pauley raising his hand palm open and gesturing small to Frankie. "Don't go there."

"But they only get bigger until he shoots his wad." Said Frankie.

"Stop it!" Said Pauley with coffee coming out of his nose.

CHAPTER 32

Frankie and Pauley went to the Bayonne docks because who ever it was that called them, told them to go there. Three containers were coming in from Taiwan that were supposed to be loaded with condoms.

Frankie and Pauley were to verify the contents of each container, accept shipment of the condoms, and pay the man for the goods. If everything was kosher Pauley would arrange for two of the containers to be picked up that day and one would go home with them.

The Boss stocked all of the central Jersey whore houses and beer joints with condoms. The one that you paid a buck for in the machine next to the pisser. Or the condom that you didn't see until after the fish you paid to suck your dick made you go cross-eyed. They were his.

Ribbed, twisted, glow in the dark even condoms that taste good right there on the shelf in front of you in your neighborhood Walgreens. Not in those days back then condoms came only one way, with guilt and worry.

Now you don't have to feel guilty about using a condom you get to feel socially responsible.

All sizes, small, sorry I mean large, who would buy a condom if it had the word small printed anywhere on the carton. Large, larger and more larger?

Most guys just buy the biggest condom they can find and cuff it once at the bottom if they have to. Maybe they sell a pair of suspenders that you… nah, that was going to be a terrible joke I will let you off the hook this time. Imagine though a tiny pair of suspenders that strap you into your condom.

Anyway, I think Sal charged a nickel apiece for them things back then, only he didn't pay more than a nickel for a hundred of them.

The quality was good enough more or less. You still had to worry some. Sure they would stop you from getting the clap most times and keep you out of the way of the midwife if you were lucky. So I guess you got your nickel's worth.

I did see them things in the dollar store one time. Irregulars, the seam not straight, a button missing, off color, what?

With STD's still knocking people dead, and girls still getting pregnant, why don't you do yourself a favor and pay the full price for first quality protection. Penny wise and seven pounds six ounces foolish.

Pauley took a crowbar to a crate pulled from one of the containers by a longshoreman he knew very well. This particular longshoreman never did nothing that Big Nas didn't tell him to do.

The top of the crate came loose easy enough but the rubbers that were supposed to be inside were not. Dildos all shapes, all sizes, every color you can think of. Red dildos, blue dildos, black dildos dozens of them. They were made of rubber, but they were not rubbers.

"What am I supposed to do with these things?" Said Pauley to the longshoreman who didn't say anything. He just shrugged his shoulders. Pauley looked at Frankie and repeated himself. "What am I supposed to do with these things?"

"Well, I can tell you what to do with one of them." Said Frankie trying not to laugh.

"Don't say it. I will shoot you I swear to god I'll do it." Said Pauley.

"Hey Pauley maybe we can sell them door to door, or into the plumbing business," Said Frankie.

"You ever seen one of these things Frankie?" Said Pauley.

"No, but I think I know what the blacksmith thought when he saw his first automobile." Said Frankie.

"Pauley?" Said Frankie.

" Have you ever seen a guy with a dick this big Pauley?" Said Frankie holding up a pea green twelve-inch example of what the most fashionable young men are definitely not wearing in New Jersey this season.

"Yeah sure every time I look down in the shower." Said Pauley grinning.

"That's funny Pauley because I never seen nobody go in there with you." Said Frankie.

CHAPTER 33

It turned out that those crates of dildos were nothing to worry about since only three of them were filled with sex toys. It was the three hundred crates of rubber bands what were a problem.

"Three hundred crates of rubber bands. Jesus Christ, what are we going to do with three hundred crates of rubber bands?" Said Pauley.

Frankie was standing next to Pauley when the last crate was unloaded from the boat, opened and nearly thrown into the water by Pauley who called upon, "Jesus Christ," every time he opened one of them crates.

"Maybe we can send them back to where they came from." Said Frankie.

"Haven't you figured out how this thing works yet." Said Pauley.

"I don't follow you" Said Frankie.

"Frankie, let me ask you a question. Do you think, that I bought these things from the Woolworth's?" Said Pauley. Frankie shrugged.

"I made a deal with a guy, a very well connected guy, who did something bad to another guy who was also well connected, but was not a very good friend of Mr. Nasorosso. So I was given the opportunity to fix the thing. For a fee of course and That's what I did."

Pauley's fee was three containers of condoms.

"You see it clear yet?" Said Pauley.

"Is it possible that he misunderstood what it was you wanted." Said Frankie.

"The guy, he asks me what I want, I say rubbers. What is there to misunderstand?" Said Pauley.

"This guy, the one you said did the thing to the other guy, who is this guy, and why can't you call him." Said Frankie.

"Because that isn't how it's done. I don't want to show no disrespect to the guy because even though he did the thing to that other guy he is still a good friend of the Boss and I don't want that Sally should get pissed at me." Said Pauley.

"I thought you said that you fixed it." Said Frankie.

"I did fix it."Said Pauley offended.

"So how does sending you three hundred crates of rubber bands and three crates of them other things make it stay fixed?" Said Frankie

"Maybe he thought I wanted rubber bands." Said Pauley.

"So maybe it was an honest mistake." Said Frankie.

"A mistake, maybe, honest? I don't think so." Said Pauley.

"This thing smells so bad I am going to nickname it Your Asshole. This thing is so crooked that when I look straight at it I see the back of my head." Said Pauley.

"I get it, but it was either done straight which don't say much about what this guy thinks of you, or maybe he didn't intend to do it, and you should give him a chance to fix it." Said Frankie.

"Maybe your right, but do I really want to know if this guy tried to fuck me over, because then I got to do something which isn't a good thing." Said Pauley.

"Or do I just find something to do with three hundred crates of rubber bands and three crates of them other things, leave well enough alone. Because if I go pissing up that tree shit will fall down on me big time." Said Pauley.

"Piss." Said Frankie.

"What about piss?" Said Pauley.

"Piss, if you piss up a tree then piss not shit will fall down on you. How can you piss up a tree and have shit fall down on you? It doesn't make any sense. Piss goes up. Piss comes down." Said Frankie.

"Your sister's ass!" Said Pauley.

"My sister's ass? What does my sister have to do with shit falling out of a tree?" Said Frankie laughing.

"Please shut up." Said Pauley.

"I will shut up if you call the guy who did this thing." Said Frankie.

Pauley called the guy.

There was a diner near the Bayonne docks that served it up hot to the longshoremen around the clock seven out of seven. The food was good and it didn't cost too much.

The Boat diner, named after what was always floating in front of it, was a good place to meet girls, behind the Dumpster, under the lamppost, in the alleyway. I didn't say it is a place to meet nice girls.

The pay phone in the Boat Diner hung next to the cigarette machine. And the cigarette machine stood quiet next to a door with M E N spelled out on it in black grease pencil.

The machine was standing there all by itself because it was all out of cigarettes and was giving away only matches through the hole in the bottom.

Frankie could hear Pauley on the phone, one sided but clear enough to get most of what was passing through the wire. "Yeah, I got the things today. Three hundred crates. Oh yeah, no kidding, I was hoping you might say that." Pauley was smiling. "Tomorrow, 12:00 noon, by the big nose fish guy on Broadway. No problem, by the way, what are you going to do with them things anyway? Yeah? Good, I'll see you tomorrow then." Said Pauley.

"Who were you talking to, and what did he say." Said Frankie.

"Who he is, is none of your business, and what he said was there was some kind of mix up, and he is glad that I called him and so on and so forth." Said Pauley.

"What kind of mix up?" Said Frankie pushing a little bit. "You ask too many questions, you know that?" Said Pauley irritated.

"I don't get it Pauley. You tell me about every other thing, most of which I don't want to know about but this thing which isn't something I have to worry about, you don't say anything. What the hell?" Said Frankie. Frankie, not really pissed just curious as to why secrets do not pass between them.

"Forget about it for now." Pauley picked up his hat, lying flat on the cigarette machine, held it between his thumb and index finger, and walked to a table at the back of the dining room.

Pauley pulled a chair and sat down, his back was to the wall, and his eyes were facing the entrance. Frankie following two steps behind him took a seat opposite and to the left of Pauley.

Frankie, in the mirror behind Pauley's head, could see the front entrance, a back entrance to his left about ten yards away, and the beginning of a bald spot that maybe Pauley didn't know about yet.

The Boat Diner wasn't crowded as it was late in the day and between shifts which were eight to four, four to twelve, and twelve to eight by way of the union.

Eight hours a day unless you want to pay time and a half. A sweet deal at the time. These guys were already pulling down more than a living wage, and if things got a little slow and some things didn't get stowed or towed then the timecard got green paint job.

A job on the docks, a real job not a sublet for a percentage, came up through the roots. If you look just like your father, your Uncle Tony, or your sister Connie's husband Gino, etc., you would get placed. Otherwise just fill out an application and we'll call you as soon as we get something.

Pauley ordered a hamburger with fried potatoes, three pickles, Cole slaw on the side, and brown gravy so he can dip his spuds. I don't like brown gravy on French fries, or barbecue sauce, or vinegar and salt. I like ketchup or nothing.

Frankie ordered a BLT club sandwich on toast, no mayonnaise, one pickle, no French fries, no Cole slaw, and a coke.

The waitress, a short stack of tip bait, carrying more than just a tray of sandwiches in front of her, leaning forward because she can't help it, showed Pauley something that made him smile for the first time that day.

Pauley cracked wise with a, "Hey toots." The waitress Phyllis so says the name tag pointing straight up to the ceiling smiled but didn't stop to make small talk with him. She dropped her load and went.

"What's wrong with her?" Said Pauley. The look on his face was not pleasant.

"Maybe she doesn't go in for that kind of thing Pauley." Said Frankie.

"I was just being friendly." Said Pauley.

"You were pitching." Said Frankie.

"Yeah, so I was pitching, so what." Said Pauley.

"Maybe Phyllis is a nice girl who doesn't want to get mixed up with a bum like you." Said Frankie, taking a bite of BLT, and losing half of it to the plate.

"You're not supposed to take the toothpicks out stupid." Said Pauley. "Unless you want to end up eating that thing with a fork and that isn't no way to eat a sandwich."

"You can't eat a sandwich with a toothpick sticking in it. What do you want to do puncture yourself?" Said Frankie.

"Then tell me this? Why do they put the toothpicks in there in the first place if you're not supposed to leave them in there?" Said Pauley, throwing half his hamburger down his throat before he remembered he had teeth.

"The toothpick supports the sandwich from the time it leaves the kitchen until it has to look at your ugly mug. Then it drops dead." Said Frankie, using his fork, and smiling crooked.

"That just isn't right." Said Pauley.

"Who is Phyllis?" Said Pauley.

"Phyllis is the waitress." Said Frankie.

"You know her?" Said Pauley.

"Her name tag Pauley. You stare at tits all day long and you never see a name tag?" Said Frankie.

"I got priorities. If the tits you are talking about would stay still long enough then maybe I would have time to read a name tag. Anyway, you read all you want to. I just want to look at the pictures." Said Pauley forgetting to chew the other half of his hamburger.

Phyllis came back to see if there was anything else they needed, and would they like a refill on their drinks.

"No thanks." Said Frankie.

Pauley, never one to give up easy made another pass at the waitress.

"Hey Phyllis why don't you sit down with us for a minute? You know you look like you could use a break." Said Pauley, palming vinyl and throwing a hundred watts at the poor thing. Pauley pulled the chair next to his closer turning it out.

Phyllis smiled nervous, looking at her pad and pencil all the while she was asking whether they would like, "Pie, or coffee, the pound cake is nice."

"Hey Frankie Phyllis says the pound cake is nice, it sure looks nice don't it Frankie?"

Phyllis went red in the face and not smiling this time asked again if they would care for anything else.

"Coffee," Frankie said. "Pauley you want something?" "How about a piece of Phyllis's pound cake, and make it to go because I can do better than this dump. Can't I Frankie?" Said Pauley pausing big between the Phyllis and the cake. "Bring him some pound cake, and a coffee." Said Frankie.

"Cute kid." Said Pauley.

"You were breathing a little heavy on her don't you think?" Said Frankie, leaning in an inch.

"So I was breathing heavy, so what?" Said Pauley, knitting two brows into one.

"The kid is scared of you ease up a little." Said Frankie pulling that inch away.

"She isn't scared of me. Not used to getting the business is all." Said Pauley pausing.

"Waiting tables is like walking the street. Every dick looks too big when you first start sucking them, then after a while, they are just another dick." Said Pauley philosophically.

"Is this something I should write in my journal, or should I scribble it next to the toilet? You would be right up there on the wall with that girl from Nantucket." Said Frankie, laughing.

"Laugh, go ahead, but everything in this world is like what I just said. You haven't seen enough of it yet." Said Pauley, serious.

Phyllis came back to the table with coffee and cake, but no smile. She set a mug in front of Frankie turning the cup right-handed, the second mug and the pound cake went wherever.

Phyllis asked nobody in particular if that would be all, and left the check to rot.

"She doesn't like me too much." Said Pauley.

"You think?" Said Frankie.

"I don't feel like cake no more. Let's get out of here." Said Pauley.

"Pauley the fish doesn't want cake?" Said Frankie. "You have got to be kidding me."

"I'll take it with me." Said Pauley.

Frankie smiled.

"Hey you know something. The pound cake was nice." Said Pauley emphasis on was. The pound cake was gone. Gone before the door hit Frankie on the ass when they were leaving.

"You do know that you have teeth in that head of yours don't you?" Said Frankie.

" Better to eat you with my dear." Said Pauley quoting.

"A fan of the classics I see." Said Frankie.

"Huh?" Said Pauley.

"Never mind." Said Frankie.

CHAPTER 34

Twelve O'clock Noon by the big nose fish guy on Broadway in a nice part of Bayonne. Shops that sell all kinds of things. Hardware in the hardware store, flowers in the flower shop, and booze in the drug store.

Booze by the case, cigarettes by the carton, condoms under the counter, and penicillin in the back for men that spend all their dough on booze and cigarettes and have no money left to pay for the rubbers.

When I was a kid if you called the doctor to the house you had better be dying, or close to it.

For three dollars the doctor would come to the house. Bringing everything he needs in a little black bag to do whatever he has to do, and you didn't have to wait in a lobby for two hours reading last weeks Daily News, or a June issue of The Saturday Evening Post on the third Tuesday in December.

"Go and see the druggist," My mother would say. "Tell the druggist what's wrong with you." Whatever it was that was wrong you the druggist would give you something. What it was he would give you was up to him.

If you had a pain the foot, the head, or up your ass, the druggist was going to sell you some ear wax remover or hemorrhoid cream or maybe give you some sugar pills but he wasn't going to give you medicine, not real medicine, but then again he didn't charge three dollars.

Doctors do not come to your house anymore. Why not? Why should they wear out their shoes for you? You who is too lazy to go and see a doctor at his office.

Is he a plumber, or an electrician? No, and let me tell you something else, if the pipes in your kitchen or the wires in your wall came out easy and you could bring them to him to be fixed, then believe me you would be reading a three month old copy of Popular Mechanics right now.

The big nose fish guy was standing outside of his fish market leaning on a broom and sweeping nothing when Frankie and Pauley pulled to the curb in front of his place. From where they parked Pauley and Frankie could see a warehouse with a green door.

The building was old brick and falling to the ground in places but the door solid and secure looks painted fresh and of corse was their destination. Otherwise why would I waste your time talking about it.

I apologize I must be getting a little tired from sitting, no worries there is plenty of coffee to drink here. I will be fine in a minute.

Anyway, a platform used for loading and unloading came up out of the cement four feet high and ten feet across. It was front and to the left of the green door. It had two truck tires, with no rims, hanging to the left and right and just below the platform so that trucks backing into it did not send any more of the building crumbling onto the pavement.

The truck that Frankie and Pauley brought with them was big enough to hold three hundred crates of rubber bands and the infamous three crates of dildos.

"I hope nobody can smell the horse that dropped dead in the back of this truck last week. They did the best they could to get the stink out, but I could still smell it this morning when they were loading the crates." Said Pauley.

"They" are any number of nameless boys that hang around looking for handouts from the guys who work the trucks. They are mostly neighborhood ruffians with no inclination to be good, pure or wise. Spending money is all they require and hey keep their mouths shut.

"Did you smell the thing too when you was back counting rubber bands?" Said Pauley.

"What horse?" Said Frankie.

"You don't know about the horse?" Said Pauley.

"I don't know anything about a horse." Said Frankie.

"You don't know about that horse that Joey Spoons liberated from that racetrack up near Syracuse. Only the horse didn't make it all the way back to Yonkers where he was supposed to run the mile and a half with a name that wasn't his to begin with?" Said Pauley.

"No, I did not." Said Frankie.

" I thought you knew about that. Anyway, did you smell something back there or not?" Said Pauley.

Before Frankie could answer Pauley this giant human type thing came walking through the green door waving a hand the size of a tennis racket and smiling like he just ate a whole pig or something?

"What is that?" Said Frankie. I don't think Frankie blinked one time since just before the guy came through the green door and when he opened his mouth.

"You piss up that tree? I told you that didn't I?" Said Pauley. "Seven feet six inches of fucking tree."

"How you boys doing?" Said the tree, but he, did not wait for an answer. "Hey Pauley is this the kid what you tell me about when you was putting the order through?"

"Tree how you doing?" Said Pauley losing his hand in flesh through the window on the driver's side.

"Let me get out of the truck so we can talk about things." Said Pauley.

"Do I have to get out of the truck?" Said Frankie.

"What, are you scared?" Said Pauley, smiling like a father smiles when his kid falls on his ass.

"Yeah, a little bit." Said Frankie.

"Good, now get the fuck out of the truck so I can introduce you to the Tree." Said Pauley who got out of the truck first.

The big nose fish guy disappeared into his market when the Tree came into the light. He knows that the Tree doesn't like anybody looking at him.

Seven feet six inches, although The Tree will only admit to less. And four hundred and thirty-three pounds of muscle, old muscle, old muscle what done things.

The Tree had been dispensing mayhem on the poor unfortunate townspeople of Bayonne since Doctor Frankenstein screwed the bolts in his neck.

When the Tree turned fourteen years old, he was already too big for the house he was living in. So his father, A man of normal height, took him to the warehouse he owned, threw two pallets on the floor, end to end, and told the Tree that he should make himself comfortable.

The Tree did not say anything as he was sick and tired of knocking shit over. His mother was sick and tired of feeding him. The Tree would eat continuously and she wanted to do something besides cook.

The Tree lived in an open space above the warehouse. A Treehouse? Anyway, he got enough room up there so he doesn't knock anything over that isn't his to knock over.

The Tree's mother used to come over to the Tree's house to clean it for him, but she got old.

The top floor of the Tree's house had one of those doors that open up to the outside, but doesn't have any stairs under them. I don't know what they call a door like that or what it was used for. It had a block and tackle held by large hooks over the top of it.

Maybe they used to drop hay out of door when vehicles were only one horsepower.

So now whatever it was that got in the Tree's way went out through that door. Maybe whatever it was hit the pavement or maybe whatever it was landed on someone who was stupid enough to walk under it. Either way when that door flew open you didn't want to be anywhere near it. That is for sure.

"Tree, this is Frankie Migliori from Jersey City." Said Pauley throwing a finger at Frankie.

"How you doing Frankie Migliori from Jersey City?" Said the Tree. "I hear good things about you."

The Tree swallowed up another hand. "Glad to know you." Said Frankie.

"I hear you are keeping company with Sal's little girl." Said the tree.

"Sir I am." Said Frankie.

"Risky business that?" Said the Tree. Frankie smiled at the Tree.

"Enough bullshit. Is that truck full up? None of them crates got lost I hope." Said the Tree.

"They are all there." Said Pauley.

"What about them three crates what we talked about?" Said the Tree looking at Pauley with a squared jaw.

"They are right in the ass." Said Pauley, going flush.

"Pauley you turning all red in the face from them things?" Said the tree, giving Pauley an elbow, and almost knocking him over.

"And you can send them things through the mail?" Said Pauley continuing a telephone conversation he and the Tree had had the day before.

"Pauley them things are nothing to be ashamed of. They are just tools no different from a hammer or a screwdriver." Said the Tree. "And we don't put a return address on the box."

The dildos were in the ass and three hundred crates of rubber bands were stretched to the head.

"Big money in them tools. One hundred and twenty at fifteen bucks a piece, plus shipping. And they don't cost me more than two bits to produce." Said the Tree.

"So why you only get three crates?" Said Pauley. "It's the rubber, you can't get enough of it." Said the Tree. "American rubber is still wrapped up in the flag not like when we were fighting in Europe and Japan, but almost." Said the Tree.

"No kidding?" Said Pauley.

"The rubber we use for them things come through the jungle on somebody's back. Things are looking up though, I think we will be up to twelve crates a month by the end of next year." Said the Tree enthusiastically.

" Is There really a market for this kind of stuff? A woman got to ask twice to get fucked?" Said Pauley pointing to three crates sitting on the back of the truck.

"This thing?" Said the Tree holding a dildo from one of the crates, a red one. The Tree pulled the top off the crate with two fingers, no claw no crow. "This thing never treated a woman like shit after some asshole blew his wad down her throat."

"This thing, doesn't care if you get fat, get a hairy lip, or a pimple on your ass."

"It also doesn't drink too much and slap you around, and it doesn't sleep with one of your girlfriends and then lies about it afterwards." Said the Tree. The Tree held aloft a pink dildo in his large right hand and said. "This my friends is the perfect man. And one day when women wise up they will ride this thing until mankind masturbates itself to death."

"So you think there is a market for these things." Said Pauley.

"I do." Said the Tree.

CHAPTER 35

"Don't let me forget them rubbers is coming in next Tuesday." Said Pauley.

"Hey Pauley, them rubbers are coming in next Tuesday." Said Frankie.

"I just said that." Said Pauley.

"I know it was a joke." Said Frankie.

"I don't get it." Said Pauley.

"Forget about it." Said Frankie.

"You buy the skates yet?" Said Frankie.

"What skates?" Said Pauley.

"For the kid?" Said Frankie. "Fuck me up the ass, son of a bitch I forgot about them things. What day is it?" Said Pauley with holy shit all over his face.

"It is Saturday." Said Frankie.

"What time is it?" Said Pauley.

"Ten passed eleven. And you promised Naomi that you would be there when the kid wakes up." Said Frankie.

"Suck my fucking ass, you're right." Said Pauley now rubbing his face with his hands stretching the skin all over the place.

"Give the kid some money so he can buy his own skates." Said Frankie.

"Seems like a good idea don't it but it's not. Money will not buy you an inch with that broad. She knows it don't mean nothing to count bills. I go there I start peeling, the kid is happy, everybody is happy right? No, the kid, he is smiling like he is getting his dick sucked by Miss America, but she is growling like a junk yard dog." Said Pauley. "We got to get some skates."

"Hey Pauley, where do you buy skates?" Said Frankie. "I am not sure a toy store maybe, or a sporting goods store, why?" Said Pauley.

"I have never had skates." Said Frankie.

"I never had any skates either." Said Pauley scratching his head with two fingers.

"I think they got one of them toy stores not too far from here."

Frankie and Pauley spent more time with the Tree than they wanted to, and maybe they had a few too many cocktails.

The Tree didn't like to drink alone, and he never drank with less than two other guys in the room because it would take that many men to drag his ass upstairs when the curtain came down.

The Tree's capacity for booze might have been big, but his tolerance for standing up afterward, was not.

The Cadillac crossed the line between Bayonne and Jersey City. The Hudson Boulevard, a main street that passed through both of those places, was wide. Wide enough to handle a little give and take to the left and right when you were not seeing things too clearly.

Hudson Boulevard also passed through Journal Square, Jersey City's main shopping area at that time. It was and still is square like it says in the name.

The Jersey Journal was a local newspaper that had been planted on that same plot of land since they had sheep cutting the grass where they now have parking meters. And until the internet took a paring knife to its circulation.

The Jersey Journal named the place. I think? I could look it up for you if I had one of those smart phones like everyone else. But I don't. Uncle Frankie doesn't pay me enough to buy one. My phone still flips I am sad to say.

Journal Square, in its heyday held hundreds of stores and restaurants, some decent size buildings most of them banks, two or three movie palaces built in the twenties long before television made them say uncle, all gold leaf and leaky ceilings. Some of them are still around today only I don't think they show movies anymore. One of them is a Jehovah's witness hall, and the other one has been empty since I was a kid.

"There goes one." Said Pauley slowing down as he passed a toyshop.

"It doesn't look open." Said Frankie.

"We will see about that." Said Pauley.

Pauley made a right turn at the corner and parked next to an alleyway which ran behind all of the stores on that block. The alley was big enough to drive through, but had two padlocked wrought iron gates at each end to discourage through traffic.

"We got to hop this thing." Said Pauley looking at Frankie and then looking at the gate when he said it.

"Climb the gate?" Said Frankie.

"We do." Said Pauley.

"Why do we have do that?" Said Frankie.

"How else we going to get on the other side?" Said Pauley.

"What are we going to do once we get over there?" Said Frankie.

"Maybe the toy man left the back door open or something." Said Pauley.

"What are the odds that he did that?" Said Frankie.

"I say the odds are pretty good." Said Pauley.

"Put your knee over here so I can stand on it." Said Pauley with one hand high up on a cross section of iron two feet above his head. The vertical bars were too close together for either of them to squeeze through otherwise they would have tried that first, it being easier to go through than over.

"Why do I have to put my knee there?" Said Frankie. "Why don't you put your knee there and let me stand on it?"

"Because you are taller than I am. And I can't get over the thing without you, but I think you can get over the fence without me." Said Pauley.

There were two crossbars, one at the top and one at the bottom, six inches up from macadam and six inches down from spikes lined up looking sharp and fearless. The gate was at least seven feet high with no foothold going up.

A padlock and chain pulled tight left no loose end to step into.

The hinges were both on the inside so they would make it easier to get out, one being ten inches higher than the crossbar at the bottom, the other ten inches below the crossbar at the top and not so high that it wouldn't make for a good enough foothold.

Frankie set his right knee tight to the iron and held firm to the crossbar while Pauley put a shoe to Frankie's pants leg.

"Hold still I don't want get stuck like a pig on them pikes." Said Pauley.

"It's a pig in a poke." Said Frankie. "What's a pike?"

"Shut up for a minute I can't concentrate." Said Pauley.

Pauley stepped up, grabbed hold of the crossbar and tried a kind of side step up the wall. Pauley somehow got his one knee between the spikes at the top and was trying to swing his other knee up into the same position.

Frankie held one hand to Pauley's back as he went up. And one more hand on Pauley's ass when he fell over the top of the gate, and nearly lost one of his testicles through his inseam as one of the spikes ripped through his pants and cut through his ball sack. Did Pauley scream like a girl? What do you think?

Pauley hit the ground hard and immediately went into a fetal position and started balling, no pun intended. If Pauley had had three hands they would have all been holding his crotch.

The blood was seeping through what was left of his pants.

Seeing Pauley like that on the ground reminded Frankie of a time in the not so distant past when he lay in a similar position beneath the neck of a frozen giraffe. How the wheel turns he thought. Empathetically of course.

Pauley's hands were red from blood trying to find the quickest way the ground. The color had run out of his skin, and his body had begun to shiver.

Not a good thing to lose your balls when perpetrating a crime both figuratively and literally. Almost losing them is not good either.

"Pauley should I get an ambulance, or a doctor or something?" Said Frankie. The blood did not bother Frankie much as he has seen some of it in that Army hospital he worked in. So he didn't get too excited when he saw a puddle forming midway between Pauley's hat and his shoes.

Frankie put two hands to the wrought iron, chinned up and went over. He almost landed on Pauley during the free fall but quickly shifted position so as to avoid causing any more damage to the poor bastard.

Only Frankie didn't land flat. He either twisted, or broke something he didn't know which. Frankie did see a bright white light for a few seconds when he hit the ground. The light show subsided and when his vision cleared Frankie found himself lying next to Pauley.

Frankie tried to stand up but stumbled he couldn't put any weight onto his right foot. And his shoelaces were already being pulled taut due to swelling.

Frankie knew better than to take his shoe off so he just kind of watched it swell for a couple minutes. Then he remembered that he was someplace he wasn't supposed to be with a guy who still hasn't made a coherent noise since he went all white in the face.

"Pauley you got to get up. We got to get out of this place before somebody calls the cops." Said Frankie while shaking Pauley by the lapels of his Navy blue pinstripe suit jacket.

Frankie didn't get anything out of Pauley that he could understand so he slapped him one time hard in the face. Pauley blinked his eyes two times and then went to babbling again.

Frankie hit Pauley again, slapping him harder this time. Pauley came to and said, "What are you slapping me for?" Said Pauley raising his upper body so he is almost sitting up.

"I thought you were unconscious." Said Frankie.

"Help me up." Said Pauley.

Frankie got behind Pauley and put his hands to Pauley's pits and lifted.

Frankie discovered that he could put some pressure on his foot, but the weight was dead.

"Pauley you got to help me help you. You got to let go of your balls for a minute and try to lift yourself up." Said Frankie.

Frankie counted softly one, two, and three and pulled up on Pauley. This time Pauley let go of his balls and palm pushed the ground until he was almost upright.

Pauley was bent crooked at the waist but standing which Frankie took to be a good sign.

"How we going to get out of here?" Said Frankie leaning left to avoid putting all of his weight on the right foot.

"We're not leaving yet." Said Pauley.

"What do you mean we are not leaving yet? You are bleeding to death through your balls, and I think my foot is broken. Look at the thing." Said Frankie.

"I got my own problems." Said Pauley.

"Listen to me. We are going down this alley to the back door of the toy place, we are going to open the door, and we're not leaving until we get some skates. You got it?" Said Pauley determined, or pigheaded, "Start walking."

Pauley put his hand on Frankie's shoulder for support. The two of them were walking slow, but making progress. The back door to the toyshop had a sign painted on it. Toyshop Delivery Entrance, it said.

Pauley tried the handle one time. It was Locked. "The gate isn't enough? They got to lock the door too." Said Pauley.

Pauley reached into his right pants pocket and took out a pocketknife, brown, not too big, more of a penknife.

Pauley opened the knife and slipped it between the door and door-frame. He flicked his wrist and the door opened. It took two-seconds.

The back door opened into a storeroom and office. One desk, a file cabinet, a chair on wheels, cardboard boxes stacked to the ceiling along a back wall, and an adding machine.

On the other side of the room there was second door. It had been left open so Frankie and Pauley could see that the door opened onto the shop floor.

They went through the door and then split in two, Frankie going left and Pauley to the right and circling through each of the aisles.

Three aisles in Frankie, limping, found the skates.

"Hey Pauley." Said Frankie in a loud whisper. "I found the things."

"I'll be there in a minute." Said Pauley at normal volume.

Pauley was in the next aisle but it took him a minute or two to get to Frankie. He wasn't walking too good, and his balls were still bleeding. Pauley could feel that his sock was soaked with blood and that his shoe was filled with the sticky liquid.

"What size foot does Junior have?" Said Frankie.

"How should I know, Naomi buys his shoes, what sizes do they got?" Said Pauley. "They don't have sizes. The box just says youth." Said Frankie, straining his eyes to read in the dark.

"Open one of them things up and lets see what they look like." Said Pauley.

Frankie pulled the lid. The skates were wrapped in tissue paper. Two metal shoe like things with rubber wheels. Each one had a cap at the toe, with a half cap at the heel, a slotted center strips, adjustable when unlocked at the bolt underneath.

"These things, they adjust to fit. They got a key, like a ratchet wrench. I guess they have one size for everybody." Said Frankie.

"Put the lid on that box and let's get out of here." Said Pauley.

With the box now closed Frankie tucked it under his left arm and with his right arm held up Pauley who was stumbling.

If it took less than five minutes for the two of them to make it back to the office I would be surprised.

"Hold up a second." Said Pauley standing next to the desk in the office. Pauley, now leaning on the desk for support, reached into the front left pocket of his blood soaked pants, took out a roll of bills held together with a rubber band and peeled off a wet fifty-dollar bill. He tossed the bill onto the desk. "Let's go." Said Pauley.

They pushed out through the door and into the alley.

The lock had been jimmied but not broken so it locked when Pauley pulled it closed. He tried the door knob one time, it stuck, so he turned (with the help of Frankie) facing the gate which separated them from the street.

"It would be a miracle if we got you out of here before you bleed to death." Said Frankie.

"Thanks for the encouragement." Said Pauley with very little breath left to carry the words from his throat.

"You don't look so good Pauley. You lost a lot of blood." Said Frankie.

"Don't worry about it, in a few minutes we will be out of here." Said Pauley.

"I don't think so Pauley." Said Frankie who was pretty much carrying Pauley now.

Frankie carried/dragged Pauley to the gate and put him down with his back to the wall sitting up.

"Get over the gate and start the car." Said Pauley in a whisper.

Pauley held a bloody key ring in his hand with his palm open and rating on his thigh. Frankie took the key ring and put it in his pocket.

"What about you Pauley? I think I should get you over the gate first. There is no way that you are going to get over that thing by yourself." Said Frankie.

"Just do what I tell you." Said Pauley.

Frankie, with a bum foot had some trouble getting to the other side of the gate. The hinges made it easier to get a foothold as they were large enough to get half a shoe onto.

Frankie took a look at Pauley before he pulled open the door to the Cadillac and started the engine. Pauley was crawling and clawing his way to the gate.

Frankie was about to get out of the car again when he heard Pauley tell for him to stay in there.

"Stay in there and put your head down." Said Pauley who made it to his feet and was pointing his revolver at the padlock.

The Padlock took one to the gut, but stayed in one piece. The noise from the gun was loud. Pauley shot it again, and this time, it came loose. The mangled lock and chain fell to the ground.

Pauley grabbed the gate and pushed it away from him hanging on to it as it swung outward.

Firing that revolver must have pumped some adrenaline into him. Pauley hobbled over to the passenger side door of the Cadillac which Frankie kicked open from the driver's seat as soon as he realized what was happening.

Pauley fell knees to face into the car and went black.

Pauley's feet were hanging out over the doorframe so Frankie lifted himself up by grabbing hold of the seat back cushion, taking Pauley by the seat of his pants and pulling on him until his feet cleared the door.

Frankie had to put his full weight onto Pauley to reach the door handle as Pauley was splayed out before him. He slammed the door shut, flung himself into driving position and hit the gas.

CHAPTER 36

Frankie drove the Cadillac to the Jersey City Medical Center and was pulling into the emergency room parking lot when Pauley came to.

"Are we back in Elizabeth yet?" Said Pauley sand papering the words before he let them go.

"Jersey City, we are just pulling into the Medical Center parking lot." Said Frankie.

"Are you crazy? We can't go in there. That's like pleading guilty to something they don't even know we done yet." Said Pauley exasperated.

"Pauley you have to see a doctor right away." Said Frankie.

"They see the powder on my hand they know I shot something, only they don't know what. IF anybody has been shot around here tonight they will hold me until the cops get here. And when the cops see I got a record I will not get out of here at all." Said Pauley.

"Plus we are carrying stolen property and I'm not giving up them skates." Said Pauley.

"So what do you want me to do with your body when you drop dead in a few minutes. Do you have any last requests?" Said Frankie.

"I request that you shut up and get me home." Said Pauley.

Twenty-five minutes later they were in front of Pauley's house in Elizabeth. Frankie put the Cadillac to the curb, got out of the car and ran to the passenger side. He opened the door and took hold of Pauley's belt and pulled with whatever strength he had left.

Frankie slid Pauley until his knees were out of the car and touching the ground. He grabbed onto Pauley's collar and yanked him up by it. Frankie put both of his hands under Pauley's arms and pulled until Frankie was dragging Pauley along the ground.

Up the stoop and into the doorway, Frankie leaned Pauley against his legs as he finagled with the doorknob.

Frankie was able to get Pauley into the house and onto the couch before he collapsed onto the floor. The pain in his foot was almost intolerable.

Next to the telephone not far from where Pauley was lying in his own blood on the couch was a notebook. And written in pencil under the letter S Frankie saw the word Spoons with a number next to it, so he called the number.

Three rings and a voice came up swinging.

"Who the fuck is this?" Said a voice Frankie assumed belonged to Joey Spoons.

"Spoons, Frankie Migliori from Jersey City, you got to get over here to Pauley's right away he has been hurt real bad and he is not looking so good." Said Frankie.

"Hurt bad how? Has Pauley been shot, stabbed what?" Said Spoons.

Frankie was not about to take the long way around this story so he said what seemed to be closest to what actually happened. "Stabbed." Said Frankie.

"I'll be there in a few minutes with the Doc." Said Joey Spoons before he hung up the phone.

The Doc turned out to be the dentist cousin of Sammy Graves, and a few minutes turned into three-quarters of an hour.

"I didn't find the Doc too quick." Said Spoons to Frankie. "Doc you got to give me the number at your girlfriends house. Your wife, doesn't have it, and she was not so crazy about me asking for it neither." Said Spoons to Sammy Graves' cousin the dentist.

"Fuck her. If She would suck my dick once in a while I might stay home now and again." Said the Doc to Spoons. "Hello." Said the Doc to Frankie.

"Tony Graves and you must be Frank Migliori."

"Frankie"

Tony Graves, AKA the Doc, is tall, about six foot three inches, blue eyes, an olive tan, graying brown hair slicked back, khaki pleated casual slacks, Italian loafers with no socks and cashmere every where else.

"Tell me what happened to Pauley." Said the Doc to Frankie. The Doc was holding Pauley by the wrist and taking his pulse.

"Pauley got his balls caught on some spikes when he was climbing a gate." Said Frankie to the Doc.

"I thought you said Pauley had been stabbed." Said the Doc looking at Spoons. "That's what the kid tells me on the phone." Said Spoons looking at Frankie.

"I didn't say somebody stabbed him, only that he was stabbed, which he was. Are you going to look at his balls or what?" Said Frankie irritated.

The Doc pulled a pair scissors from a black leather pouch he had carried under his arm into the house, and started cutting Pauley's trouser leg up from the shoe to his nuts. It looked to Frankie that the bleeding had stopped, but it was not a pretty sight when what used to be Pauley's balls, was uncovered.

The Doc knew what he was doing. In ten minutes Pauley was all sewed up, and breathing sweet.

The color had come back into Pauley's face. The Doc gave him a shot of something for tetanus, and another one for infection, and waved smelling salts under Pauley's nose to rouse him. Pauley came around pretty quick.

"Well, if it isn't the anti-whop. How you doing Doc?" Said Pauley.

"Better than you." Said the Doc.

"Am I going to live?" Said Pauley.

"I suppose" Said the Doc.

"Thanks Doc." Said Pauley.

"You lost a lot of blood, but you will be up and around in a few days." Said the Doc.

"Take me to Helen's will you, Spoons."

"Is that your wife, or your girlfriend?" Said Spoons.

"What do you think? Let's go." Said the Doc.

"Pauley you take these pills," The Doc handed Pauley a vial. "Take them four times a day. I will look in on you tomorrow." Said the Doc.

"Not tomorrow Doc, leave me to sleep it off a day or two and I'll give you a call on Monday." Said Pauley.

"You had better take care of those stitches Pauley, no horseplay. Bed rest until I say so, from the bed to the bathroom, that's it. No showering until I remove the stitches, sponge baths only." Said the Doc.

Before the Doc could leave Frankie took off his shoe and presented his foot to him.

"I don't think your foot is broken, but without an x-ray I cannot be sure. You may have a stress fracture, or just a sprain, but in any case you should stay off of it for a few days," Said the Doc. He smiled at Frankie with a beautiful set of teeth.

"I can give you something for the pain if you like, or swallow a couple of aspirins every four hours to take the edge off."

"Thanks Doc, the aspirins will be fine." Said Frankie, putting his sock back on, but leaving his shoe off.

"Spoons." Said the Doc with volume. Spoons had fallen asleep.

"We out of here?" Said Spoons.

"We are." Said the Doc.

"Hey Pauley it will cost you if you want I should keep quiet about this." Said Spoons.

"How much?" Said Pauley.

"I will let you know." Said Spoons.

"Can we leave now?" Said the Doc.

"Sure Doc"

Spoons gave a wave to Pauley and a nod to Frankie as he tried to catch up with the Doc who had cut and run.

After the door was shut behind the Doc and Spoons Frankie limped over to the sofa where Pauley was sitting on one cheek.

"We got to get you to the bed." Said Frankie.

"What time is it?" Said Pauley. Pauley was wearing a watch, but he couldn't open his eyes.

"Three-thirty, why?" Said Frankie.

"Just leave me here for now. You go to bed and set the alarm clock for six. We got things we got to do in the morning." Said Pauley.

"Pauley you heard what the Doc said you got to stay in the bed until he says so." Said Frankie.

"He is a fucking dentist what does he know?" Said Pauley.

"What do we got to do tomorrow that you want to risk popping that seam?" Said Frankie.

"The skates? Did you forget why we got all banged up in the first place?" Said Pauley.

"The kid, I forget about him." Said Frankie.

"Look, we get there before the kid wakes up, we give him the skates, have breakfast, stay for an hour or so, and then we come back here and take it easy. Ok?" Said Pauley.

"You are making the call on this one, I vote with the Doc, but he's your kid, and since I don't know nothing about being a father I'm going to keep my mouth shut on this one." Said Frankie.

"Thank you" Said Pauley.

"Six o'clock?" Said Frankie.

"Yeah," said Pauley.

"You want me to clean you up now so we have less to do in the morning?" Said Pauley.

"Don't worry about it you go to sleep. Make sure you set them alarm." Said Pauley.

"The alarm, got it." Said Frankie.

CHAPTER 37

Six o'clock came quick. Frankie got out of the bed slow. His foot was swollen, and his disposition was poor, but he was determined to make the best of it for Pauley and the kid.

Pauley was not on the couch when Frankie entered the living room. Frankie had heard the water running in the kitchen so he went to the sound. Pauley was standing lopsided in front of the sink filling the kettle with water.

Pauley was dressed in a gray worsted suit and patent leather shoes. His hat was behind him on the table, brushed and creased.

"You want some coffee?" Said Pauley.

"Yeah, thanks." Said Frankie. There was a pause before Frankie spoke again.

"Pauley you look good for a guy who was almost dead a few hours ago." Said Frankie.

"Don't make the story bigger than the fish." Said Pauley.

"How did you get cleaned up and dressed by yourself?" Said Frankie impressed. "You know when I told you to go to bed?" Said Pauley.

"Yeah," said Frankie.

"I started then, and I finished a few minutes before them bells started screaming at you. My balls, are getting bigger by the minute, another hour and I will be carrying them in a suitcase." Said Pauley.

"Swollen?" Said Frankie.

"You could say that." Said Pauley.

"Pauley this is not good. You should get some rest, at least a couple of hours. And you need to put ice on them things " Said Frankie concerned.

"What are you my mother now?" Said Pauley.

"I am worried about you that's all." Said Frankie annoyed.

"Just get dressed so we can do this thing. You can be mad at me when were finished." Said Pauley.

"Give me twenty-five minutes. Thirty if I can't get a shoe over this thing." Said Frankie pointing to his enlarged foot.

"Put that dog on a leash." Said Pauley.

"Big isn't it?" Said Frankie.

In ten minutes Frankie had showered and shaved his face. He put on his clothes in five minutes, and spent the next fifteen minutes trying to stuff his foot into a shoe.

The pain was tough, the four aspirins he swallowed helped, but the shot of whiskey he washed them down with helped more.

"Drink some coffee and let's get this side show out of here." Said Pauley.

Pauley was sitting half off the chair and holding his balls through the zipper hole of his pants.

"Your balls are sore, huh?" Said Frankie pouring a cup of coffee from the pot Pauley left on the burner at low gas. Frankie turned off the heat and placed the coffeepot onto the avocado tile on the counter top.

"What do you think?" Said Pauley pulling an ice pack from his trousers.

"They are not still bleeding are they?" Said Frankie.

"They are just swollen, and sore as hell."

Frankie finished his coffee, rinsed out his cup, placed it upside down onto a folded dishtowel, a practice of Pauley's he was fond of, and turned to Pauley who dozed off with his hand in his pants.

Frankie tapped Pauley one time on the shoulder.

"Pauley, you ready to go?" Said Frankie, softly into Pauley's ear.

"Yeah, yeah, let's go." Said Pauley, groggy.

"Help me up." Said Pauley after he removed the icepack from his crotch, and zipped up.

Frankie put his arm around Pauley, cupping his hand into Pauley's armpit, and lifted him until he was standing.

Frankie and Pauley baby stepped their way out the door, down the steps and into the Cadillac. Pauley sat in the back so he did not to have to sit on the dried blood he had left on the front seat the night before.

Twenty minutes later Frankie and Pauley were in front of Naomi's house.

Pauley grabbed the skates from the floor in front of his feet. The box was covered in blood so Pauley took the skates out, and held them in his left hand while he tried to lift himself out of the car.

Frankie was having a hard time too. His foot was killing him from working the pedals. The gas wasn't too bad, but the brake was a bitch.

By the time Frankie got around to Pauley he was holding onto the doorframe and the skates were in the gutter.

"You Ok Pauley?" Said Frankie getting behind Pauley.

"I got woozy a little bit. Pick up them skates will you." Said Pauley.

Frankie picked up the skates and held them. Pauley got his balance and shut the door to the Cadillac.

Pauley looked toward the house and saw Naomi peeking out through the blinds.

Pauley straightened up and began to swagger, but not too much. And walked up to the door like his balls weren't torn apart. He was leaning to the left, but only slightly.

Frankie on the other hand moved like a one legged man in a dance contest. He took twice as long to get to the front steps as Pauley did.

Naomi came to the door and right away took an interest in Frankie's foot. She didn't spend any time on Pauley except to peck him on the mouth.

"What did you do to this boy?" Said Naomi scolding Pauley.

"I didn't do nothing to him. Can I help it if he's clumsy?" Said Pauley.

"Is that right boy? Is you clumsy?" Said Naomi.

"I guess I am." Said Frankie.

"You come inside and put your foot up in my lap. I will give it a rub, make it feel better." Said Naomi.

"You are not rubbing none of that horse shit on him are you?" Said Pauley.

"Horse shit?" Said Frankie.

"It's not horse shit. It just some liniment we use down home. It will Make you feel like dancing in no time at all." Said Naomi.

"That shit smells bad, and burns like hell. You tell her you don't want no part of that stuff." Said Pauley.

"Hush up, and leave me to do this boy some good." Said Naomi.

"Your son isn't up yet so go into the kitchen and help yourself to the fritters I fried up this morning." Said Naomi.

"What is a fritter?" Said Frankie.

"They are like a calzone only they got fruit inside instead of mozzarella." Said Pauley.

"Do they taste good?" Said Frankie.

"Hell yeah they taste good." Said Naomi before Pauley could open his mouth. "They are no calzone, but they are pretty good." Said Pauley.

Frankie and Pauley went into the kitchen and sat down at the table. The fritters, were there under a napkin, so Frankie took one.

Pauley reached across Frankie to a napkin holder that was behind the salt and pepper shaker, and laid it down under Frankie's chin. "Them things make for a lot of crumbs." Said Pauley.

"Thanks." Said Frankie leaning over the napkin and taking a bite of his fritter. It was a little greasy, but tasty.

"I like this thing." Said Frankie.

"Good you eat them." Said Pauley relieved. "I'm so sick of them fritters that I don't want to eat no more of them things, ever. Just don't tell Naomi I said that, she would kick my ass." Said Pauley.

"Why?" Said Frankie.

"Fritters are her specialty. Her mother gave her the recipe, or taught her how to make them when she was a kid." Said Pauley, now sweaty, and growing pale. "Naomi grew up on a farm in North Carolina. Her father held paper on the land."

"Why did they come up here?" Said Frankie.

"The farm got played out, or the mortgage dropped dead. I don't know, but the father, he dragged everybody up here when he found work as a machine operator in a box factory in Newark." Said Pauley.

"When was this?" Said Frankie.

"Jesus Christ Frankie can't you see I'm dying here. Drop the third degree and eat the fucking fritter." Said Pauley closing his eyes and putting his head into his hands.

"Sorry," said Frankie.

Naomi came into the kitchen carrying a quart size bottle of a yellow liquid. The top was open, and Naomi had a cork between her teeth. Naomi spit the cork into her free hand, and then dropped it onto the table.

Naomi grabbed a chair by its back and moved it to face Frankie.

"Move your chair so you facing me." Said Naomi. Frankie did what he was told. "Lift that foot up and give it to me." Said Naomi, forceful. Again Frankie did what she said.

Once Naomi took Frankie's foot into her hands, she turned gentle when she saw how swollen it was. Naomi, placed Frankie's foot onto her lap, pulled off his shoe and let it fall to the floor. She peeled down his sock extra careful so she didn't make it hurt more than it did already.

Frankie's foot was black and blue, bloated and didn't smell so good. I don't think it ever smelled, good, but Naomi took no notice of it.

The bottle of yellow liquid got tipped and Naomi put some into her hands. The smell was strong, a heavy menthol, a real sinus clearing aroma. She rubbed her hands together to warm the horse liniment up.

Naomi worked that piss water into pure heat and began to knead it into Frankie's foot. The pain Frankie was feeling before the rubbing wasn't anything compared to the pain that he was feeling now.

Frankie's eye's stung, his nose was running, and his reason for living had escaped him for the moment. And then it was over. The pain went away.

"I think that should do you." Said Naomi.

"It doesn't hurt anymore." Said Frankie.

"It is not done hurting yet. You are going to take home what's left of this bottle and rub that foot twice a day, one time in the morning and one more time again in the evening and in a few days you be, good as new." Said Naomi, washing her hands at the sink.

"Where does this stuff come from?" Said Frankie.

"We used to use it on horses down home when they came up lame." Said Naomi.

"Kind of like me," said Frankie.

"Yeah, Kind of like you," Said Naomi, smiling.

"You stink." Said Pauley.

"It doesn't smell so good does it?" Said Frankie.

"I never get used to that smell" said Pauley."It does work though."

"Hey you want me to rub some of this horse shit on your balls?" Said Frankie.

"What's wrong with my Baby's balls?" Said Naomi, turning away from the sink, and moving in on Pauley.

"Oh shit." Said Frankie realizing what he had done.

"You hurt yourself Baby?" Said Naomi, looking hard into Pauley's face.

"It's nothing." Said Pauley, looking hard into Frankie's face which decided to look hard into an empty shoe.

"Let me see your balls." Said Naomi, pulling at Pauley's belt buckle.

"I am not going to show you my balls, so fuck off." Said Pauley.

"Since when I can't see your balls when I want to." Said Naomi, still tugging at Pauley's waistband.

"Since right now." Said Pauley, going weak, and turning pale from the struggle.

"Baby, you turning white. Please tell me what is wrong with your balls." Said Naomi going soft, and tearing up. "You are scaring me."

"They are just a little tender, that's all. Now don't worry about me, and what's say you wake the kid so I can give him his present." Said Pauley his money spent.

"Pauley come with me into the bedroom for a minute will you Baby?" Said Naomi not waiting for an answer, and walking into the bedroom which was just off the kitchen. "Oh man, see what you did." Said Pauley.

Frankie was still staring into his shoe. Pauley gripped the back of his chair and set himself flat footed. He waited a minute for the haze to burn off then took it slow to the bedroom. He closed the door.

A couple of minutes went by before Naomi screamed. Frankie expected it sooner, but maybe Pauley didn't give in to the pressure right away.

Another couple of minutes passed before Pauley came through the door alone. He shuffled himself back to the same chair he left five minutes earlier, and sat down easy. He didn't say a word, but he was sweating like a pig.

A couple of more minutes went by before Pauley had enough wind to blow words out of his mouth. "Well, that didn't go too good." Said Pauley.

"She upset with you." Said Frankie.

"I don't know, I'll have to ask her when she wakes up." Said Pauley.

"She fainted?" Said Frankie.

"A little bit, yeah." Said Pauley.

"Should we do something?" Said Frankie.

"Like what?" Said Pauley.

"I don't know. Throw water on her?" Said Frankie.

"You can if you want to, but I think she is better off the way she is." Said Pauley.

"Maybe you got a point." Said Frankie.

Naomi woke up, but she, didn't ask to see Pauley's balls no more. I guess one time was enough.

Naomi was good and kind to Pauley for the rest of the time they were there. She, didn't make him get up to do anything. Naomi just let him sit there while she was buzzing around the place. Frankie, he was good for nothing, so he just sat there while she buzzed around him too.

The kid woke up an hour into the visit, and when he saw his old man sitting at the kitchen table he took flight. If Frankie didn't pull the kid out of the air Pauley would be dead right now.

Frankie put the kid into Pauley's lap as far away from the balls as he can but the kid would not sit still. So Naomi came over and with some difficulty pulled the kid off of Pauley and sat him down in the chair next to him.

Pauley wrapped the kid up in his arms every time he looked at him, giving him lips until the kid made a face, then Pauley didn't kiss him for a while.

Happy birthday was said, and sung. The fritters, were eaten, and the skates were tried on and discarded by junior when the television crossed his mind.

Pauley could take no more of being conscious, and Frankie was about finished too, so the two of them gave eyes to each other and made for the door with goodbyes and kisses.

Naomi kissed Pauley on the mouth, and told him she wanted to come to his house and look after him, but he said it wasn't such a good idea, and she cried, but he didn't change his mind.

Naomi gave Frankie a kiss on the cheek, and reminded him to take the bottle of horse liniment with him when he left.

"Thanks again." Said Frankie.

Frankie could see the Cadillac, only twenty feet from the door, but he could not see any way Pauley was going to get there by himself. So Frankie got up under Pauley and took half his weight onto his good foot and with a shuffle and a hop in ridiculous succession made it to the car.

"Why do you have to be so damned short?" Said Frankie. "You are giving me a hunched back."

"I think it will look good on you." Said Pauley.

"I'm glad you think so." Said Frankie.

"Don't mention it." Said Pauley.

CHAPTER 38

"Hey Pauley the Jersey Journal says that we are vandals." Said Frankie.

"What else does it say about us?" Said Pauley.

"Two fucking morons who can't climb a stupid fence shoot and kill a padlock while trying to steal a four dollar pair of roller skates." Said Frankie.

"What does it really say you wise ass?" Said Pauley.

"Vandals destroy public property in Journal Square shopping district, blah, blah, shots fired, blah, blah, blood found at the scene, blah, blah, nothing reported stolen, blah, blah, police have no leads at this time." Said Frankie.

"What's with this blah, blah shit?" Said Pauley.

"Don't ask me read the whole thing it's embarrassing." Said Frankie.

"Maybe you are right." Said Pauley.

"Anyway I guess the guy pocketed the fifty bucks and kept his mouth shut."

"One good thing," said Frankie.

"We better get dressed we got to be at Sal's in an hour." Said Pauley.

"I forgot about that. Maybe we should skip it this week." Said Frankie.

"Dinner at Sal's every Sunday, did he stutter when he told you that?" Said Pauley.

"No, but," said Frankie.

"But nothing," cut Pauley. "Unless you are dead. Are you dead?" Said Pauley.

"No, but," said Frankie.

"Again with the but? And what about Sophia are you not in love with her no more? That right there could get you killed. Maybe you want to die from a sudden ass kicking?" Said Pauley.

"From you? Right now my mother could kick your ass, and she's drunk most of the time." Said Frankie, smiling at Pauley.

"Don't you smile at me you, you, you. You better get dressed. We got to be at Sal's in less than an hour." Said Pauley.

"I will be ready in twenty minutes, but you? I'm not so sure." Said Frankie.

Twenty minutes later Frankie was ready to go but Pauley still hadn't found pants big enough to hold his swollen balls, and an icepack. "All these fucking pants are too tight, my balls are like grapefruits, and grapefruits are not going to fit in none of these pants." Said Pauley.

Pauley was in his room standing in front of his closet, his one hand holding onto the doorframe, the other pressing an icepack to his balls. He was wearing a pale blue oxford style shirt, the collar button threaded, pushing up the apple in his neck, black silk double Windsor, a pair of black socks, and the icepack.

"Must be twenty pair of pants in there, you going to tell me that none of them things will hold a couple of grapefruits?" Said Frankie.

"I tried almost every one of them." Said Pauley.

"We got enough time to go to the warehouse?" Said Frankie.

"No," said Pauley. "We got to be at Sal's in half an hour."

"Pauley, how far down your pant leg do your suit jackets go?" Said Frankie,

"Which suit?" Said Pauley.

"The longest one you got." Said Frankie. "The gray, double breasted is long, I haven't had it altered yet." Said Pauley.

"The jacket, or the pants?" Said Frankie.

"Both," said Pauley.

"Put it on." Said Frankie.

"But it doesn't fit." Said Pauley.

"Put the fucking thing on. You got any safety pins?" Said Frankie.

"There is three or four of them in that drawer behind you." Said Pauley.

Behind Frankie was what looked to be a mahogany side table. Next to the side table was a medium sized chair covered with a white sheet. The chair was brown leather, but Pauley doesn't like the way the leather feels on his back.

Pauley put on the gray suit. He wasn't kidding, the thing didn't fit. The pants were six inches too long, and the inseam, it went downstream swimming around his knees.

The jacket sleeves fell below his hands on their way to the floor, and the cut was just above the knee. The chest and waist fit perfectly. Go figure.

"I look like a gorilla." Said Pauley.

"The pants do they cover your balls?" Said Frankie, "Yeah, but." Said Pauley.

"But nothing, hold still while I pin you up."

Frankie turned under Pauley's sleeves until they were just below the wrist, then he pinned them up.

He cuffed Pauley's pant legs until they were just above the heel, then he pinned them up like the sleeves.

The jacket's length hid the extra cargo space Pauley needs for his balls.

"Let's get out of here. We got fifteen minutes to get to Sal's." Said Frankie.

"Can you see the pins?" Said Pauley.

"Not so much," said Frankie, lying a little.

"Good, Let's go." Said Pauley.

"If you were wearing a tuxedo you would look like a penguin." Said Frankie.

"If you was wearing a tuxedo I would ask you what the dinner specials are." Said Pauley.

"If you was wearing a tuxedo I would hand you the keys to my car, and tell you not to scratch the paint." Said Frankie.

"You got a car?" Said Pauley.

"You win." Said Frankie.

CHAPTER 39

Sophia and Frankie kissed like they meant it.

"I never see you, and you don't call me." Said Sophia.

Frankie and Sophia were alone in the kitchen of her father's house. Italian tile from floor to ceiling, white enamel painted stove with a double oven, and a matching white enamel double basin sink and drain board.

"I call you every day." Said Frankie, leaning against the yellow ceramic tile counter top, opposite a center island, also yellow tiled. Sophia had chin to his chest and was whispering up.

"Only once a day," said Sophia, in low tone.

"Will it make you happy if I call you twice a day?" Said Frankie.

"Four times." Said Sophia, holding four fingers against his chest.

"Twice," said Frankie, kissing her two times just below the hairline on her forehead.

"Three times." Said Sophia, tilting her head back and lifting her lips to touch his three times.

"Twice," said Frankie, kissing each of Sophia's eyelids making a small noise with his mouth.

"Twice?" Said Sophia, pouting.

"Three times." Said Frankie, kissing her soft and long on the mouth breathing heavy on the intake.

"Three times then?" Said Sophia, smiling, satisfied.

"Three times." Said Frankie.

The smell of food filled the kitchen even though it had been over two hours since they had finished eating.

The usual suspects, Sal of course, the two boys, Peter and Little Sal, Sophia, Frankie, and Pauley. They all ate like pigs with the exception of Sophia who ate like a piglet. And afterwards retired to the living room. Sal, on the red velvet plastic covered couch sleeping with his left hand in the waistband of his unbuttoned trousers.

Pauley, on a matching side chair sleeping with his left hand cupping his balls. The two boys, they left the house right after the food ran out.

Sophia and Frankie took advantage of the situation and went into the kitchen to be alone.

"Do you still love me?" Said Sophia, pressing herself into Frankie, accepting all of her that he possibly could.

"Yes, I do" Said Frankie, desperation tinged.

"But?" Said Sophia, expecting.

"But what?" Said Frankie. "Tell me what's wrong, something is wrong." Said Sophia, stiff grained.

Frankie, weary, rubbing his face and talking through his hands.

"I'm tired." Said Frankie.

"And?" Said Sophia.

"And, and I wish we were more than a couple of hours of whispering in a kitchen. And I wish we were more than a five minute telephone call when I'm trying to fall asleep, thinking about what I am not doing with you." Said Frankie, eyes peeking over fingers.

"So this is about fucking." Said Sophia, straight edged.

"Why do you have to talk like that?" Said Frankie off balance. "That mouth of yours is too pretty to say words like fucking."

"It's always about fucking with you isn't it?" Said Sophia.

"How do I answer a question like that? Sure I wish we were intimate with each other, but we are not, and maybe it bothers me a little." Said Frankie.

"So it is about fucking." Said Sophia.

"It's more than that." Said Frankie.

"Like what? Not fucking?" Said Sophia.

"The before and after," said Frankie.

"I'm not sure I understand." Said Sophia.

"Before sex there's the anticipation of sex, a good thing, and after sex there is the satisfaction of having had sex, and the anticipation of having more sex in the future, another good thing." Said Frankie.

"So it is about fucking." Said Sophia. "Yeah, it's about fucking." Said Frankie.

"So what do we do about it?" Said Sophia.

"What can we do about it? We got to wait until we get married." Said Frankie.

"You masturbate don't you?" Said Sophia.

"Jesus Christ, how can you ask me something like that?" Said Frankie, going crimson.

"I have two older brothers that almost made a career out of doing it. They're twins. If you see one without the other you have a pretty good idea where, and what the other one is doing. You walk through enough doors in this house without knocking and you see things." Said Sophia.

"So do you?" Said Sophia.

"Not enough I guess." Said Frankie.

"Why do you say that?" Said Sophia. "Because all I can think about is you and me, and you know what." Said Frankie.

"Fucking?" Said Sophia. "Yes, fucking," said Frankie.

"When are we getting married?" Said Sophia.

"You tell me?" Said Frankie.

"You have to talk to my father about that." Said Sophia.

"Maybe we should elope." Said Frankie.

"Sure, how much money do you have?" Said Sophia. "About an inch and a half," said Frankie.

"Huh?" Said Sophia.

"Long story, about Seven hundred dollars." Said Frankie.

"That's not so much, is it?" Said Sophia.

"No, it isn't." Said Frankie.

"I have some money." Said Sophia.

"How much?" Said Frankie.

"About twenty-thousand dollars," said Sophia. "Twenty-thousand dollars!" Said Frankie in a high-pitched whisper and almost swallowing his tongue.

"About that much," said Sophia.

"How?" Said Frankie.

"You know, birthdays, first communion, confirmation, sweet sixteen, stuff like that." Said Sophia.

"That's a lot of money," said Frankie, impressed.

"Is it?" Said Sophia.

"Yes," said Frankie.

"It doesn't seem like a lot." Said Sophia.

"It's a lot of money believe me. People don't make that in three years working straight." Said Frankie.

"When we get married you get to take that money with you?" Said Frankie.

"It's my money." Said Sophia.

"Yeah, but, I mean, do they know you got that kind of money?" Said Frankie.

"My Father?" Said Sophia.

"Yeah," said Frankie.

"I don't know, maybe." Said Sophia.

"A person could do a lot with that kind of money." Said Frankie.

"Like what? Give me a for instance." Said Sophia. "Start a business, buy a house, start a family." Said Frankie smiling sideways and winking.

"It's still about fucking isn't it?" Said Sophia. "It's all inclusive" Said Frankie.

"Now are you going to tell me what's wrong with Pauley, and why you have been trying to hide a limp since you got here?" Said Sophia.

"Don't ask." Said Frankie.

CHAPTER 40

It was a week before Pauley could wear anything except the gorilla suit which he had professionally altered and another week before the stitches came out.

Frankie was feeling so good after two days of using the horse liniment that he put the laces back on his shoe.

Things, were slow around the office, so the mending was convenient.

Pauley was back at the wheel when the stitches were pulled. The Cadillac was washed inside and out. The carpeting, seat cushions were now bloodless, and business was usual.

"Hey Pauley? Don't you think its about time me and Sophia got married already?" Said Frankie.

Frankie and Pauley had just left the office and were driving down Route nine in clean tanker number four moving south on their way to Old Bridge.

A blanket suds deal twice a month, a tanker of beer, delivered to a restaurant/nightclub called Vino e Bello. Whether or not there was ever an Vino e Bello I, I don't know. Anyway, they were driving suds south.

"This is about fucking, isn't it?" Said Pauley. Frankie sighed.

"Does it always have to be about fucking?" Said Frankie, exasperated.

"Of course." Said Pauley. "What's the matter, your hand getting tired?"

"Pauley, I got to get laid." Said Frankie.

"I can understand your problem, and I can sympathize, but I am not going down that road with you. You know I can't let you do nothing.

Remember one thing, it's my neck lying next to yours. One of them gets cut, they both get cut." Said Pauley.

"Then how do I get Sal to push the wedding?" Said Frankie.

"You don't. Don't nobody put things in Sal's head except Sal." Said Pauley.

"What about Sophia? What if she asks him?" Said Frankie.

"Why would she? Sophia waits until next June, or whenever, has a big wedding with lots of people, get lots of presents, make lots of dough." Said Pauley making sense.

" If it moves too quick, there has to be a reason. No?" Said Pauley, easy to understand so far.

"You don't want people to talk about you. With Sophia everything has got to go smooth, otherwise she isn't any better than those two tramps what belong to Jackie." Said Pauley.

"It's too bad you don't run into one of them at the Beach. As long as you pushing smack they give you something."

"Yeah, too bad," said Frankie.

Fifteen minutes later Pauley pulled the tanker into Vino e Bello's parking lot. Next to the side entrance, under a portico there was a cap stuck into the asphalt.

The cap says, "Oil," on it. Pauley lifted the cap, Frankie attached the hose, opened the valve, and the beer, three hundred and fifty gallons, went into the ground.

"Why do they keep the beer in an oil tank?" Said Frankie.

"Under the ground, cooler down there." Said Pauley.

"Makes sense." Said Frankie.

"Yeah it does, don't it?" Said Pauley.

"You want to go get a drink before we head back to drop the tanker?" Said Pauley.

"Only one stop today?" Said Frankie.

"Yeah, were done." Said Pauley.

"Sure, why not?" Said Frankie.

The Cozy Couch, a dive bar and grill, in Woodbridge, behind the ESSO station on route nine going north.

The couch sells Beer, two kinds of sandwiches, one with mustard, one without mustard, and girls what don't wear too many clothes. The girls are rentals.

"This joint one of Sal's?" Said Frankie.

"Nah, the Moose, he runs it." Said Pauley.

"Who is the Moose?" Said Frankie.

"You got to say what, not who, when you ask that question." Said Pauley.

"What do you mean?" Said Frankie. "You remember the Tree how tall he is? Well, the Moose, he isn't so much tall as he is wide." Said Pauley.

The Cozy Couch was dark inside, but cool. The place was empty of patrons except for two guys in their mid forties, wearing white shirts buttoned to the neck, and tied off with silk. One red solid and the other blue monogrammed.

The bartender, tall, thin, and gray skinned, wore his hair flat on top, and his sleeves rolled up past his elbows.

"Hey Tim, what's doing?" Said Pauley to the gray skin.

"Pauley, how you doing? I don't see you in a long time, where was you in jail, or something?" Said Tim, laughing at his joke.

"Hey Tim please give my thanks to you're lovely wife for making visiting day so much fun. Tell her I still owe her two cartons of cigarettes." Said Pauley.

"You could have had her for one." Said Tim.

"Now you tell me." Said Pauley, laughing. "The Moose, is he here?"

"In the back, you want I should get him?" Said Tim. "Thanks." Said Pauley.

"Pauley is that you out there?" Said, a-fat soaked throat from the back room behind the bar.

"Moose, you come out of there so I can see you." Said Pauley.

Pauley held two fingers up to Tim who returned to his spot behind the bar. Tim acknowledged, and brought two frosty mugs from inside a waist high freeze box next to a sink filled with soapsuds and mugs.

The frosty mugs were topped off and placed on the bar one in front of Frankie and the other Pauley.

Frankie took a pull from his glass first, and then Pauley.

"Thanks Tim." Said Pauley.

The Moose came through the door slapping his fat into everything he passed until he was in front of Pauley smiling big enough to close his eyes from the fat pushing on them.

Smiling the Moose looked like a Buddha. Not smiling, the Moose, he still looked like a Buddha.

"Good to see you Moose." Said Pauley.

"You looking good Pauley, you putting on weight?" Said Moose.

"How can I when you got it all?" Said Pauley. The Moose, he laughed until you don't see his eyes again.

"Nobody working the floor tonight Moose?" Said Pauley.

"On a break, they're always on a break." Said Moose.

"Who you got working tonight?" Said Pauley. "Candy, and that other one, Liz." Said Moose.

"Moose this here is Frankie Migliori from Jersey City." Said Pauley. Pauley threw his chin at Frankie.

"You the kid marrying Sal's little girl?" Said Moose.

"Yes, I am." Said Frankie.

"Good to know you." Said Moose.

"Like wise." Said Frankie.

"Moose, Is it Ok we go in the back, and see the girls?" Said Pauley.

"Yeah sure Don't make them stay back there too long otherwise I pay them for nothing." Said Moose.

"You paying them now?" Said Pauley.

"Yeah, we don't draw the crowds like we used to, and they not making nothing on the rub no more." Said Moose.

"The rub?" Said Frankie.

"You tell him, or better you let the girls show him. They can use the practice in case we ever get busy again." Said Moose.

"I'm way ahead of you Moose." Said Pauley.

"Listen, what happens here, stays here, you got that." Said Pauley.

"Sure thing, but what's going to happen here, that has to stay here?" Said Frankie.

"Never mind, just do what I tell you." Said Pauley.

"Sure thing Pauley," said Frankie.

On the other side of the bar was a door. And inside that door was the cozy couch, like it said on the sign in the parking lot.

The room was painted black with a tin tile ceiling, also black. The light from a lamp next to the couch gave off a pinkish light which made the room look more purple than black.

The lamp was decorated with beads hanging down around the shade, and what looked like a doorknob dangling on a pull string.

The couch itself was not black, but brown corduroy. But in this light who could tell.

Frankie followed Pauley into the room. Candy and Liz, were sitting cozy in their g-strings and pasties on the couch smoking cigarettes, and whispering into each others ear.

"Hey Liz you still wishing Candy had a dick?" Said Pauley, when he cleared the doorframe.

Candy was a tall blonde with freckles, blue eyes, red sequins, and buxom. Not much ass, but enough for a reasonable man.

Liz on the other hand had enough ass for two men. She was short, brown eyed, with brown hair, full lips, dimples, green tit covers, a matching pussy hammock, and like I said carrying more than her share.

"Pauley with tits like she got, Candy don't need a dick to make me happy." Said Liz, smiling sly.

"Candy don't you get tired of just squeezing that ass? Don't you just want to fuck it one time?" Said Pauley, biting his bottom lip.

"You make a good point." Said Candy giggling.

"How you girls doing?" Said Pauley.

"Things are slow Pauley, are you going on the clock?"

"No babe, not this time, but he is. Girls meet Frankie." Said Pauley.

"Hi Frankie," said Candy and Liz in stereo.

"Pauley, what are you doing?" Said Frankie.

"Don't worry about it, just do like I tell you." Said Pauley.

"Hey girls, you got a man here needs a rub real bad." Said Pauley.

"Oh yeah?" Said Candy.

"Which one of us do you fancy Frankie?" Said Liz, ass showing.

"Pauley I can't do this." Said Frankie.

"You can, now shut the fuck up, and sit down on the couch." Said Pauley.

"Frankie can't decide which one of you two lovely ladies he likes better, so I guess he got to have the both of you." Said Pauley.

"Ooh," Said Candy.

Frankie sat on the couch, there were three cushions he sat on the middle one. Pauley put a knee into the cushion on Frankie's left side. He went to Frankie's ear and told him to sit still with his hands at his side and under no circumstances was he to touch either of the two girls.

"As long as you don't touch nothing, I can live with this." Said Pauley.

"Pauley, you sure this is Ok?" Said Frankie.

"The way I see it, you are just an innocent bystander, maybe you are a guy on a city bus, and some broad rubs herself against him, it can't be his fault, now can it?" Said Pauley.

"This is not a city bus Pauley." Said Frankie.

"Ok, so you are in a crowded bar, and in this case two broads, they bump into you and maybe rub the package a little, is it your fault? It's not a crime is it?" Said Pauley.

"Pauley, there isn't but five people in the whole place including you." Said Frankie.

"It's a small couch?" Said Pauley.

Candy and Liz, they went side dish on Frankie. They got one hand each on him. Liz was working the chest, and Candy was working the inner thigh. And Pauley, from behind the couch, whispered some instructions to Liz, who nodded her head and whispered to Candy what Pauley said to her, only she used more tongue then what Pauley did.

Pauley went back through the door to the bar and sat down. The less he saw the better he would feel about the whole thing.

"Hey Frankie, you remember what I told you, and keep your hands to yourself." Said Pauley with enough volume to carry through the wall.

Frankie kept his hands at his side. Candy, and Liz kept their hands moving.

Liz unbuttoned Frankie's shirt to his waist, and was pulling at the hair around his nipples, and putting the squeeze on them things while she was in the neighborhood. Candy was blowing into Frankie's ear, rubbing his thigh, and waiting.

Frankie hadn't had a woman in a long time, and it was plain, and prudent that he didn't have one that day either, but nature, being what it is, uncontrollable and what not, was doing stuff to him, and Candy, she saw what happened.

Candy gave Liz a wink, and Liz started to work on Frankie in a more direct fashion. Candy put her mouth in close to Frankie's ear, saying whatever, while Liz took a seat in Frankie's lap.

Frankie went stiff legged, and Liz put her palms flat to Frankie's thighs and lifted herself up enough to set the action on her ass. Fucking pistons didn't move like that ass. Frankie's hard on didn't stand a chance. Two, maybe three minutes, and Frankie was rolling his eyes.

Frankie couldn't talk right away, but he smiled a lot. Liz and Candy gave him a kiss on the cheek and then went out to the bar room to do some fishing.

Pauley came into the room with the cozy couch while Frankie was taking a handkerchief to the front of his pants.

"Spill something?" Said Pauley.

"Very funny, hey Pauley thanks. I needed that." Said Frankie.

"I thought you did." Said Pauley.

"And what they did, it wasn't cheating?" Said Frankie.

"Did you have sex with anybody?" Said Pauley.

"No?" Said Frankie.

"Are you asking me, or telling me?" Said Pauley.

"I don't know." Said Frankie. "Did you fuck anything?" Said Pauley louder.

"No," said Frankie.

"Did you touch anything you were not supposed to?" Said Pauley. "No," said Frankie.

"Did you exchange any fluids of any kind with anybody?" Said Pauley.

"Huh?" Said Frankie. "Did you shoot your load into anything other than your own boxer shorts?" Said Pauley.

"No, I did not." Said Frankie.

"Then it's not cheating, not in my book." Said Pauley.

"Then what do you call that thing those two ladies did to me?" Said Frankie.

"I call it the rub." Said Pauley.

"What do they call it?" Said Frankie.

"They call it a way in which two dikes can make dough off a guy's joint without having to touch it, suck it, or fuck it." Said Pauley.

"How much it cost you?" Said Frankie. "I threw the girls a ten spot." Said Pauley.

"Moose, he get any of that?" Said Frankie.

"Half, I guess." Said Pauley.

"How many girls does Moose got working for him?" Said Frankie.

"Five, or six, Why?" Said Pauley.

"They all do the rub?" Said Frankie. "You kidding? Guys don't want that shit. They want their dick sucked, or they want to get fucked, or maybe if they still fuck their wives they just want to see the girls dance, but nobody is going to pay good money for a dry hump on a couch." Said Pauley.

"I think they will." Said Frankie.

"You are fucking nuts. Who is going to pay ten-bucks for a fucking lap dance when they can get their dick sucked for half of that?" Said Pauley.

"A, lap dance Pauley?" Said Frankie.

"A, rub, whatever." Said Pauley. "I like that, a lap dance. Makes it sound harmless, innocent." Said Frankie, his wheels turning.

"It doesn't make any difference what you call it, it isn't the same as seeing lips on your cock. And maybe you haven't noticed but this joint isn't exactly jumping." Said Pauley.

"Hey Pauley, what do the girls look like who usually work a joint like this?" Said Frankie.

"Well, with the exception of those two," Said Pauley, making reference to Candy, and Liz. "Your typical dog and pony variety, I guess." Said Pauley.

"Why is that, I mean, the money is pretty good, the hours are light." Said Frankie.

"Because they are whores that dance a little, they are not by any stretch of the imagination beauty queens. What's your point?" Said Pauley.

"Candy, and Liz are beautiful girls, right?" Said Frankie.

"Yeah, so?" Said Pauley. "Why do you think they work a dive like this?" Said Frankie.

"The money's not bad the hours are good, everybody knows they are dikes, so they don't have to fuck you, and they look good without their clothes on. Oh, and once in a while they kiss each other so that makes them fun to watch." Said Pauley.

"The lap dancing, it doesn't bother them?" Said Frankie.

"It isn't fucking." Said Pauley.

"So, let me get this straight. They don't have to fuck anybody, they get to keep some of they clothes on, and men actually pay to be in the same room with them?" Said Frankie.

"Some guys go in for that kind of thing, I guess." Said Pauley.

"And they are not breaking any laws?" Said Frankie. "Not with the rub, no," said Pauley.

"The cops are not getting paid off to keep the place open?" Said Frankie. "Well, yeah, but not for the rub, for other things."

"The Moose he pays a couple of them, to keep the peace, not look too close at the liquor license, and to turn their heads when the girls are busy doing stuff, but for everything else all you got to have, is a cabaret license." Said Pauley.

"What stuff?" Said Frankie.

"Say there isn't but a couple of guys in here and the girl what is dancing isn't making no tips, so she shows her stuff, or maybe she gives a guy a whiff, you know.

Remember these girls are not that good looking, but a pussy is a pussy no matter who it belongs to, and any pussy will get a guy going if that's all he's looking at. So the girl, she puts her thing up in the sucker's face, and then she waits for the dough to keep it there. Maybe the guy, he's pulling on his dick under the bar, but if the dough doesn't keep coming then the pussy goes away. The dough comes, the pussy stays, and little dickie wins the race. Kind of like them nickelodeon's when we were kids." Said Pauley.

"Risky?" Said Frankie.

"Only if somebody complains, and who going to complain? The guy with a pussy in his face and a wife waiting at home or the pussy that isn't where it's supposed to be. Well, maybe the cleaning lady, she complains." Said Pauley.

"What about the good looking ones?" Said Frankie.

"They don't have to do much, except smile, and shake their ass." Said Pauley.

"They don't have to show their stuff?" Said Frankie.

"Why should they? They are already making good money with only their teeth showing. The really good-looking Dames, they make chumps fall in love with them, it pays better, and it keeps paying as long as the string has got some slack in it." Said Pauley.

"What about the girls that are not so good looking?" Said Frankie.

"That is the funny part." Said Pauley gathering his thoughts.

"The good looking babes, they string a guy along until he don't have a pot left to take a piss in and then they cut him loose." Said Pauley before taking a pull on his beer.

"The other ones, they are the ones who fall in love, and lose their pot, but nobody seems to care about them too much. They come and go." Said Pauley.

"What about the beauties Pauley, what happens to them?" Said Frankie.

"The beauties, they either strike-gold or they don't. But Sooner or later they all get used up, and got to show their stuff to some lowlife for a buck. Only with the good-looking ones you got to wait longer to see it" Said Pauley.

"But the house always gets a piece?" Said Frankie.

"The house is the house, isn't it?" Said Pauley.

"Does it cost a lot of money to own a place like this?" Said Frankie, looking around the bar.

"A tits bar?" Said Pauley.

"Yeah, a tits bar " Said Frankie.

"A place doesn't start showing tits until it can't make money no other way, why you want to own a dive for?" Said Pauley.

"What if we took it to the high side?" Said Frankie.

"What, like a burlesque house?" Said Pauley.

"A high class strip joint." Said Frankie.

"This is New Jersey, it's not Vegas. There is no such thing. Not here anyway," said Pauley.

"You said the good-looking women do not have to show much to make a man go all wall eyed." Said Frankie.

"Yeah, I said it, so?" Said Pauley. "So we only hire that kind of women." Said Frankie.

"I told you, they don't stay in a place like this too long, and once they get a guy's number the house goes shy." Said Pauley.

"Listen for a minute, will you?" Said Frankie, excited.

"We set up a nice place, I mean real nice, high class all the way, first rate meat, thoroughbreds only, no nags, and we collect them see, and then we parade them up and down like they were horses giving the players a peek before the gate goes up." Said Frankie with a glint in his eyes.

"Then what do we do with them, and how do we make money with a horse what doesn't play itself out in a week, or two?" Said Pauley.

"Let me finish." Said Frankie.

"Sorry, go on" said Pauley.

"All the while we are parading these girls, we are selling booze right?" Said Frankie.

"Naturally," said Pauley.

"And the prettier the girls the more we can charge for the booze, right?" Said Frankie.

"I suppose." Said Pauley.

"And where do we get the booze from?" Said Frankie.

"We already got the booze." Said Pauley.

"Exactly, the booze is cheap, but the girls are not." Said Frankie.

"They are still strippers Frankie, you can't just repaint them, and mark them up." Said Pauley.

"You are not getting it, these girls are not used cars selling cheap. They are new cars. Creampuffs, fresh out of the box." Said Frankie.

"Frankie, the girls you are talking about, they don't work in places like this. They get paraded all right, but by their mother's, and only until some rich guy comes along and buys them. I mean marries them" Said Pauley.

"Candy, and Liz, they ever getting married?" Said Frankie.

"No, but they are not normal." Said Pauley.

"They are beautiful, are they not?" Said Frankie.

"They are that." Said Pauley.

"They didn't have any trouble getting me off, did they?" Said Frankie.

"But you were holding your breath for a reason." Said Pauley.

"I bet there are a lot of guys not breathing right for one reason or another." Said Frankie.

"I don't know." Said Pauley, talking slow, and pausing between words.

"Pauley, these girls, they don't have to fuck anyone and they don't have to let a guy stick a dick in their mouth. All they got to do is blow in a guy's ear and rub him up like they did to me." Said Frankie.

"How you going to stop a guy from taking liberties?" Said Pauley.

"We tell them they can't touch the girls." Said Frankie. "Better yet, let the girls tell them. We just enforce." Said Frankie.

"Tough job, we better hire big." Said Pauley.

"Big and beautiful inside the room, and big and ugly on the chair outside the room," said Frankie.

"No fucking?" Said Pauley.

"Nope," said Frankie.

"No blowjobs?" Said Pauley.

"No blowjobs," said Frankie.

"What if a guy don't want to come in his pants?" Said Pauley.

"Not our problem," said Frankie.

"Could be though. Maybe the guy, he doesn't want to pay after he comes, maybe he is embarrassed and wants to get the fuck out of there before somebody sees the stain on the front of his pants. Or maybe the guy, don't want to pay if the broad don't make him come. I bet there would be more of them than the other." Said Pauley.

"Maybe so, but it is still not our problem." Said Frankie.

"We will have music playing, right?" Said Frankie.

"Of course." Said Pauley.

"Ok then after we parade the girls, we circulate them through the place, smiling big, wiggling their ass when they walk, making eye contact, pushing drinks, being sociable." Said Frankie, still making the rules up as he goes along and hoping that they make sense.

"These are beautiful girls, knockouts, and they are being nice, real nice to a guy, any guy, every guy, and maybe this one guy, he has never seen a real doll this close up before." Said Frankie with more confidence in his voice.

"And maybe this one guy has never had any luck with the ladies, or with nothing in his life, but with these ladies every guy has got the goods, every one of them is a ladies man." Said Frankie.

"So far I like how it sounds." Said Pauley. "Keep it going."

"Everybody knows a dance is one song. If the guy comes during that song he's a lucky guy and he gets away cheap, but if the girl, she works him up real good, but knows how to bring him down a little before the song finishes then he has to buy another dance, right?" Said Frankie.

"More money for her, and more money for us, right?" Said Pauley. "Frankie, it sounds like a regular come on, scheme. The guy still gets took. Only we don't pick his pocket while we blowing him, we, let him give us his money, and maybe he don't even shoot his load, and get to feel bad about it later." Said Pauley.

"I'm telling you Pauley, that guy will leave with a smile on his face, he'll be broke, but smiling." Said Frankie.

"But why is he smiling?" Said Pauley.

"Pauley, you have Naomi, but you do not have her, so you feel Ok about screwing around with other broads, like that waitress, what's her name, Sheila, down Long Branch."

"I got Sophia, but I can't have anybody else, otherwise I got trouble." Said Frankie.

"You better believe it." Said Pauley.

"If I was to go and get a blow job from some whore, it wouldn't mean nothing, but it would make me feel like shit. And it would cause you to have to hurt me some." Said Frankie.

"Hurt you a lot." Said Pauley.

"Don't you think there are a lot of guys like me who love their wives, their girlfriends or whoever, but want to screw around a little, on the side, but can't do it for one reason or another?" Said Frankie.

"Yeah, I guess so." Said Pauley.

"Pauley, I just had a hell of a time, with two beautiful women, and I don't feel all that guilty about it." Said Frankie. "Don't you think that kind of fun is worth something to somebody?" Said Frankie.

"So what do we do about it?" Said Pauley.

"We put it in a bottle, and try to sell it." Said Frankie.

"Maybe you got something there," said Pauley.

CHAPTER 41

"The boss says he don't care if we open a place as long as he gets a piece. Oh, and that it don't interfere with what we are doing already. " Said Pauley.

"How much he taking?" Said Frankie.

"The Boss isn't taking nothing, we are giving him a third." Said Pauley.

"That's not too bad," said Frankie.

"Bad enough," said Pauley.

"Could be worse." Said Frankie.

"How?" Said Pauley.

"He could say no, altogether." Said Frankie.

"The boss don't never say no to free money." Said Pauley.

"Where is this place of ours going to be, you got any ideas?" Said Pauley.

"How much money do we have?" Said Frankie.

"We, or Me?" Said Pauley.

"I got about a grand, cash, three Rolex watches, two platinum, and four gold set engagement rings, and one Hamilton wrist watch with a leather band." Said Frankie.

"That the one you wearing?" Said Pauley.

"Yes," said Frankie.

"That's about Two and a half, maybe three G's," said Pauley.

"How much you got?" Said Frankie.

"None of your business," said Pauley.

"What?" Said Frankie, taken aback.

"We don't need money to do this thing." Said Pauley.

"Well, maybe a little bit, for the permit, and the inspectors and shit." Said Pauley.

"How do you open a joint without money?" Said Frankie.

"The shit hole, the building, sorry, is easy enough. You tell me where you want this place to be, and maybe the boss, has something there already." Said Pauley.

"I told you, it's not going to be a shit hole." Said Frankie.

"Whatever," said Pauley.

"Jersey City?" Said Frankie.

"The boss has a building down by the river, next to the train station, in Hoboken. Close enough?" Said Pauley.

"I guess so, what's it look like?" Said Frankie. "What does it matter? Whatever it looks like now, it isn't going to look like that later." Said Pauley.

The building in Hoboken was a red brick, two-story, walk up with a flat roof. There was an entrance into the basement accessible from the street. And a fireplug in front of the building, but Pauley parked the Cadillac in front of the building anyway.

"Pauley, there is a fireplug in front of the place. Said Frankie You are going to get a ticket."

"I don't see no fireplug. And the next time we come here you won't see a fireplug either." Said Pauley.

"Who lives here, Pauley? Whoever it is they have a Cadillac like you do." Said Frankie.

A Cadillac, same make, same model, different color, red, was parked just ahead of the fireplug, out of range of a ticket.

"Charlie Chili dogs, he lives upstairs." Said Pauley.

"He going to get mad, we messing up his house?" Said Frankie.

"Who do you think is going set straight the assholes trying to get fresh with the girls?" Said Pauley. "Charlie Chili dogs?" Said Frankie.

"You got it." Said Pauley.

"Charlie is a little old isn't he?" Said Frankie.

"No, he is just seasoned." Said Pauley.

"With what formaldehyde?" Said Frankie.

"I'm going to tell him you said that." Said Pauley. "No Pauley please, I was just kidding." Said Frankie.

"I thought so." Said Pauley.

"The basement, and the first floor apartment are not occupied. And the empty lot next to the place belongs to Sal, so we have ample parking." Said Pauley.

"So far so good," said Frankie.

"A shit load of people go in and out of that train station every day, so we got customers," said Pauley.

"But what about the neighbors, what are they going to say?" Said Frankie.

"Well, we don't have any, so make all the noise you want." Said Pauley.

"That over there is a bank, and they close at three o'clock." Said Pauley, pointing to the granite, and marble opposite the building. " And that over there is a mechanic's garage, Sal, he owns a piece of it." Said Pauley, pointing to the gray corrugated, and poured concrete building next to the granite, and marble.

"So I say this place is good to go. What do you say?" Said Pauley.

"All of that empty space behind the apartment building, who does it belong to?" Said Frankie, looking at about ten acres of weeds, and old tires.

"The railroad, they own it." Said Pauley.

"I say we are good then." Said Frankie.

"I thought I heard you guys out here. How you doing Pauley, and you too Frankie?"

Charlie Chili Dogs came through a door from the basement. He looked pretty good for an old barroom brawler. Aside from the vegetation above his eyes, and around his ear holes, he, don't look so bad.

A blue pinstriped suit, white shirt, too tight in the neck and a powder blue tie. Charlie wasn't wearing a hat, or shoes.

"Charlie, how you doing?" Said Pauley, looking down at Charlie's bare toes.

"I'm Good. Did you come to look at the place?" Said Charlie.

"Yeah, who told you I was coming?" Said Pauley.

"The Boss, he called twenty minutes ago, and told me to look out for you." Said Charlie.

"Charlie, where are your shoes?" Said Pauley.

"Jeez, I must have left them in the house." Said Charlie.

"Why don't we go inside before you hurt yourself, is it Ok with you that we do that Charlie?" Said Pauley, still looking at bare toes.

"Yeah, sure thing, only come in through the basement on a count of that door, it don't open from the outside." Said Charlie, waving at the front door one flight up from the street.

"What's a matter with it?" Said Pauley.

"It doesn't have a key." Said Charlie.

"What happened to the key, Charlie?" Said Pauley.

"I think maybe I lost it. I got one for the inside though. I keep it in the lock so I don't lose it like I lost the other one." Said Charlie.

"That lock got a dead bolt on it Charlie?" Said Pauley.

"Yeah, how you know that?" Said Charlie.

"Because I'm a magician. Charlie the lock on the outside is the same as the one on the inside." Said Pauley.

"No kidding?" Said Charlie.

"Charlie, how many times you get knocked in the head?" Said Pauley.

"Too many, I think." Said Charlie.

"I think I agree with you." Said Pauley.

The basement was twelve feet floor to ceiling, and seventy feet, by thirty, front to back, and side to side.

"This place is huge." Said Frankie.

"We used to stack and store the booze down here, back during the prohibition years." Said Charlie. "Is that why the ceiling is so high?" Said Frankie.

"Yeah, we dug it out of the ground to make room for the cases of hooch we can't fit on the truck." Said Charlie going back, way back.

"We never took more than one truck out of here at a time." Said Charlie.

"But why here?" Said Frankie.

"The booze, it came down from Canada crooked, so we had to hide it someplace, and we pick this place because it was so close to the rails." Said Charlie his eyes squinted trying to recall.

"The Boss, I think he used to buy the booze from that guy what dated Gloria Swanson you know the Ambassador to them Limeys and had it shipped here, but we always had to order more than we could use, so it had to be stored for a while until we needed it."

"Makes sense." Said Pauley.

"Ambassador to them Limeys, that's funny," said Frankie.

"He is talking about Joe Kennedy." Said Pauley. "Before he went to Hollywood he used to run whiskey for us, and just about everybody else," Said Pauley. "oh, and he was the Ambassador to the United Kingdom before the war, the big one, not that skirmish you was in. I am surprised that you didn't know that you being so smart and all." Said Pauley with a grin on his face.

"OH, That Joe Kennedy, yeah, yeah, I remember him." Said Frankie with a red blush around the ears.

"So how long you living here Charlie?" Said Frankie.

"Since when they say it's Ok to drink booze again." Said Charlie.

"That's a long time." Said Frankie. "It goes fast, especially when you don't remember most of it." Said Charlie.

"Hey Charlie, what say you, me, and Frankie, we go to the Clam Broth House for some clams?" Said Pauley.

"They got good chicken there too Pauley." Said Charlie.

"Charlie, you go find your shoes, and then we will go and get you some of that chicken." Said Pauley.

"Sounds good to me." Said Charlie.

Charlie climbed a staircase to his apartment. Frankie and Pauley could hear his bare feet flapping on the wood as he went up.

"Is he all right?" Said Frankie.

"About half all right." Said Pauley.

"Is that enough?" Said Frankie.

"Look, he isn't counting the money, and he doesn't have to do much more than stand there and be." Said Pauley.

"Be what?" Said Frankie.

"Charlie, he got a face like a road map, and knuckles the size of your belt buckle. He doesn't have to be or do nothing except be what he is, and if somebody steps out of line, then Charlie, he just has to be what he was for a minute, or two. I think he can handle that much." Said Pauley.

"Did that Kennedy guy really date Gloria Swanson?" Said Frankie.

You bet he did, and a bunch more of them starlets too. I hear his kid is a real horn bag just like he was. Said Pauley. "Good looking Kid, I hope he stays out of the rackets."

CHAPTER 42

The Depot is what Frankie and Pauley called the place. It turned out good, better I think than even they thought it would. A nice joint they made.

The wood-workers union, Hoboken local 200, they donated all the manpower needed to panel the walls, and rebuild the front of the place so it looked like something.

The plumbers, whatever local they were refit the place, and put in the toilets.

The masons, they finished off whatever the wood workers didn't do, and the teamsters, they stood around and did nothing, but they didn't want to be left out of the thing.

Four weeks after the first nail got hammered the joint was ready to open. They got enough booze to drown an elephant, and they got more girls then Heinz got varieties.

Liz and Candy came to help out with the girls, teach them things. It turns out the rub isn't so easy to do, and the ladies they got tired easy. Also it turns out that beautiful girls are lazy.

It was a Friday night when the doors opened. The place was packed tight right away, and things started to go sour quick.

There wasn't a regular Joe in the place, and since it was the grand opening, all the boys, they showed up to have a good time.

The cocks were out of the coop more than they were in. And the girls who were promised that they didn't have to see any cocks start walking out of the joint, with most of what little they had on to begin with still sticking to some parts of what they intended to keep covered.

The boys were not accustomed to there being any strings attached where strippers were concerned tried to do as they please, and since they had an in with the Boss, and knew the guys who ran the place they didn't come across with no dough neither.

Liz and Candy, already disgusted by the sheer number of cocks they were seeing, couldn't get a good rub going. So they walked out of the joint too.

Charlie Chili dogs was so happy to see so many of his old pals he forgot what it was he was supposed to be doing, so he didn't do nothing, except chew fat, and try to remember some of what the boys were reminiscing about.

Pauley tried to set everybody straight, but the whole idea didn't make sense to any of them.

"What do you mean that whore don't got to suck my dick? I give her five bucks didn't I?"

"What do you mean she's not a whore? She's a stripper, no?"

"Maybe you are just ahead of your time Frankie. The world is just not ready for a lap dance, or stripper's what don't suck cock." Said Pauley with his arm around Frankie.

"So now what do we do?" Said Frankie.

"There are two things we can do. One, we close the place down, and reopen at a later date as something else, or two, we get some hookers down here right away so some dick's get sucked and these, hoodlums don't trash the joint." Said Pauley.

"Then what do we do?" Said Frankie.

"After which part?" Said Pauley.

"The second part." Said Frankie.

"We lose the filet, and buy ground beef." Said Pauley.

"I think we lost it already." Said Frankie.

"These guys, they don't know what to do with good piece of meat, they put ketchup on it, might as well be hamburger." Said Pauley.

"This a tits bar now?" Said Frankie.

"It sure looks that way." Said Pauley. "A very nice tits bar, but yeah."

CHAPTER 43

Pauley telephoned about a dozen hookers that he knew, and they came down to The Depot and saved the joint from destruction. Some of them broads hired on as entertainment that night, none of them were too good looking, but maybe they are not supposed to be.

Charlie Chili dogs, he stayed on, as the whatever, only because he don't have to go so far to get to work, and it was good for him. Otherwise he would just stay upstairs and look for his shoes all day.

The Depot made good from the beginning, the second day anyway. The Boss, he said, "You did good," each week when they brought him his cut.

Liz, and Candy went back to the couch, to do whatever with each other to the appreciation of nobody much, since they still don't want to suck dick.

Frankie, he went to the couch a couple of times to get the rub because none of the whores they hired wanted to spend any time doing it to him since they said blowing a guy was quicker, and they didn't have to work so hard at it.

The Depot wasn't open more than two months before Pauley had the idea that they should open another joint closer to where he lives so he don't have to drive all the way to Hoboken so much.

Frankie didn't think it was such a bad idea as two joints was better than one when the money was counted.

Frankie moved into the empty apartment upstairs from the tits. The rooms go six in a row, like ducks. You can stand at one end and see the other end without moving an inch. He painted it only one color all the way through, beige, it looked nice.

The furniture was picked up from here and there, this truck, and that truck. Brown, or off brown, or off beige.

A couch, two chairs, assorted tables, all earth tones, more or less.

The music from the band playing the walking music for the girls, was loud enough to make you go deaf, but the noise didn't bother Frankie too much since he was not home half of the time. Him and Pauley kept busy with all the shit they had to do for the boss, and what it was they had to do to keep their two joints up in the air at the same time.

The boss took Charlie's Cadillac away from him and gave it to Frankie, because Charlie kept forgetting where he parked it, and the boss was tired of sending people out to look for it every time Charlie claimed that somebody had swiped it.

Charlie, he didn't mind giving up the car because he was tired of calling the boss every time he thought somebody stole it from him, which was once or twice a week.

When the boss wanted to see Charlie, Frankie would take him, or Charlie would the train, which was never more a hundred yards away from the house.

Things were going pretty good for Frankie and Pauley. Not necessarily a good thing because while they were not really bad guys, life was not supposed to go well for them what don't deserve it.

Three days after Pauley opened up the second tits bar six blocks away from where he lived, the boss decided to come and see the nipple he was sucking, so he drove his Cadillac from his house in Linden to the tits in Elizabeth. But the boss, he don't get more than three blocks from his house before he put his face through the windshield.

The boss's Cadillac didn't know how to drive itself so it hit a telephone pole. The boss was dead before he could hit the brakes.

The Doctor who read the report to the immediate family, said that the boss didn't feel a thing when he died. He had had a massive Arterial embolism. Anyway, one minute the boss was driving to the tits and the next minute he was dead.

As you can imagine this turn of events hit hard and everyone who loved and cared about the boss was broken up in one way or another.

The two boys who lost their father wanted to avenge him in some way, But who were they going to punish? A roasted pig, a plate of ravioli, or the eight thousand packs of cigarettes the boss smoked in his lifetime? "Vendcarsi Niente!" Said nobody.

Pauley, he felt like he had lost a father when Sal went through that windshield and landed on his face. But didn't dare show it too much. He had no way of knowing who the next boss was going to be, and you never know who maybe didn't like Sal so much and was glad he went out the way he did.

Sal went through the windshield, but his shoes didn't go with him. Those big shoes they didn't fit through the hole that Sal made in the glass, and was sitting on the dashboard when the cops got to the scene.

Sophia didn't have to go through this ordeal without Frankie by her side all the way to the cemetery.

Frankie wondered for a moment right before they started shoveling dirt onto the casket whether maybe a dead cockatoo, or a capuchin monkey was inside the box keeping company with the boss. Frankie didn't ask.

After the wake and funeral was finished. Jackie N jumped to the front of the line and tried to pull strings, but the two boys, Peter and little Sal, put up a fuss.

Peter and little Sal ran the yard in Linden, and didn't want anybody telling them what to do, except the guy, who can't tell them nothing no more.

Jackie N didn't waste any time before he laid down the law for all the particulars, Pauley, Joey Spoons, Sammy Graves, Philly, Charlie Chili dogs, and Frankie.

The meeting took place at the Linden Yard and it didn't go well.

Jackie N wearing a camel hair coat covering black pin stripes with a double breast, was waiting, when Pauley, and Frankie come through the door to the inner office.

"Who the fuck broke the lock on that closet?" Said Pauley before he saw Jackie N sitting comfortable at the desk with his ass on the cordovan leather chair that used to belong to his brother.

"The lock was broke when we get here, and that, I mean, him, he was sitting in the chair when we come through the door." Said Joey Spoons, biting his tongue.

"How you doing Pauley?" Said Jackie N when Pauley came through like a bull, snorting through his nose.

"What's a matter, them chairs are not good enough for you?" Said Pauley panning the room, folding chairs scattered.

One of the mugs that Jackie N brought with him took a step at Pauley, but thought better of it.

"A little respect." Said the mug what stepped.

"What's a matter with you Pauley, a guy can't sit on a comfortable chair?" Said Jackie N making light.

"That is the boss's chair, and." Said Pauley cut off.

"And the boss, he isn't here any more, so shut up." Said Jackie N asserting him self. Pauley, he didn't say nothing in response, but he did give eyes to Jackie N who didn't like it, but left it alone.

"We are here to talk, not fight, so everybody calm the fuck down," said Jackie N.

"Pauley, you and Frankie pull a chair to the desk, and the rest of you guys go outside until I tell you to come back."

"If Any of you guys have a problem with this arrangement you can go fuck yourselves."

"Ok, let's do this thing." Said Jackie N, loud.

Charlie, Joey, Philly, Tony, they didn't move a muscle until Pauley, he threw them his chin.

The door to the office was shut by the last guy out the door.

"Pauley, I know it hasn't been but three days since we put my brother to rest, but things have got to be put in order quick so business can get done, and the shit can move smooth. You understand?" Said Jackie N, in a kind of dramatic low talking.

"If You want your shit to move smooth take some fucking Ex-Lax." Said Pauley getting one in before he had to go along.

Jackie N, he smiled at Pauley.

"That was a funny one Pauley. I didn't know you was such a comedian." Said Jackie N.

"I have my moments." Said Pauley.

"Well, make that your last moment, Ok." Said Jackie N, this time he wasn't smiling.

"Pauley you are upset, and I can understand that." Said Jackie N softer this time.

"You lost someone that was close to you, so did I. And maybe you are a little bit worried that things are not going to be so good for you no more. But I am here to tell you that even though you got a fucking attitude problem, I am not going to take nothing away from you, the tits bars, the tanker deal, the truck stops, none of it. All of that is Ok by me, you can keep them, but." Said Jackie N, and then he paused. "The terms are getting a bump on my side. I know you, was kicking a third upstairs, and while that was a generous contribution you were making, it is not going to be enough no more. Starting today we go to fifty percent." Said Jackie N.

"Fucking half, you want fucking half of what I earn?" Said Pauley shaking his head, no anger, almost like he was expecting something like this to happen.

"That's right" Said Jackie N picking his teeth with a toothpick he pulled from behind his ear.

"What if I say no?" Said Pauley.

"Then today you are out of business, and everything that you got, it goes to the next guy, whoever the fuck that is. Maybe it's the kid here, or one of them fucking morons you got working with you, but somebody is going to pay me what I want, or don't nobody get nothing." Said Jackie N, his face all pinched.

"Why you doing this? Your brother, he never did nothing like this." Said Pauley.

"Fuck him, he's dead, and I am not. I say what goes, and I say it goes up. Half is the deal. Take it, or get the fuck out of the way." Said Jackie N.

"Take it or leave it, is that the deal?" Said Pauley.

"Take it, or drop dead." Said Jackie N.

"You threatening me?" Said Pauley.

"I don't make threats, I make deals and I offered you one. Take it or not, it's your decision, and maybe it's your funeral too." Said Jackie N.

"You think you got the muscle to drop me Jackie N?" Said Pauley, leaning in on Jackie N, his hands on the desk fisted, and going white in the knuckles.

"I think I do." Said Jackie N still picking at his teeth.

Pauley's disposition changed all of a sudden, he smiled, showing teeth to Jackie N, which made Jackie N nervous.

"Ok Jackie, you got a deal." Said Pauley, pink knuckles on the desk.

"Good" said Jackie N, arrogant. "And it's Jackie N or Boss from now on you got that Pauley." Said Jackie N.

Frankie kept his mouth shut all the time he sat there. "Frankie, now you and me, we got something in common." Jackie N smiled like the cat that swallowed the canary. "Sophia, my niece, she's a good kid and I like her and son of a bitch if I don't wish my girls were like her, but they are not." A slight cringe from Jackie N when he mentioned his two girls. "Anyway, out of respect for my brother I am going to keep an eye on the both of you until you are married."

"Pauley Her Aunt Sophia is on her way up here from Long Branch, and should be here soon, but until she is, watch your step." Said Jackie N flashing the dead eye at Pauley.

"Whatever it was that you were doing to make sure these kids didn't get in any trouble keep doing it."

"By the way kid," Jackie N turned his head to face Frankie and forced a smile.

"The wedding is in three weeks. I know it's soon, but get used to the idea. I already told Sophia, and it don't seem to bother her none, so there it is," said Jackie N.

Frankie heard the words that Jackie N said to him, but they didn't sink in right away. Marry, three weeks, huh, what? Jackie N, since he didn't hear no complaints, he says, "Ok then. Three weeks, I let you know where, and when. Pauley, make sure the kid shows up." Jackie N, he laughed at that last remark.

Jackie N got up from the cordovan leather, pulled down the creases in his pant legs, and went through the door.

All of Jackie N's boys were standing on one side of the outer office staring at Sal's boys, who were on the other side staring back at them.

"Let's go." Said Jackie N when he passed between them.

Jackie N's boys, they followed in a line behind him like ants marching. The last of them bugs went through the door slamming.

Sal's boy's, with Philly up front, went into the office one at a time. Pauley was still sitting at the desk, but Frankie got up to walk off what he heard from Jackie N.

The boys kept it down until they got the Ok to pipe up. Pauley gave the signal to speak after he heard Jackie N's car pull away from the front of the garage, splashing gravel as it peeled out.

"You guys, you want the good news, or the bad news first?" Said Pauley smirking. Pauley was rubbing his eyebrows like he did when things were making him uncomfortable.

"The good news first Pauley," said Charlie Chili dogs.

"Yeah, the good news," said Spoons.

"Everybody take a chair, we got things we got to talk about, and none of them but one is good, so sit down and get comfortable, and don't nobody say nothing until I finish. You got it?" Said Pauley.

Grunts all around as they were dragging chairs, until a half-circle of wood slats surrounded the desk.

"Pauley, Ok I sit in the Boss's chair, my hemorrhoids is burning, and these wooden slats, they are not helping." Said Charlie Chili dogs who don't like to sit on folding wood when his ass hurts.

"Don't nobody sit in that chair no more." Said Pauley.

Pauley reached into his pocket and produced a pocketknife. He pulled the blade from the casing and gripped the handle tight like he was going to stab somebody.

Pauley ripped into the cordovan leather with the knife, pulling the blade down from top to bottom, popping some buttons that got in the way of the sharp edge.

"Pauley, What the fuck are you doing." Said Spoons.

"The boss, he can't sit in this chair no more, so don't nobody sit in this chair no more." Said Pauley, determined.

"Hey Pauley, slice me off a piece of that leather will you." Said Sammy Graves.

"Yeah, hack me off a piece too." Said Philly.

"And one for me," said Charlie.

Pauley cut some squares from the leather, and handed them out to all of them what was there.

They all put the leather into their pockets, or they wallets, or wherever.

"Jackie N, he is not going to like what you done Pauley." Said Philly's cousin Jimmy No Neck, who didn't say a word until now.

"Fuck him." Said Pauley.

"Yeah, Fuck him," said Philly's cousin No Neck.

"Fuck him." Said everybody else.

Pauley, after he finished murdering the chair, turned its back to him, and kicked it through the door into the outer office.

"Spoons, you and Charlie get rid of that thing tonight. Throw it in the river, take it to the dump, I don't care where you take it, but make sure it goes away." Said Pauley.

"Sure thing Pauley," said Spoons.

"Spoons, give Charlie a ride home after you get rid of the chair, he don't drive no more." Said Pauley.

"No problem," said Spoons.

Charlie, he smiled.

"Everybody shut up now, so I can tell you what gives, now that the boss is not living no more." Said Pauley pausing.

Pauley reached with one arm over the desk, picked up an empty folding chair and lifted it up and over and set it down behind the desk and sat down.

Everybody else in the room did what they could to get close enough to Pauley so they could hear what it was he was going to say to them.

"First the good news," said Pauley, smiling at Frankie. "Three weeks from now, Frankie and Sophia, are getting married."

Spoons, Charlie, Sammy, Philly, and the rest of the guys made a happy noise when they heard what Pauley said. Congratulations passed from one to the other until Frankie had been wished well by all.

"Now the bad news," said Pauley after everybody shut up again. "Jackie N has made himself the boss, and I don't think we can do nothing about it."

"What about Peter, and little Sal, what do they got to say about all this?" Said Spoons.

"I haven't seen either one of them since the funeral, and anyway, they can't do nothing about it, they don't have seniority or the wherewithal." Said Pauley.

"If you mean brains I agree, but didn't nobody hear me say that." Said Spoons.

"I was being kind I love those boys like they were my own kids." Said Pauley dropping his lids for a second.

"We all feel the same way." Said Charlie, while the rest of them, moved their heads up, and down.

"So maybe it isn't such a bad thing," said Philly, thinking positive.

"I am not finished yet. Jackie N, he says his end is going up. He is taking half, or he will be after today." Said Pauley rubbing his head with both hands through his hair.

"Are you kidding? We do all the work, and he collects half the dough. That is not right Pauley." Said Spoons.

"Is that just on the booze, and oil deal, or is that everything?" Said Philly.

"Everything," said Pauley.

"So maybe we don't pay, what happens then?" Said Spoons.

"I get dead, and it still don't change nothing." Said Pauley.

"We got to do something." Said Spoons, his face red, and his expression dark.

"We are going to do something, but not yet. We got a wedding to get through first." Said Pauley.

"Why the wedding? I love Sophia you all know that I do, but why now? I thought I had to wait until next year for her sake and the family's. So why the change?" Said Frankie.

"Jackie N needs something big, something happy, something that will bring the family together, make people forget." Said Pauley.

"Forget what?" Said Frankie.

"Forget that he isn't Sal." Said Pauley.

CHAPTER 44

"So, are you good with this?" Said Sophia.

"What choice do I have?" Said Frankie.

Frankie and Sophia sat under one of the fig trees in her backyard. Sophia, doesn't see any reason why Frankie shouldn't come to her house. Her father isn't there any more, and Pauley is worrying about other things right now, and doesn't have any time to worry about whether or not Frankie and Sophia are doing stuff to each other.

"You don't want to marry me?" Said Sophia, tearing.

"Sure I do, but," Said Frankie.

"But, what?" Said Sophia, going stiff.

"Is this the way you want it to be, on the run, like we are in a hurry to get it over with, or something?" Said Frankie.

"I thought you would be glad, I mean, now you only have to wait a few weeks before you can fuck my brains out." Sophia was crying, she put her face into Frankie's chest, her palms cradling.

"I never thought of that." Said Frankie, trying to go light. Sophia laughed, and cried at the same time.

"Sophia, please, tell me the truth, this cannot be the way you wanted it to go. You deserve more than this. And I can't help but." Said Frankie, stopping short.

"What? You can't help but what?" Said Sophia, doe eyed and damp.

"I can't help but think maybe I kind of know what my father felt when the old Don pulled a shotgun on him, and pushed him down the aisle." Said Frankie, stuttering.

"It isn't that way, and you know it." Said Sophia, insulted.

"Sophia please, don't get mad at me, I know it isn't the same with us, but, well, maybe it is a just a little bit." Said Frankie.

Sophia, didn't answer Frankie, maybe because she thought he was right.

Sophia put her arms around Frankie, and squeezed him hard. Frankie did the same.

"So what do we do?" Said Sophia.

"We get married." Said Frankie.

"Are you sure you want to?" Said Sophia.

Frankie put Sophia at arm's length, and stared into her face. "You listen to me. Maybe this is going too fast, and maybe it isn't. Who knows, but the one thing I know for sure is that I love you more than anything in this world, and the when, and where, and how doesn't mean a thing to me, but you, you mean everything to me." Said Frankie, serious.

Sophia turned on the waterworks again, and buried her head into Frankie, and maybe she blew her nose on his shirt too, I'm not sure. Anyway, Frankie and Sophia hugged some more, and kissed, and maybe Frankie, he felt her up a little.

Now Sophia had a good body, and Frankie, he could feel it through the gray cotton dress she was wearing. And for a short while Frankie forgot Sophia had just lost her father through the windshield of a Cadillac, and felt guilty.

"What's wrong?" Said Sophia when Frankie pulled away from her.

"This isn't right." Said Frankie.

"What's not right?" Said Sophia.

"This what we're doing, it's not right. Sal, your father, he hasn't been dead three days, and we are here doing stuff that maybe he would think we shouldn't be doing." Said Frankie.

"Frankie, I loved my father, and I miss him, but if it was only him, and his rules that said that we shouldn't be together, then those rules don't matter any more.

There isn't anyone here that can stop me from doing anything I want to do, if I really want to do it." Said Sophia.

"Then why you letting your Uncle Jackie N force you to marry me?" Said Frankie. "He is not forcing me to marry you, he is forcing you to marry me." Said Sophia.

"Did Jackie N, your Uncle, did he discuss it with you." Said Frankie.

"He asked me if I had a problem with it, and I said no." Said Sophia.

"This is about fucking, isn't it." Said Frankie.

"Maybe a little bit." Said Sophia, giving space between her thumb, and forefinger.

"But not until we are married." Said Frankie.

"Why, don't you want to fuck me under the figs?" Said Sophia, smiling sideways.

"Not the worst idea I ever heard." Said Frankie.

"Not tonight honey I have a headache?" Said Sophia, testing.

"Gee, that's a new one. You got any more of those?" Said Frankie.

"I have to wash my hair?" Said Sophia.

"Do my nails?"

"Ok, I get it, no fucking under the figs." Said Frankie.

"Hey, where are we going to live after we get married?" Said Frankie, a thought crossing.

"I thought we could live here." Said Sophia.

"In your fathers house?" Said Frankie, forgetting that Sal was dead.

"Why not?" Said Sophia.

"What about your brothers?" Said Frankie, remembering they also lived in the house.

"They are moving out tomorrow." Said Sophia.

"Why?" Said Frankie.

"Uncle Jackie told them to." Said Sophia.

"Why?" Said Frankie.

"Because I asked him to." Said Sophia.

"Why?" Said Frankie.

"So we can live here, by ourselves." Said Sophia.

"Oh," said Frankie.

"But what if I say I don't want to live here?" Said Frankie.

"Believe me, you want to live here." Said Sophia.

"Why do I want to live here?" Said Frankie.

"Because I do." Said Sophia.

"You spoiled brat." Said Frankie.

"Maybe a little bit." Said Sophia, again making space between her thumb, and forefinger.

"What's a matter, you don't want to live over a tits bar?" Said Frankie, referring to where he, lives.

"Maybe I don't want you living over a tits bar." Said Sophia.

"Why, are you jealous of all those tits?" Said Frankie.

"Temptation" said Sophia. "For you, or me?" Said Frankie, smiling crooked.

"You are disgusting." Said Sophia.

"I don't know, you seem to be enjoying yourself in my head." Said Frankie, a dreamy eyed expression.

"Pig." Said Sophia, with mock disgust.

"Sophia, what do I have to do for the wedding, I mean is there anything special I have to do to prepare? I guess I should go and rent a tuxedo, and what about the honeymoon, I better get something set up. Where do you want to go? What about the reception, do we have to set that up, we don't have much time." Said Frankie, getting nervous and showing it.

"Relax, everything is being taken care of, my grandmother, my aunts, and my uncle are working on it. My dress is being sewn, the hall has been arranged, the caterer has been hired, the band, the flowers, done. So take it easy, you don't have to do anything except buy a tuxedo, and show up." Said Sophia.

"No kidding? Well, that takes a load off. But what about the honeymoon, do we have a say on it, or do we have to follow the line on that one too?" Said Frankie.

"Where do you want to go?" Said Sophia.

"I don't know, have you ever been anywhere?" Said Frankie.

"No, you?" Said Sophia.

"Except for fort Dix New Jersey, and Korea, no. I was in Long Branch one time, met a nice girl there too." Said Frankie.

"Oh yeah, what ever happened to her?" Said Sophia.

"I hear she's getting married to some two bit hood." Said Frankie.

"Gee, that's funny So Am I." Said Sophia.

"I feel sorry for the both of you." Said Frankie.

"Hey, why do I have to buy a tuxedo?" Said Frankie.

"You should have one, in case you ever go into politics, or become a waiter." Said Sophia, smiling.

"No really, why do I have to buy one of them things?" Said Frankie.

"Would it kill you to own a suit that doesn't make you look like a gangster?" Said Sophia.

"I got a blue blazer, but don't tell Pauley."

"Why?" Said Sophia.

"He says a blue blazer makes me look stupid." Said Frankie.

"Buy a tuxedo, for me, Ok." Said Sophia, with a kiss, and boo face.

"All right for you I will buy a tuxedo." Said Frankie.

"And after the wedding, we will buy you some nice clothes, suits, a top coat, good shoes." Said Sophia.

"Did you say buy?" Said Frankie.

"If you want to look like a gangster." Said Sophia going up register.

"No, really I don't, it's just these clothes, they were free, and I didn't have any money at the time, and Pauley, he brought me to this warehouse, and it was dark, and maybe I couldn't see very well when I was pulling suits from the rack." Said Frankie sputtering.

"Are you done?" Said Sophia.

"Yeah," said Frankie.

"Have you ever heard of Brooks Brother's, or Barney's?" Said Sophia.

"Who are they?" Said Frankie.

"They are Men's clothing stores, in Manhattan. My Father bought all of his suits there, and so will you." Said Sophia.

"Fancy?" Said Frankie, making a face.

"Sensible, and classy," said Sophia. "Expensive?" Said Frankie. "Yes," said Sophia, emphatic.

"I told you I don't have a lot of dough saved, not yet." Said Frankie.

"Don't worry about it, we'll manage." Said Sophia.

"How?" Said Frankie.

"Don't worry." Said Sophia, patting his arm.

CHAPTER 45

"Pauley, who are you bringing to my wedding?"

"I don't know yet, maybe nobody." Said Pauley.

Frankie, and Pauley were at the Depot, sitting at the bar having a cup of coffee, and a sandwich. The Depot, didn't sell food, so Pauley brought it in with him.

"Good sandwich," said Frankie.

"Yeah it is, I bought it from a guy up the street, on Washington, he made it, he said to say hello." Said Pauley.

"W I don't know, I didn't ask him." Said Pauley, his mouth overflowing.

"The delicatessen on the corner, three blocks up, on the right?" Said Frankie.

"Yeah, that's him, what's his name?" Said Pauley.

"How do I know, I didn't ask him" said Frankie. A "Good sandwich though" Said Frankie.

"Yeah," said Pauley.

"Why don't you bring Naomi?" Said Frankie.

"Ancora co questo?" Said Pauley exasperated. "How many times are you going to push this dead horse?"

"You don't push a dead horse Pauley, you beat a dead horse." Said Frankie.

"That don't make sense, why would you beat a dead horse? What good would that do?" Said Pauley. "It's already dead."

"That's the point of it Pauley, you don't want to beat a dead horse." Said Frankie.

"I should hope not," said Pauley with an air about him. "That would be stupid."

"Do you mean stupid, like you not bringing Naomi to my wedding?" Said Frankie.Sal is dead, and who else is going to give a shit?"

"Everybody else, who isn't dead." Said Pauley.

"I think you are wrong." Said Frankie.

"How do you figure?" Said Pauley.

"I like Naomi, and I am no different from everybody else." Said Frankie, speaking up. "I would like her to be there, the kid too, and I bet Sophia, if she knew about them, she would want them there too." Said Frankie.

" If I bring her, and the kid to the wedding, it would be the end of me." Said Pauley, saddened. "It's one thing to screw around with a black woman, but it's another thing to throw it in peoples faces, and at a big deal like this," Pauley was shaking and stirred up by emotion.

"Sarebbe suicidio, forse per entrambi" Pauley put his head to his chest and began to breath slow, steady and deep. "Se solo, pace."

"I guess it don't matter what I think then, and maybe I think I don't care what anyone else thinks, but I do care about you, Naomi and the kid." Said Frankie determined to give his opinion on this racial question.

"One more thing, I have every expectation that I will be happy with Sophia and she will be happy with me, and we will be fucking delirious together." Said Frankie now with a head of steam.

"So if you think I am going to suffer through all of this fucking happiness by myself you are the crazy one here not me." Said Frankie. "And one more thing," began Frankie.

"No, no more things you made your point. And thank you" Said Pauley.

"I still think you wrong about this. People will get used to anything, and I don't think this situation is any different." Said Frankie.

"Let us put this to bed, it should sleep for a while. Ok?" Said Pauley, in a quiet even tone.

Frankie nods.

Pauley sees Liz, who came down to the Depot to pick up a few hours of shake and take.

"Hey Liz, you want to go to a wedding with me?" "Open bar?" Said Liz. "Absolutely," said Pauley.

"Sure, why not," said Liz.

"Maybe I will get you drunk, and we can forget I have a dick for a few minutes so we can do stuff. What do you say?" Said Pauley, sleazy.

"For you Pauley, no" said Liz, laughing.

"But for your friend, maybe?" Said Liz to Frankie.

"He is the one getting married." Said Pauley.

"Oh yeah that's right, to Sal's kid. Hey Frankie what happened you knock her up?" Said Liz, serious.

"No, why you asking?" Said Frankie. "You just got engaged, like twenty minutes ago?" Said Liz.

"It's a long story." Said Frankie.

"No it isn't." Said Pauley. "Jackie N wants to tie up some loose ends, and make nice with the big shot." Said Pauley.

"What big shot? He is the only big shot I know about." Said Frankie. The music started, so Liz made with the shaking.

She waved to the both of them from the stage like she was a kid on a merry-go-round. Frankie and Pauley waved back.

"What are you talking about Pauley, what big shot?" Said Frankie.

"Sal was the boss of us. And Jackie N, he worked under him. But Sal wasn't the top banana. There is one guy that I know of was over Sal, and he is who Jackie N wants to make nice with." Said Pauley.

"So who is he that would make Jackie N sell off his niece just so he can kiss his ass?" Said Frankie.

"The Mayor of Jersey City" said Pauley.

"Get the fuck out of here." Said Frankie, dumbstruck. "But he's not Italian."

"He's not?" Said Pauley.

"The mayor is Irish, or something, but he isn't Italian." Said Frankie.

"What he is now is different from what he was." Said Pauley.

"What, he changed his name?" Said Frankie.

"Among other things" said Pauley.

"Like what?" Said Frankie.

"His nose." Said Pauley.

"Anything else?" Said Frankie.

"Yeah, he made his dick smaller, so he would be more Irish. Jesus, what else you need, the guy changed his name, his nose, his family background. That's enough don't you think?" Said Pauley.

"Pauley, how can a guy get away with something like that?" Said Frankie.

"Harder now then it used to be, but forty, or fifty years ago, the day you got off the boat was page one. If You were healthy they would let you in." said Pauley.

"Just like that?" Said Frankie.

"Pretty much." Said Pauley.

"Immigrants were like so many water bugs coming up through the drain, millions of them clogging the thing up, so you had to keep them moving."

"Back then there wasn't no passports, social security numbers, just what's your name pal, and welcome to America." Said Pauley.

"So Pauley, the Mayor, what was his name before he changed it?" Said Frankie.

"Nazione, Vito Nazione," said Pauley.

"Hey, you know something Pauley, my mother, her maiden name was Nazione, maybe me and the mayor are related." Said Frankie.

"No kidding, That would be funny, if." Pauley pulled up short. "Hey who did you tell what your mother's maiden was, anybody?" Said Pauley.

"Sophia, she asked me who my mother and father is where did they come from, you know my life story. She said her father would want to know, but I don't know if she ever told him." Said Pauley.

"Your mother, is she coming to the wedding?" Said Pauley.

"I don't know, I haven't told her anything about it." Said Frankie.

"Her father, who was he." Said Pauley.

"Some local Don back in the old country, grew olives, made people nervous, you know, goon shit." Said Frankie.

"The old Don have any brothers?" Said Pauley.

"I don't know, maybe." Said Frankie.

"Can you ask your mother if he did?" Said Pauley.

"Are you thinking maybe I got some kind of connection to this guy, the mayor." Said Frankie.

"It makes sense, don't it." Pauley was scratching his head, lowers his index finger and points it at Frankie. "You, who don't have a pot to take a piss in meets a girl with connections up the wazoo, and three months later you walking her down the aisle." Said Pauley with curiosity.

"The princess can't marry a fucking frog. Somebody had to make the connection, I don't know if it was Sal, or Jackie N who put it together, but either way it pays off for you, and for Jackie N if he plays this wedding deal right." Said Pauley.

"It still doesn't tell me why I got to get married now, and not later." Said Frankie.

"The big boss, the mayor, he don't like Jackie N, and he never did as far as I know. He always went through Sal, and that is how Sal went one up on his brother, but if Jackie N, or the Nasorosso's, become part of your family, the Nazione's, or Migliori's in your case, then how is he going to tell Jackie N to get lost." Said Pauley, putting pieces together.

"This is a nice story, a fairy tale, but what if none of it true?" Said Frankie.

"Where is your mother, right now?" Said Pauley.

"What time is it?" Said Frankie.

"Seven thirty, why?" Said Pauley.

"I'll show you." Said Frankie.

Frankie called Charlie Chili dogs from the backroom.

Charlie thought maybe he left his shoes in the backroom the last time he saw them, and was searching high and low.

Charlie appeared sans footwear.

"Charlie, we are going out for a while, will you keep an eye on the place for us?" Said Frankie.

"Sure thing,"said Charlie.

"Hey Pauley, how you doing?"

"Good Charlie, how you doing?" Said Pauley, looking down at Charlie's feet, but not saying nothing about them.

"Ok Charlie, we'll see you later." Said Frankie.

"Ok I'll see you." Said Charlie.

"Where we going?" Said Pauley, sitting next to Frankie in what used to be Charlie Chili dog's Cadillac.

"You want to talk to my mother don't you?" Said Frankie.

"Oh, Ok good," Said Pauley, angled on the seat, relaxing.

It took five minutes, to get from The Depot in Hoboken, to The Hole in the Wall Pub in Jersey City.

A local dive, an old man bar around the corner from where Frankie's mother lives.

A bar, and nothing else. The Hole in the wall Pub looked more like the hole in your ass pub. Booze, and a seat to drink it on, if that's important to you.

Not a Television on the wall, no juke box, no class whatsoever.

Shellac on the walls, tin on the ceiling, and sawdust on the floor. Spit buckets at both the ends of the bar, no barstools so belly up, six tables, and four booths. Frankie's mother was in one of those.

Frankie's mother Maria wasn't bad looking, she still had a shape to her. The brown dye in her hair looked fresh, but so did the bags under her eyes, and the red lines in her eyeballs.

"Look what the cat dragged in." Said Maria to her son.

"Hey Mom, how you doing?" Said Frankie, leaning in to peck at her.

"Watch my makeup." Said Maria, bringing her hands up fast to block.

Frankie kissed the air around his mother's cheek.

"Do you mind if me and my friend Pauley here talk to you for a couple of minutes?" Said Frankie.

"Buy me a drink, and I got all the time in the world." Said Maria.

Frankie left Pauley alone with Maria, went to the bar and ordered two beers, and a screwdriver.

The bartender told Frankie to go sit down, he would bring the drinks around when they were ready.

Frankie walked back to the table, and sat next to his mother. Pauley sat across from Frankie.

Pauley, and Maria were pals by the time Frankie came back to the table, throwing words at each other in Italian, and flirting dirty, or she was flirting, and Pauley was going along.

Frankie can't help but be disgusted by his mother, but he didn't care enough to care enough.

"Mom, Pauley and me, we work together." Said Frankie thinking maybe filling her in would stop her from grabbing at Pauley from under the table. It, didn't.

"So he was saying." Said Maria, her hand reaching.

The drinks came to the table on a tray, with a bowl of peanuts. The bartender smiled at Maria, like he knew things about her, which he probably did. Seeing, as he was the man with the bottle, and she was the one with a problem.

"Thanks Chick," Maria says to the peanuts, picking up a couple, or three and tossing them in her mouth.

Maria's lipstick was a deep red, her teeth were red from the lipstick, and also her face was red from the booze, so when she tossed the nuts, Frankie thought she looked like the back end of a baboon that was sucking peanuts up through it's asshole.

"Is This your kid, Mary?" Said Chick, the bartender.

"Yeah, he's a good looking kid isn't he? Takes after his mother." Said Maria.

"Name's Chick, glad to know you." Said Chick, holding out a hand to shake after wiping it on an apron he was wearing around his waist.

"Frankie, and this is Pauley, nice to meet you." Said Frankie, taking Chick's hand.

"Your mother, she talks about you once in a while, says you was over in Korea. I guess you are back from there, huh?" Said Chick.

"Been back a few months." Said Frankie.

"Well, I better get back behind the bar before somebody dies of thirst. Hey Mary, will you be around at closing time tonight?" Said Chick.

"Are you going to run out of booze before then?" Said Maria.

"There is Not much of a chance of that happening." Said Chick. "What are the odds Chick?" Said Maria.

"70 to 1 Mary." Said Chick.

"I'll be here then." Said Maria.

"Maybe we can do something after I close the place, what do you say?" Said Chick.

"Chick, unless Tyrone Power walks through that door before you turn that lock, I'm yours." Said Maria pointing to the door.

"Ok Mary then I will wait over by that door there and keep him out of the here." Said Chick, with mock determination.

" Now don't be rude Chick. If Tyrone Power tries to get in here you let him." Said Maria, fixing her hair as if to freshen up her look.

" Ok Mary, Nice meeting you guys." Said Chick.

"Why does he call you Mary?" Said Frankie.

"He thinks I'm Irish, can you believe it." Said Maria.

"You don't have much of an accent." Said Pauley.

"In a place like this you don't need to know more than a few words to get by, so I guess I learned the few words I know real good. Anyway, I'm here more than twenty years, it don't take that long to learn enough English to get by." Said Maria.

"So, why are you here Frankie, I thought you don't like me no more?" Said Maria to Frankie.

"I, we want to ask you something, Ok with you?" Said Frankie.

"Buy me another drink first, my mouth is too dry to talk." Said Maria. Frankie held up a finger to Chick, who nodded.

"Your father, did he have any brothers?" Said Frankie, not waiting for Chick.

"He had one brother, but he left the old country before I was born, I seen his picture when I was small. He was younger than my father, by a couple of years, but he, don't like olives, or he don't like his brother, one or the other. Why you asking?" Said Maria.

"What was his name?" Said Pauley.

"I'm thirsty, where's my drink? Chick!" Said Maria, more than loud enough for the smitten.

Chick came around the bar quick. "Here you go Mary, I brung you one extra, so you don't have to wait next time, it's on me." Said Chick, trying to please.

"That not all what's going to be on you Chick." Said Maria, all Come-hither like, and then laughing.

Chick blushed up, and ran away. Frankie closed his eyes, and shook his head.

"What was his name, Mom?" Said Frankie, breathy.

"Who?" Said Maria, before putting half the tumbler into her throat.

"Your Father's brother Ma," said Frankie irritated.

"Who you talking about, Uncle Vito?" Said Maria, slurring her words.

"His name was Vito?" Said Frankie.

"I just said that didn't I?" Said Maria, reaching again under the table for Pauley's knee.

"What do you know about him?" Said Frankie. "

"Nothing, except that he lives around here someplace, or he used to at one time. That's why we came here, and didn't go to New York City like everybody else. But Uncle Vito, he didn't want nothing to do with me, us, so we didn't bother him no more after he told me to leave him alone." Said Maria, now angry, and drunk.

"What did he look like?" Said Pauley.

Maria, her head, it bobbled some before she spoke.

"He looked Irish, hey maybe that's why Chick thinks I'm Irish. Hey, Chick!" Said Maria, not so loud that Chick could hear her, or before she could forget why she was calling him.

"Did you ever see him any more after that?" Said Frankie. "

"I think I see him in the paper all the time, the mayor, he looks a lot like your great Uncle Vito, but the Mayor, he got a funny nose. Uncle Vito, he had a normal nose, Roman" Said Maria, before going empty times two, and looking for her Chick.

"Mom, I'm getting married in two weeks." Said Frankie, but Maria was too busy craving to hear him.

"Mom!" Said Frankie, louder this time.

"What?" Said Maria, annoyed.

"Mom, I'm getting married in two weeks, and I want to know if you want to come to the wedding." Said Frankie.

"Why do you want to go and do that for?" Said Maria, still looking for Chick, who was in the back room pulling ice into a bucket from a box, what makes ice.

Maria gave up her quest, and paid attention to Frankie.

"Get married, or invite you?"" Said Frankie.

"The first one," said Maria.

"I love her." Said Frankie.

"And?" Said Maria.

"And what?" Said Frankie.

"Is She pregnant?" Said Maria.

"No, she isn't" Said Frankie.

"Then why do you want to go and marry her? How old are you?" Said Maria, tired.

"Twenty-one, why?" Said Frankie.

"You" Said Maria, to Pauley, squeezing his knee.

Pauley forgot her hand was there.

"Yeah?" Said Pauley.

"How old are you?" Said Maria. "Thirty-two" said Pauley. "Are You married?" Said Maria.

"No" said Pauley.

"Are you happy?" Said Maria. "I suppose" Said Pauley, shrugging small.

"There you go." Said Maria.

"Chick!" Said Maria, screaming desperate.

Chick dropped the bucket with the ice, and came out of the back room on the fly.

"Yeah Mary, what can I get you?" Said Chick, out of breath, and sweating from pulling ice, and carrying heavy.

"Now isn't that a stupid question." Said Maria, eyes rolling.

"It is isn't?" Said Chick, smiling, and wiping sweat from his brow by pulling up his apron, and crouching, pink belly showing. "Right away Mary." And away he went.

"So, who is this tomato?" Said Maria.

Chick brought two more screwdrivers, only this time he didn't say that they were on the house so Frankie, he figures they are on him this time, these and two more beers, that Frankie didn't order.

"You are my prince, Chick baby, kiss, kiss." Said Maria smooching air.

"Her name is Sophia Nasorosso." Said Frankie.

"Like the gangster?" Said Maria.

"It's her Father." Said Frankie, no apology.

"You marrying the daughter of a gangster?" Said Maria, concerned, maybe.

"She is not the daughter of a gangster any more, Sal is dead." Said Frankie.

"Who killed him?" Said Maria.

"It wasn't a who, it was a what." Said Frankie.

"Ok then what was it that killed him?" Said Maria.

"It was a heart-attack and the sidewalk. Mr. Nasorosso was driving his car when it happened, and he went through the windshield" Said Frankie.

"Better that way." Said Maria. "Your Grandfather, he used to feed people to the pigs." Said Maria, no apology either.

"You a gangster?" Said Maria.

"Yes," said Frankie.

Maria, gave a tear to the tabletop, and shrugged.

"It's The family business."

"I guess so, yeah." Said Frankie, he shrugged too.

"So you making good?" Said Maria, rubbing her thumb, and forefinger.

"Not bad," said Frankie.

"Can you spare a little something for your poor old mother?" Said Maria.

"Mom, you are not even forty yet." Said Frankie.

"Don't be a cheapskate, give your mother some money." Said Maria, smiling, and drooling at the same time.

Frankie went into his pocket and took out three twenty-dollar bills and handed them over.

"Thanks honey, kiss, kiss." Maria kissed the air two times, rolled the bills tight and slid them between her tits.

"Mom, we got to go." Said Frankie, standing. "You coming to the wedding?"

"Sure thing sweetie, let me know again when it gets close. And pay Chick will you. Give him a nice tip. I don't want him to think my son, the gangster, is a gyp. Better yet leave me another twenty, and I will pay him myself later." Said Maria.

Frankie pulled another bill, and passed it over to his mother's tits. Frankie dropped a ten spot on the bar in front of Chick when he passed.

"Thanks, kid." Said Chick, wiping his hands again, before going to the cash box with the bill.

"Your mother, she's a piece of work." Said Pauley, rolling the window down in the Cadillac before Frankie hit the gas.

"Isn't she now?" Said Frankie, giving no weight to the pedal and creeping while he ponders.

"Hey are we driving, or walking, because I don't see no difference." Said Pauley, sarcastic.

Frankie leaned in, and the Cadillac went faster, Pauley felt a breeze and smiled.

"She's not bad looking, beautiful almost, or maybe she used to be." Said Pauley with his head back against the seat, his hat off, and his hair blowing.

"Yeah, I think maybe that was her problem, always catching flies when she should have been doing other things." Said Frankie.

"Like what?" Said Pauley. "Being a wife, and mother." Said Frankie, quickly.

"Oh, them things?" Said Pauley.

"Them things, yeah" Said Frankie, slower, airing out the words.

"Your mother likes them high balls don't she?" Said Pauley.

"Screwdrivers, and yeah she does." Said Frankie. "

"She's got it good." Said Pauley.

"No, she got it bad." Said Frankie. "And that ain't good," said Pauley.

"She has been drinking non stop since I come out through the in door, maybe before, maybe during, maybe the bartender, he pulled me out, maybe the bartender, he put me in too." Said Frankie.

"Now that you bring it up, what about your father, do we have to buy him a few drinks too?" Said Pauley.

"I don't know where he is, or who he is, but if you mean the guy who closed the book on me when I was a kid, fuck him." Said Frankie, a bitter taste in his mouth.

"Now I'm not defending the bum, but" Pauley paused considering, but giving up after trying to find something inoffensive to say. "If I was shackled to a broad who kept dropping babies around what didn't look like me I would have lit out quick, a lot quicker than he did that's for sure." Said Pauley.

"I would probably have done the same, but it doesn't change nothing about me, or the way I had to grow up without a father." Said Frankie.

"You're right. So, are we going to go find the bum, or what?" Said Pauley.

"Fuck him." Said Frankie.

"Fuck him then." Said Pauley. "So, are we going to go find this bum or what?"

"No!" Said Frankie.

"All right, all right let's not get our panties in a twist." Said Pauley laughing. Frankie was also laughing, he couldn't help it. It was all so ridiculous to him.

CHAPTER 46

Vito Nazione was young, but not stupid. His older brother was an asshole with a pig obsession, and he had better things to do than take orders from an idiot. So, before he suffered too much, Vito took off for America.

Along the way, Vito somehow ended up in Dublin Ireland, maybe the boat stopped there to get gas, or coal, whatever it was they used to keep the boat afloat.

Vito, while he was in Dublin he met up with an Irish lass who liked him immediately. She couldn't understand a word he said, but she liked the sound of his voice and look of his face enough to keep him close when the boat got going.

Remember this was the early days of the twentieth century, and being a woman and Irish usually meant that you were poor, stupid, and starving half to death. If you were married then you were all of that, and pregnant.

Patricia Doyle, fairly educated, reasonably well off, attractive, but alone after her father, Patrick Doyle passed away trying to free Ireland from the British.

Patricia, green eyes, dirty blonde curls, delicate features, and an ambitious nature saw something worth the effort in Vito right away, and stuck with him. By the time the boat was tugged and tied onto Ellis Island they were inseparable.

Patricia and Vito fell in love somewhere in the middle of the Atlantic Ocean.

Five weeks after they landed Patricia and Victor Doyle was married. Patricia's Uncle, Mike Doyle, her only living relative, lived in Jersey City, and was the reason why she came over in the first place.

Mike Doyle was a freeloader, I mean freeholder, a duly chosen and paid for in cash thermometer who takes the temperature on the street and provides vital statistics to the up and comers and the incumbents.

Patricia thought that the name Doyle would be a more acceptable name than Nazione if Victor were to go into politics, her family business, so to speak.

Victor learned two words of English right away, Vote Doyle, and having gotten that out of the way he got a job pulling in votes for Uncle Mike.

Victor did OK, and with him pulling the neighborhood into the ballot box, Uncle Mike became City Councilman Mike Doyle, and Victor was chosen to fill the Uncle Mike's vacant Freeloader spot.

So without saying too much, having chronic Italianitis, and with Patricia seducing her half of the glad hands while he smiles through his, Victor somehow became an up and coming Irish politician.

Everything would move smooth as long as Victor, didn't open his mouth, and look sideways into the camera. The nose job he needed came courtesy of a whiskey bottle, and a shot of what was in it.

His new nose didn't look any better, but it did look different. Later on when the money came easier Victor would go away for a few weeks, and come back with a nose like Maureen O'Hara.

The english came easy to Victor, and after three years of intense harassment you could not tell that Victor didn't grow up on the same street as Patricia did, almost.

When Mike Doyle died about five years later, Victor, didn't lose or miss a step on his way to the City council. It was during those council years, seven, or eight of them when Victor met the late great Salvatore Nasorosso.

Victor was taking a few minutes off from baby kissing and hiding out in the back room of a little beer-joint in one of the lower Jersey City neighborhoods when Sal came through the side door pulling a hand truck with Six cases of whiskey balancing precariously.

When the side door tried to close up on Sal as he was backing through. Victor gave a hand to the door, and Sal went on in like it was nothing.

Hands were shook, two beers were ordered, and an enduring partnership was started.

Sal and Victor got along well, and the time moved quickly. After an hour, or two of throwing words around, Victor used up all the words in English he could remember, and dropped a few meatballs into the pot. And Sal being Italian himself didn't notice the switch, maybe, he still thought in Italian, I don't know.

After a few minutes of speaking in tongues, Sal says, "Hey, you speak good whop for an Irishman." Victor all of a sudden realized what he's doing, and went all pink.

"I'm not really Irish." Said Victor, now Vito again.

"What are you?" Said Sal.

Victor thought about it for a minute, and decided to go around the mulberry bush until his life story fell out. Sal, he did the same.

All said and done the two men had an idea that together they could go places, so both Sal and Vito made a pact, and formed what would become a very profitable partnership.

Victor, he came out the "lead" dog, his connections making it so, and Sal he stared sniffing ass, but the 60/40 worked.

Victor went behind the scenes and stayed there while Sal took a seat at the head table.

All told maybe three people, Sal, Jackie N, and Pauley knew about the partnership and no beans got spilled, ever.

Sal, and Vito, kept their distance, thirty years in business together, and Sal didn't see Vito more than three, times.

It was three times I'm sure of it. Once that first night, again on the day that Mrs. Nasorosso died and the last time was when Patricia Doyle passed away from cancer of the Pancreas a few years after Mrs. N.

Sal and Vito in turn sat alone in their cars and paid their respects from the back seat, Sal in his Cadillac and Vito in a borrowed Lincoln. His government issue Limousine and driver would have made to much of an impression.

CHAPTER 47

"So why is it that you have to buy a tuxedo when we got a shit load of suits in the warehouse what don't cost no money?" Said Pauley.

"I told you once already Sophia asked me to buy a tuxedo like the one her father used to wear." Said Frankie.

"Sophia, she wants you to look like the cheese, not the rat, is that it?" Said Pauley, giving it to Frankie.

"Yeah, She doesn't want me looking like any of you bums." Said Frankie.

"Oh, so now it's you bums, is it. No more us bums, it's you bums."

"Maybe I should pull the Cadillac to the curb so you can plant your ass in the back seat." Pauley laughed while he slowed the Cadillac for effect.

"You jerk" said Frankie.

"So now it's you jerk and not..." Pauley was stopped short by a fist to his jaw. Placed in advance by Frankie.

"Ok, Ok I'll shut up." Said Pauley shamefaced.

"Hey, where we going again for this store bought monkey suit?" Said Pauley.

"Some guy named Barney, on Madison Avenue, in Manhattan. Sophia wrote down the address for me, I got it in my pocket, I'll take it out when we get through the tunnel." Said Frankie.

"I hate going through the tunnel, can't we go over the bridge?" Said Pauley.

"We are in Hoboken, the Holland tunnel isn't even five minutes from here." Said Frankie.

"But I don't like going through them things." Said Pauley.

"It will take us thirty minutes to get to the George Washington Bridge, and when we get to New York, it will take us another half hour to go downtown, this way we are there in fifteen minutes and back here before lunch." Said Frankie.

"Ok, but you got to drive, I can't drive with them walls around me, and all that water over my head." Said Pauley.

"What water?" Said Frankie.

"The Hudson River, the Holland Tunnel, it doesn't go over the thing, that would make it a bridge! The tunnel has to go through the Hudson, no?" Said Pauley, confused.

"The Holland tunnel, it goes under the water, through the bedrock. You got rock, not water over you." Said Frankie.

"No kidding?" Said Pauley.

"Yeah, what do you think, they held their breath the whole time they were building the thing?" Said Frankie, laughing.

"Fuck you. I thought they lay like a big garden hose on the bottom and build the tunnel inside the thing." Said Pauley.

"That doesn't sound so stupid." Said Frankie, thoughtful, "Maybe they done that."

"It seems like the thing to do, don't it?" Said Pauley.

Pauley stopped the car about four blocks from the Holland tunnel.

"Why you pulling over?" Said Frankie.

"You're driving through the tunnel, remember?" Said Pauley.

"I thought you were fine with it now?" Said Frankie.

"I never said that." Said Pauley, getting out of the car, and walking around to the passenger side. Frankie slid across the leather bench into position.

"Chicken shit." Said Frankie, when Pauley slammed the door.

"You want to do this thing by yourself? No, then shut up, and drive." Said Pauley.

Frankie was shaking his head, and smiling.

"You know that sitting on that side of the car will not save you when the water starts rushing in". Said Frankie pointing at Pauley.

"What do you mean when the water starts rushing in?" Said Pauley with a look of genuine terror on his face.

"Hypothetically speaking," said Frankie.

"Impoticio" Said Pauley, only mildly comforted."Vuole spaventare a morte"

"I am not trying to scare you to death don't be so dramatic." Said Frankie still amused.

Frankie paid the toll, and sent the Cadillac through the chute.

Pauley closed his eyes, and told Frankie to let him know when the Sun was showing through the windshield again.

"Hey Pauley, will you stand up with me when I do this thing?" Said Frankie.

"If Sophia don't trust you to buy your own suit, she definitely don't trust me, That's why we got to go see this Barney character?" Said Pauley, his eyes shut tight.

"I'm not talking about the suit, the wedding, will you stand up with me at the wedding?" Said Frankie.

"What, like be your best man?" Said Pauley opening his eyes and looking at Frankie.

"Yes," said Frankie.

"Of course," said Pauley with pride. "Come se fossi mio fratello."

"Thank you Pauley." Said Frankie tearing up a little. "You are like my own brother, I don't really know what that really feels like but my guess is that it feels pretty much like this."

Pauley smiled and shut his eyes again.

"We are out." Said Frankie, only a few minutes after Pauley closed hi eyes.

"No kidding, that was certainly faster than I thought it would be." Said Pauley.

Frankie coughed.

Frankie handed Pauley the slip of paper Sophia had given him.

"Which way do we go?" said Frankie.

"It says on this note that we go uptown, six blocks, and turn right." Pauley took out a pair of reading glasses from his inside breast pocket.

"I have never seen you wear those." Said Frankie.

"Did you ever ask me to read something?" Said Pauley.

"No," said Frankie.

"Then that's why you have never seen them." Said Pauley.

"Good point," said Frankie. "So which way do we go next?"

"We go straight until we hit Madison Avenue." Said Pauley. "Then we got to turn left and go straight until we see it, it's on the right side." Said Pauley.

"Sophia said her father shopped at this place, and another one called Brooks Brothers, all the time. How come you don't know anything about them?" Said Frankie.

"I didn't say I don't know nothing about these guys, I just never went with the Boss when he went to see them." Said Pauley.

"Because of the tunnel thing?" Said Frankie. "The tunnel thing," said Pauley discomfited.

"Did The Boss drive himself there?" Said Frankie. "Yeah, or Spoons, he took him a couple of times, but I think Barney, and Brooks, they used to send the clothes to the Boss when he needed something." Said Pauley.

"What about shoes, where did the Boss buy his shoes?" Said Frankie, in earnest.

"He bought his shoes at the Clown College, at the school store with a pendant for the wall in his bedroom, he was an alumnus" Said Pauley, laughing so hard he had to grab his balls, still a little tender.

"I needed that." Said Pauley. "Thank God the Boss is dead, otherwise he would kill me if he heard what I said."

"Hey Pauley, this guy Barney, he's not doing too bad, look at this place." Said Frankie, when he saw the sign on the front of a building that says Barney's on it.

"Not too shabby," said Pauley. "Hey, how we going to find this guy Barney when we get in there?"

"Do we got to ask somebody?" Said Pauley.

"I guess so, he the big Boss right, somebody has to know where he is." Said Frankie.

Frankie put the car to the curb at the first parking meter he saw with an empty space next to it.

The space was two blocks away from the building.

"What do I got to do, walk all the way back to the fucking place?" Said Pauley.

"What do you want me to do?" Said Frankie shrugging his shoulders. "There was not one parking space closer than this one." Said Frankie pointing to the curb, and getting defensive.

"Park in a lot, or something. I can't walk two blocks with these balls." Said Pauley.

"I'll go around the block and drop you off in front of the place, and then I will look for a space closer." Said Frankie.

"Good enough for me," said Pauley.

Frankie pulled out from the spot, took a few right turns and then dropped Pauley in front of Barney's.

Frankie was patient but irritated, Nothing but full lots, driveways, fireplugs, and meters in use. Three times he went around the block looking for space.

Pauley flagged the car down the third time Frankie passed the front of Barney's.

"Stop fucking around and park the thing." Said Pauley, when Frankie dropped the window.

"There is no place to park this fucking boat Pauley. Every lot is full and there is not one meter open." Said Frankie.

"Leave it here." Said Pauley, pointing to the ground.

"You want them to tow the car Pauley?" Said Frankie.

"They're not going to tow it." Said Pauley.

"They are going to tow it Pauley." Said Frankie. "They are not going to tow it! Shut the fucking thing down, and get out of the car before I do something." Said Pauley, agitated.

Frankie killed the engine, and got out of the car. "What were you going to do?" Said Frankie.

"What?" Said Pauley.

"You said get the fuck out of the car before I do something, what was it that you were going to do?" Said Frankie, curious.

"Figure of speech." Said Pauley.

"No, it isn't." Said Frankie.

"Yeah, it is. You never hear that before? Do this, or I'll do something? Stop doing that, or I'll do something?" Said Pauley.

"Only from you" said Frankie.

"Well, there you go." Said Pauley.

"You don't count." Said Frankie.

"What do you mean, I don't count?" Said Pauley.

"Ok, then where did you hear it from?" Said Frankie.

"I think I heard you say it one time." Said Pauley.

Pauley reached for the door handle before Frankie could throw a raspberry at him, which he threw at Pauley's back after he passed him on the way into the store.

"That was rude." Said Pauley once they were inside the place.

"Figure of speech." Said Frankie.

"Hey Pal," Said Pauley, to a tall skinny guy in black wool with a flower in his lapel who dropped his jaw when Pauley and Frankie walked through the front door.

"May I assist you two gentlemen," said the skinny guy who smelled too much like flowers.

"Yeah, we are here to see Barney, you want to tell him we here." Said Pauley.

"Whom would you like to see?" Said the walking gardenia.

"Barney, this is his place, no?" Said Pauley.

"Perhaps I may assist you." Said The gardenia.

"Are you Barney?" Said Pauley, put off.

"No, I'm afraid, I am not, but I will only be too happy to assist you Mister Fratello." Said the gardenia. "May I presume that the gentleman accompanying you is Mister Migliori?" "

"You may, but how may you. How is it that you know who we are, but we don't know who you are?" Said Pauley, suspicious.

"I received a telephone call from Miss Nasorosso this morning letting me know you were coming." Said the gardenia.

"Oh," said Pauley. "That was very kind of her."

"Yes, I have spoken with Miss Nasorosso on several occasions, in reference to her dear departed father, a fine man, and a very good customer I might add. Also her description of you both was quite accurate." Said the gardenia.

"Yeah, he was all right. Anyway, we are here to outfit the kid with a Tux, what can you do for us?" Said Pauley, moving forward, and nodding up.

"All that you require, I pray." Said the gardenia. "Praying will not help you if you make the kid look foolish." Said Pauley.

"I can assure you that Mister Migliori will look splendid." Said the gardenia.

"For your sake, I hope you right." Said Pauley.

"Listen Pal." Said the gardenia in a whisper, pulling into Pauley's ear. "Sally, he was the guy what got me this job see, and I'm not going to hang you up, so don't sweat it. Capisci?"

"Hey Frankie, the gardenia here speaks English." Said Pauley on the wrong side of loud.

"You want to keep it down. I don't have to tell you how hard it is to keep my tongue straight in this place. So give me a break." Said the gardenia.

"Sure thing, Now, let's get this kid in a tuxedo so we can get the fuck out of here." Said Pauley. "Follow me gentlemen." Said the gardenia, phony.

An hour after watching the two of them come in, Frankie and Pauley were walking out through the front door carrying nothing, but a pair of socks, two shoes, and a bow tie. The suit, would be cut and sewed that afternoon. They could pick it up in two days.

The car it got towed.

CHAPTER 48

Wedding day, it's raining, good luck? Who knows, what with Marriage at 50/50 these days, flip a coin.

This wedding however is a lock, the only way it ends is when they pull the lid down on one of these lovebirds.

The Candlelit Palace in Elizabeth, was a place for people who spelled their name with a vowel at the end. And can afford to pay through the nose.

A Nice place, but for the kind of money they were spending anybody could have done the job.

Crystal chandeliers, mirrors on every wall, and marble on the floor, with gold plate in the toilet, nice. If maybe you were in Vegas, but not in Elizabeth, here it was too much.

Jackie N tried to get Jimmy Roselli to sing some songs for the bride and groom, but the guy said no thanks, so Jackie N found some other guy to do it, Perry Como, maybe.

Louie Cuclinare, the guy who owned the Palace, agreed to patch together this deal out of respect for Sal who fed him good over the years.

Louie had a hell of a time putting it together, but he got it done in time. The place really looked good. The flowers, the food, the band, the limousine, even the guy who snaps the pictures, Louie, he took care of everything.

Louie, He didn't do it on the cheap though, this thing was going to cost Jackie N a pile of money by the time Sophia threw her daisies.

The ceremony was sandwiched in between the deviled eggs, and the endive salad. I'm kidding, deviled eggs? Come on.

The antipasto was amazing and the Pasta Fagioli was like gas in the tank. The ceremony followed this.

The nuns thought Sophia was knocked up, so they said nix to the church, and since Sal dropped dead before he check cleared on the Buick he gave them, they didn't even show up for the free food.

The Priest, from Jackie N's parish, Father Quinn, he told the kids to break a leg, but not without a note from Sophia's doctor verifying that the her Hyman was is in tact. And a new set of golf clubs was in his trunk.

The Priest, with nothing better to do than eat and drink, showed up early, and was inebriato before the accordion started playing the wedding march. In other words the priest was snookered.

Sophia looked like an angel, her dress was pure white, and her virginity verified.

Frankie looked good in his store bought tuxedo it fit perfectly. Black suit, and shoes, a white shirt, and a bow tie, very classy. Pauley, impeccable, in gray silk top to bottom.

"Hey, where did you get the suit?" Said Frankie, when Pauley stepped up to stand behind and to the left of him.

"When I went back to pick up your Tux, I asked George to set me up. It looks good don't it?" Said Pauley.

"You pay a lot of money for that?" Said Frankie, surprised. "Not so much, George, the gardenia, he gives it to me with his employee discount." Said Pauley.

"The tuxedo too?" Said Frankie.

"I got that at cost, with a promise." Said Pauley. "What did you have to promise him?" Said Frankie.

"That we don't try to dress ourselves no more." Said Pauley.

"Too late," said Frankie.

"What do you mean, too late?" Said Pauley.

"I already promised Sophia the same thing." Said Frankie.

"I don't think we looked too bad before we meet George." Said Pauley.

"I said the same thing to Sophia, and you know what she said?" Said Frankie.

"What?" Said Pauley. "She said, that's the problem." Said Frankie.

"I don't get it." Said Pauley.

"I don't either," said Frankie.

Sophia gave Frankie a nudge with her elbow. The Priest, he was talking, and Frankie wasn't listening.

Sophia didn't have that far to walk after the music started so she stood next to Frankie until somebody thought tell the accordion player that he could stop pushing buttons and squeezing on the thing.

Jackie N walked over to the priest with her so I guess he gave her away.

Sophia, didn't have a maid of honor so her two cousins, Tiffany and Ruby, were backing her up.

The smack was sucking the life out of those two.

Their once lovely faces were drawn thin, and their bones were showing enough to count them one at a time. They looked pretty good though, almost human in matching silk lavender sheath's, with lace shawls.

Jackie N paid very little attention to his girls, maybe he finally gave up on those two.

Big Ruby seemed more interested in what Peter, and Little Sal were doing as opposed to what her two daughters were't doing, which was eating solid food, and keeping a needle out of their veins.

Big Ruby, she had an eye for the youngsters, only Jackie N, he, didn't know about it yet.

The twin boys, Peter and little Sal, they were standing next to Pauley, wearing twin sharkskin suits, and two tone shoes.

Frankie noticed the way they were dressed and caught Pauley's eye. Pauley, he saw them too, because a nod went between them. Sophia, she saw the nod, and smiled.

Frankie didn't spend much time away from the wedding party table at the front of the room, but from where he was sitting it looked as though all of the guys from both Sal and Jackie N's crew showed up for the thing.

Frankie's mother Maria, didn't show. He doesn't know why she was absent. He called her up the day before, he bought her a new dress, he even sent a car to pick her up, but the car came back empty.

Maybe Frankie's mother was at The Hole in the Wall with Chick, maybe he doesn't care why she didn't come, but Sophia was not happy.

The food was good, the band was Ok, Vic Damone, he killed it. I know I said Perry Como before, but he begged off at the last minute so Freddie Cannon, named Freddie Picariello at the time filled the spot.

To be truthful I am not exactly sure who the singer was, but I remembered so many other things didn't I? I will give myself a pass on this one.

I should really end the story right now. I have things I have to do, and the Boss, he doesn't want to know nothing about why you can't, or why you don't do what he wants.

Let me see if I can tie this thing up for you. Frankie and Sophia got married, but they never had any kids. Not that they don't get good marks for trying. During the honeymoon Frankie almost killed her, but she lived through it, and they were all over each other until the day she died or maybe the day before.

Frankie's mother ran off with Chick, after he saw her in the new dress that Frankie bought her. She ran out on him when the money and the liquor dried up. Frankie, he didn't have much to do with her after that, and then she died.

Vito, he, didn't show up at the wedding, but he sent an envelope, and an invitation to meet up with Frankie when he returned from his honeymoon. Which he did, with Pauley in tow, who found out he was the guy who with Frankie would run everything except the yard in Elizabeth, Jackie N would keep running that yard until Peter and Little Sal turned twenty-five years old, then Jackie N would step down.

Only Jackie N, he, didn't like none of this, so he caused a lot of grief for everybody and a few people got killed, but that is no way to end a story so I am not going to say another word about that.

After Frankie and Sophia got back from Niagara Falls, That is where they went on their honeymoon, Sophia gave Frankie a tour of her father's, now her house, including the vault, a six by six room in the basement that no-one besides Sophia knew about.

She said that she found the vault one night when she was eleven years old and her father was lying drunk on the floor wedged between the door to the vault, and the woodwork where the door latched.Sophia tried to wake her father, but she couldn't rouse him so she climbed over him and took a look.

Inside the vault was cash, lots of it, banded, and stacked, and papers that wouldn't make any sense to an eleven year old.

Sophia didn't take anything from the room, and was smart enough to keep her mouth shut about it.

The next time Sophia saw her father go into the basement, she followed him, being careful not to make any noise. She hid behind some twenty or so cases of Glenfiddich, Glenlivet, and several other Glen's whiskey that was littering the place.

Sophia saw her father slide a piece of woodwork from its place at the bottom corner at floor level. And take a key from his pocket and put it into the lock recessed into the woodworking.

Sal turned the key and the latch clicked. And then Sal pulled the piece of woodwork like a handle, and the wall pulled away to him.

Sal stepped inside. And a minute or two later, he came out counting bills. He pushed the wall closed until it clicked again, and slid the piece of woodwork back into place, and went upstairs.

Sophia waited a few minutes, and then followed him up. Sophia never went in there again. And she, never followed her father into the basement any more, and she never told another soul about it. But, and this is a big but, the day Sal went through the windshield, Sophia removed that key from his personal effects before anybody started to wonder what that key belonged to.

Sophia brought Frankie into the basement. Frankie had to move seven, or eight cases of booze away from the wall.

Sophia had put the cases in front of the wall by herself so nobody would go snooping around the area by the vault while she was having her honeymoon.

The general look of the basement told her that she had made a wise decision, because things were not the way she had left them two weeks prior.

Sophia slid, clicked, and pulled, the way she remembered her father doing so many years before. It all went as she remembered. Inside, on walls lined with shelves was what turned out to be three quarters of a million dollars in cash when they finished counting.

Maybe you are thinking that Frankie wanted to run out and spend that money, but he didn't. And Sophia who had come from money couldn't care less about it. It was security for their future sure, so that made it important, somewhat, but for now it was a curiosity best to be explored at another time.

Frankie had never had any money, but strange as it may seem he never wanted more than he needed. So the money stayed in the vault. They added to it of course, and took it away with them when they moved, but they didn't have much use for it.

Frankie and Pauley took over the everyday operation of what used to be Sal's with the exception of Jackie N's place, which didn't make enough money on its own to keep Big Ruby happy. Ruby ran off with the kid who used to cut the grass around Jackie N's house, when Big Ruby let him keep his pants on that is.

Big Ruby had been stashing money away for years. Jackie N, thought that Big Ruby spent all the money he gave her on foolishness, but Big Rudy spent very little of it. Only what she picked from his pockets at night when he was sleeping.

Jackie N asked Vito for the Ok to whack her, but Vito said no. When Jackie N asked Vito, "Why not?" Vito said to him, "Because I say so." And that was it.

Big Ruby took the money and the kid who cut the grass and moved into a house that she paid for in cash in Hollywood Florida.

Tiffany and Ruby junior, well they ended up turning tricks in Newark to support their heroin habit and as it turns out they weren't very good at it.

THE END